# THE DUKE

# THE DUKE

*A Portrait of Prince Philip*

## TIM HEALD

Hodder & Stoughton

LONDON SYDNEY AUCKLAND TORONTO

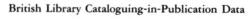

British Library Cataloguing-in-Publication Data

Heald, Tim
The Duke: A Portrait of Prince Philip.
I. Title
941.082092

ISBN 0-340-54607-7

Published by Hodder and Stoughton,
a division of Hodder and Stoughton Ltd,
Mill Road, Dunton Green, Sevenoaks, Kent TN13 2YA.
Editorial Office: 47 Bedford Square, London WC1B 3DP.

Designed by Behram Kapadia
Photoset by Rowland Phototypesetting Ltd, Bury St Edmunds, Suffolk.
Printed in Great Britain by Butler and Tanner Ltd, Frome and London

FOR ION

*Without whom this book would never have been*
*begun — let alone finished.*

# CONTENTS

# ILLUSTRATIONS

PICTURE CREDITS
(1) BBC Hulton Picture Library
(2) Private Collection – Princess Margaret of Hesse und bei Rhein
(3) Camera Press
(4) Associated Press
(5) Black Star Press
(6) Topham Picture Library
(7) The Dorchester Hotel
(8) Private Collection – HRH The Duke of Edinburgh
(9) The *Evening Standard*

(10) Author's Collection
(11) Australian Consolidated Press
(12) Press Association
(13) The Queen's Flight, RAF Benson, Oxon
(14) Rex Features
(15) Glenn Harvey Picture Collection
(16) Tim Graham
(17) *Sutton Coldfield News*
(18) Private Collection – HM Queen Elizabeth the Queen Mother
(19) Colin Jones

# PROLOGUE

PROLOGUE

# 'Two Truths'

'Two truths are told,
As happy prologues to the swelling act
Of the imperial theme'

*Macbeth*

SHAKESPEARE

'The days of our age,' says *The Book of Common Prayer*, 'are threescore years and ten; and though men be so strong, that they come to fourscore years: yet is their strength then but labour and sorrow; as soon passeth it away, and we are gone.'

This is a sombre verdict, but not without some truth. Even if there is now more to one's eighth decade than 'labour and sorrow' a seventieth birthday is still a moment for stock-taking. In the case of His Royal Highness Prince Philip, Duke of Edinburgh, that stock-taking has an inevitably public quality. He has been a very public figure ever since, soon after the war, he became engaged to the woman who would one day be the Queen of England, when he ceased to be a Greek prince and became instead the Duke of Edinburgh.

It would have been possible for the Duke to have assumed a passive role, becoming a sort of Denis Thatcher to Her Majesty, smiling and waving, giving private encouragement and comfort but never speaking out of turn, at least in public. There was never any stated requirement that he should actually do any work. He could have spent his life simply as a public symbol, accompanying his wife on ceremonial occasions, fathering heirs to the throne.

Living such a life is not in the Duke's character. He does not have it in him to be that passive. Under the unwritten British constitution the Monarch has the right, and, perhaps, the obligation, to consult, to encourage and to warn. As the Queen's consort (although he has never been formally given the title of Prince Consort), the Duke is

I

not entitled to consult Her Majesty's Ministers; he does not sit in on her weekly conferences with the Prime Minister, nor does he see the contents of those mysterious leather boxes full of Cabinet papers which pass regularly between Buckingham Palace and 10 Downing Street. Encouraging and warning, however, have always been second nature to him and he has spent his life encouraging and warning the nation on all manner of subjects in a consistently forthright fashion. He always tries, he says, to be constructive but, as he once wrote,

To do this and at the same time avoid giving offence can sometimes be a ticklish business. I have come to the conclusion that when in doubt it is better to play safe – people would rather be bored than offended.

Luckily he has not always been good at taking his own advice.

Had he devoted all his time to public exhortation and condemnation we *might* have got bored with him. Some people have. And irritated. He has never, however, been merely an armchair critic. He has always been numbingly active and busy and in his seventieth year he seemed almost to take on a new lease of life. Whenever I spent any time in his company I found it almost impossible to keep up. I am nearly a quarter of a century his junior but my experience is not unusual. It is not merely his physical energy which is remarkable. He is constantly considering, questioning and then bombarding the relevant person with sheaves of thoughts and queries. In October 1985, he wrote to a friend, 'I have just acquired this splendid gadget which is a sort of miniature portable word processor.' This was an acquisition not universally approved. He was always a prolific letter writer but the new technology has increased his output dramatically.

However, there is much more to his life than being a supportive husband and father and pumping out regular warnings and words of encouragement. If anybody else had created the Duke of Edinburgh's Award Scheme they would have been as celebrated as Lord Baden-Powell for founding the Boy Scout movement. For twenty-two years he actively ran the International Equestrian Federation and was therefore responsible for every horsey competition in the world except for racing. These two achievements are only part of the story. The Duke has become one of the most authoritative figures in the world of conservation and ecology; put together inter-faith conferences as far apart as Assisi and Amman; and was instrumental in setting up the Queen's Gallery, one of the most unusual art galleries in central London. He has also won a world championship gold medal with his horses, and cups at Cowes with his boats; he has piloted Concorde; speaks at least four languages; has published a book of theological debate with a bishop of the Church of England; and he can quote Jung.

Arguably more significant than any of this is his contribution to the Monarchy itself. Though difficult to prove, anybody who has made even the slightest study of the Royal Family will know that it is not the same institution as it was when Prince Philip first joined it. The 'Family Firm' would obviously have evolved in forty years but not in the way that it has. I doubt, for example, whether the Royal Family would have allowed the film cameras into their lives, as they did for the first time in the late 1960s, were it not for Prince Philip. When I put this to a very senior retired courtier, a man who had devoted his entire life to service at Buckingham Palace, he demurred. 'A lot of us were instrumental in that,' he said.

'Would the film have been made,' I asked, 'if the Queen had married some more conventional English husband?'

The old courtier thought for a moment.

'Fair point,' he said.

Not only did this seem an appropriate moment for writing a book about this extraordinary person, it also seemed a good time to try to put the record straight. Only once has anyone written a really informed book about the Duke of Edinburgh and that was Basil Boothroyd's biography, published twenty years ago. There have been books since as well as countless newspaper and magazine articles but they have all been more or less derivative and more or less hostile. I am not hostile to the Duke of Edinburgh, who, I believe, with a few minor reservations, to have been − and to be − an extremely good thing. I also believe that he has been widely misrepresented. When I asked one of his friends what he thought about one of the earlier biographies he said, 'I hated it because it made him seem boring and that's one thing he never is.' I agree, and I hope above almost everything else that I have not made him seem boring. At the same time I do not wish to appear sycophantic. That is the last thing he, or anyone in his position, needs.

I cut it fine. It was only at the end of 1989 that I realised that his seventieth birthday was approaching. This was, I submit, forgivable. He does not look like seventy, nor does he behave like a seventy-year-old. However, it meant that I had about a year in which to write the book. Not necessarily a problem. It would have been possible for me to have immediately embarked on a birthday book without bothering either the Duke or the Palace. After all, there is plenty of public evidence and most writers rely on that. However, I had a nagging sense that much of what had already been said about him was not quite right. I also wanted to talk to those who knew him best and I realised that without official clearance no one worth talking to would talk.

After an exploratory phone call I wrote to Robin Janvrin, then the Queen's press secretary, on 9 January 1990. I said that in order to write a worthwhile book I would like to be able to talk to such people as the Duke's ex-secretaries and to men like Lord Hunt or Lord Zuckerman who played important roles in his life. As for Prince Philip himself, I said that I would obviously like to talk to him but that, even more important, I would like him to 'vet the manuscript before it goes to the printer'. At this stage I would obviously defer on matters of fact. As for interpretation and comment, I felt sure that we could agree on a formula.

Robin Janvrin told me that there was no point in raising the matter with 'the relevant people' – by whom I presumed he meant the Duke and his private secretary – until the following month when they would be on tour in New Zealand following the Commonwealth Games. Then they could all discuss it calmly.

In mid-February Janvrin called. 'We have an amber light,' he said, 'in fact, amber to green. Can you come in for a chat with me and Brian McGrath, Prince Philip's private secretary?'

So on 24 February I found myself marching across the gravel to the Privy Purse entrance of Buckingham Palace with a Guards' band in close attendance. For a while Janvrin and I conversed, then McGrath, who had been watching and listening in silence, chipped in. Almost his first words were: 'I think you ought to talk to Prince Bernhard about the International Equestrian Federation and the World Wide Fund for Nature. I'll get on to his secretary and arrange it.'

It was obvious that I had negotiated a hurdle. But what exactly was my status? What sort of book was I writing? Was I authorised? Approved? By appointment?

'We don't authorise books,' said McGrath, 'but we want this one to be "informed". If anyone asks you, you can say that we are aware of what you're doing and we have no objection.' This is a very British way of setting out the rules. The unspoken word is almost as import-ant as the spoken. As far as the Duke was concerned, McGrath said that he was not a betting man but that he thought the odds on his seeing me were about 6–4. 'But,' he said, 'a lot of 6–4 bets don't come off.'

On this basis we went ahead.

When I started I envisaged a blow-by-blow chronological account. However, the more I got to know my subject, the less appropriate this approach appeared.

The most obvious objection is that whereas most men's seventy is a time for slippers and retrospection, the Duke remains indomitably active. His life is not a closed book; the pages are still turning; he can still surprise.

Because he continues to be an active figure in public life, no portrait of him would be complete if it were written entirely in the past tense. One needs to know what he is like at this moment in his life; how he appears to his friends, his family, his colleagues and to the world at large. For this reason I have included passages of first-person description which might seem more appropriate to the pages of a newspaper than a formal biography. The Duke is still a living person, carving out a role in the world, and I want to convey a sense of this.

At the same time there are parts of his life under which a line can be drawn. His childhood is gone, his parents dead, the most significant decisions in his life long made. It is therefore possible to apply a more conventional narrative approach to the earlier part of the book and this, for the most part, is what I have tried to do.

He was born Prince Philip of Greece, sixth in line of succession to that throne, and had a disrupted, itinerant childhood full of drama and tragedy. From birth until marriage, however, his life followed a pattern which, though exotic, at least conformed to normality enough for it to be recognisable. In 1947, however, he married the future Queen of England, was created Duke of Edinburgh and became, in many respects, a person with whom it is impossible for the rest of us to identify. Names have often proved a tiresome complication for him but it seems easiest to call him Prince Philip, or Philip, in his – relatively – private, early life and refer to him as 'the Duke' in the later, public, years. When in doubt, I call him 'the Duke'.

The premature death of King George VI in 1952 completed the transformation begun with the Duke's marriage less than five years earlier. He was barely in his thirties when he became in effect, if not in formal title, the first Prince Consort since Albert. While all his naval friends were still ambitious Lieutenant-Commanders he was suddenly an Admiral of the Fleet; while his contemporaries were battling with their first mortgages he was running vast estates in Scotland and East Anglia; while even successful men of his own generation were still struggling to make themselves heard, the Duke's every word was avidly chronicled. By 1957, when the Queen created him a prince of the United Kingdom, he was a fully fledged public figure. The basic structure of his life was established.

This inevitably affects the shape of any book written about him. Most successful public lives are a steady progress up a recognisable, conventional ladder, culminating with the ultimate rewards of office in middle age or even later. In the Duke's case, he peaked early. He arrived at the top in 1952 when he had only just turned thirty. He has remained active – some would say hyperactive – ever since. But most of the crucial appointments of his life and most of the important initiatives he launched took place in the 1950s. In his later years, when more conventional people were still struggling to the top, he was, essentially, consolidating what he had already begun. Of course he has remained busy; of course he has kept coming up with new ideas; of course he has acquired new interests and passions. But it was in the fifties that he first set his stamp on those areas with which he has since become most closely identified – with science and technology, with the environment, with youth, with equestrianism.

In more recent years his public reputation has been eclipsed by the younger members of his family, particularly the Prince of Wales and the Princess Royal. Thirty or forty years ago he was practically the only member of the Family Firm who did or said anything interesting. Nowadays they are all at it.

For this reason I have abandoned the chronological approach for his more mature years. It seemed to me that if I gave equal weight to each period of his life I would run the risk of repetition. Instead I have used the second part of the book to try to show the Duke of Edinburgh as he is today, how he functions in a number of very different roles, and to evaluate the impact that he has had on the rest of us in his full and peculiar life. It *is* a full life and, as more than one of his acquaintances observed to me during my researches, 'You can't get everything in'. If you did, you would be writing a rival to the telephone directory.

In a lifetime of sitting for portraits the Duke has never found a painter who has got him quite right. His old friend Sir Hugh Casson, artist, architect and past president of the Royal Academy, remarked apropos of this that the studies are always better than the finished article, adding 'a mercurial man like HRH needs a loose-fit portrait'. I think he is right. Someone else, probably much later, when he is dead and gone, will do a formal, stiff, comprehensive biography but full though it may be, it will fail by its very nature to capture the essence of the Duke. Following Sir Hugh's advice, a 'loose-fit portrait' is what I have tried to paint.

In relying on his own memories of himself and those of his contemporaries I have often come unstuck.

'Who told you that? . . . that's not what happened . . . he's quite mistaken.' Often memories conflict, there is no consensus and no written record to confirm or deny them. But I prefer the vivid oral evidence while it is still available. I tell the truth as best I can, I try to convey reality but I cannot be definitive. I am consoled in this failure by the words of Richard Ellmann, the great literary biographer, who wrote of the 'too early' biography, 'Even if more letters are unearthed and more memoirs written . . . the future biographer will have no more chance of being definitive. After all, what is wanted is not more incidents, or more prunings of incidents but evaluation of relationships, comprehension of motives, depictions of persons.'

The final difference between this sort of book and the posthumous biography is that the subject of the former still has a chance to answer back. In this case the Duke is clearly interested in what I have to say and has been at pains to help me get it right. At three score years and ten he can still care, but after he is dead and gone, what about his epitaph, what about his grave?

'I am not really interested in what goes on my tombstone,' he replied when I asked him this question. The tone and the content struck me as entirely typical. 'I will be dead by then and not deeply concerned about what people may think,' he said, adding as an afterthought, 'I don't take myself all that seriously.'

I am not actually quite sure about that. Or, as he himself would say, 'Yes, but . . .'

# Part One

# 1921–1947
# THE PRINCE

# 'The Grief That Fame Can Never Heal'

'They bore within their breasts the grief
That fame can never heal –
The deep, unutterable woe
Which none save exiles feel'
*The Island of the Scots*
W.E. AYTOUN

Almost seventy years on Princess Sophie could still smell the smoke as her sisters burned the documents. There was a fire in every grate. They had had very little notice of the escape. There was no telephone and the messenger had come on foot. HMS *Calypso*, a cruiser of the British Navy, would be standing offshore, and the four girls and their one-year-old brother must make their way out to the ship in a small boat with all their possessions. It was Corfu, 1922, and they were going into exile. Their father, Prince Andrew, was lucky to be spared.

'How many children do you have?' the Greek dictator, Pangalos, asked him a few days earlier.

'Five.'

Pangalos smiled and mused awhile. 'Poor little orphans,' he said.

But the family had come to the rescue. Andrew's cousin, King George V of England, had instructed the Foreign Secretary, Lord Curzon, to send the twentieth-century equivalent of a gunboat.

Commander Gerald Talbot, who had once served as Naval Attaché in Athens and is identified by Princess Sophie as 'what you call secret service', was hastily pulled out of his posting in Geneva and sent to Athens, in disguise and with false papers, to plead with General Pangalos for Andrew's release. So successful were Talbot's efforts that after Prince Andrew's trial, conviction and so-called pardon, Pangalos himself took Prince Andrew from prison, drove him to the quayside, with Talbot, and delivered him on board HMS *Calypso* and into exile.

Meanwhile word had been sent to Mon Repos, the family home on Corfu.

'It was a terrible business. Absolute chaos,' recalls Princess Sophie. 'My sisters, who were seventeen and sixteen, had to get everything ready.' It was an all-female household. 'There was a Greek lady-in-waiting, our French governess and the English nanny, Mrs Nicholas, who was a divine person, much nicer than all the other nannies. We adored her.'

The sea was very rough and the family were sick. The officers on board *Calypso* had moved out of their cabins and into hammocks so that the royal exiles could enjoy some creature comforts. 'We didn't realise what a tragedy it was,' says the Princess. The officers put on a concert to entertain the children and their parents and finally put them ashore at Brindisi where, in the small hours, they caught the train for Paris.

'Brindisi was a ghastly place,' says the Princess. 'The worst town I've ever been in.' On the train Philip crawled everywhere, making himself black from head to toe. He even spent some time licking the window-panes. His mother disapproved but nanny said, 'Leave him alone.' And she just sat there and let him get black.

'He was,' says his elder sister, 'very active.'


Princess Sophie told me the story at Buckingham Palace one June morning in 1990. They were rehearsing the Queen's Birthday Parade outside and as she talked we could hear the clatter of Household Cavalry hooves, the jingle of harness, the thump of drum and the blare of brass. Twice an almost girlish excitement and curiosity got the better of her and we abandoned the interview to go to the window and pull back the net curtain to look at the reassuring, timeless pageantry below.

The scene was so secure, so totally lacking in uncertainty that it was almost impossible to believe that all those years before she and her infant brother, their three sisters and the lady-in-waiting, the nanny and the governess had been sailing off in a small boat towards an unknown future. It had all taken place a lifetime earlier. The other three sisters are dead now. So is everybody else who took part in that adventure except for herself and her brother.

She and the baby brother are grandparents now. She has twice married German princes and he is the husband of the Queen of England. Yet she said she could still smell the smoke of the fire at Mon Repos and see the grubby child on the desolate train pulling out of the Brindisi night. It was the end of everything predictable, the beginning of another life.

# 'Something Inconceivable'

'. . . my family pride is something in-conceivable. I can't help it'
*The Mikado*
W.S. GILBERT

Royal genealogy is a complex and abstruse matter, especially post-Victorian genealogy. The Duke of Edinburgh disagrees, because it is so much better documented than most. Also because he is a part of it. Victoria and Albert had nine children and their descendants now number more than six hundred and seventy. These descendants, including Queen Elizabeth II and the Duke of Edinburgh (on his mother's side), have shown a strong inclination for intermarriage. They have also tended to follow Victoria and Albert's example by having what, by the standards of today, are large families – Prince Philip and his sisters, for instance, have twenty-one children between them. Family 'tree', as applied to the Duke, is therefore a misnomer. His pedigree is a thick, barely penetrable forest peopled with endless grand dukes and princes with multi-hyphenated German surnames all hopping from one branch to another. Unravelling it is like attempting one of those pointless old Advanced Maths exam questions:

If Ernest the Grand Duke of Hesse married, as his second wife, Eleonore, Princess of Solms-Hohensolms-Lich, and had a son, George Donatus, who married Cecile, Princess of Greece, what relation of Prince Philip was he and what did he become?

I originally thought the answer was that Cecile was one of Prince Philip's sisters and, therefore, that Grand Duke Ernest was his great-uncle by marriage. But because Ernest was also the fourth child of Princess Alice of Hesse, daughter of Queen Victoria, Ernest would have already been a distant cousin of his nephew by marriage. There is, the Duke pointed out, much more to it even than that; but by the time he had explained the full complexity of the relationship I was simply confused and certainly no wiser. I had picked an example at random and it had turned out to be even more intricate than it seemed at first glance. A simpler and more important relationship is that the Duke's grandfather, George I of Greece, was the brother of Queen Alexandra of England and that consequently her son, King George V of England, and Prince Philip's father were first cousins. That *is* helpful.

Behind all this there is, of course, deeper truth concealed. These names attached to the impersonal black rules of tables in books are not just so many chess pieces, interlocking and weaving in a dry academic game; they are real people with real lives and deaths and triumphs and tragedies, and none more so than the family just mentioned.

Seeing the wood through this kind of tree is going to demand an element of simplification on the part of the writer and of concentration from the reader. Both are essential for a clear understanding of the subject.

The overwhelming personality of his Uncle 'Dickie' Mountbatten has meant that in most people's eyes Prince Philip is first and foremost a Mountbatten. But he is only a Mountbatten on his mother's side, and in any case the Mountbattens, as we shall see, are in effect a comparatively modern invention, their origins lost – as someone put it unkindly – in the mists of the mid-nineteenth century.

So prevalent was the notion that he was, first and last, a Mountbatten that on one occasion Prince Philip said to his earlier biographer, Basil Boothroyd, 'I don't think anybody thinks I had a father. Most people think that Dickie's my father anyway.' It was not a view that Mountbatten seems to have discouraged.

However, the most important point in his heredity is not that he was a Mountbatten, but that he came from that extraordinary clan which effectively transcended nationality and whose members at one time sat on every throne in Europe. There is at least as much royal blood in Prince Philip's veins as in those of the Queen.

His grandfather was the King of Greece. Not Greek but King of Greece. Born in 1845, he was the second son of King Christian IX and Queen Louise of Denmark, and younger brother of Britain's Queen

Alexandra. In 1863 the Greeks approached this young man, Prince William of Denmark, and asked him to be their king. Paradoxically, the only people eligible for the Greek throne were those without Greek blood. Since 1832 Greece, after centuries of Turkish rule, had been a constitutional Monarchy.

William was by no means the first choice. The job was only vacant because the Greeks had dethroned the previous and only incumbent, Otto of Bavaria. They originally wanted Alfred, Duke of Edinburgh, second son of Victoria and Albert, but this was vetoed by Queen Victoria. She was, however, happy enough with the appointment of William, whose sister Alexandra had just married the Prince of Wales, to give the seven Ionian islands, including Prince Philip's birthplace, Corfu, back to Greece. The new King, George of the Hellenes, could therefore arrive in Athens bearing gifts for the Greeks.

At that stage the Prince was an eighteen-year-old lieutenant in the Danish Navy. He didn't even speak Greek. His father and mother, later, but not yet, the King and Queen of Denmark, were not keen on their son 'going to such a faraway, little-known country as Greece then was'. His grandfather, on the other hand, was enthusiastic and told Christian that if he made a fuss he would have him arrested. In the event, the boy became King of the Hellenes before his father became King of Denmark. Seasoned observers such as our man in Athens, Horace Rumbold, found the sight of this 'slight delicate stripling' swearing before an assembly of unscrupulous traitors to carry out an 'unworkable' constitution 'painful and saddening'. But Rumbold was too pessimistic.

Four years later on a trip to Russia to see his younger sister Dagmar, who married Tsar Alexander III, George of the Hellenes fell in love with the Grand Duchess Olga, eldest daughter of the Grand Duke and Grand Duchess Constantine Nicolaievitch of Russia and a granddaughter of Tsar Nicholas I. She was only sixteen but they married in St Petersburg and he brought her back to Athens with an elderly lady-in-waiting, the Countess Coucheleff, to keep her company and to instruct Greek ladies in the etiquette and manners of court life. Despite her frequently repeated remark that 'I fell in love with the man and not the King', the child bride was pathetically homesick. On one occasion when the ladies of the Court were all assembled for a formal audience she was nowhere to be found. Eventually the King and Countess Coucheleff found her under the stairs weeping copiously and cuddling her favourite Russian teddy bear. She was finally persuaded to conduct the audience — 'but with red and swollen eyes'.

George and Olga had seven children, though one died in infancy. Andrew, later to become Prince Philip's father, was the second youngest and was born in 1882. It was a curious family. King George developed a passion for Greece and its people, a patriotism which was all the more fervent for being adoptive. 'He always drilled into us,' wrote his daughter Marie, 'that we were Greek and nothing else.' The drill was so effective that when, on a foreign visit, she was told that she was a Dane and not a Greek, she actually burst into tears. At first the English nurses saw to it that the children always spoke English but then father forbad it and insisted on Greek. However, although they spoke Greek to each other, they used English to their parents. And to confuse matters further, the parents conversed with each other in German.

Of them all Andrew was the most Greek. He was the only one of the children whose first language really was Greek rather than English. He was even sent away as a child to an island where he was tutored by the military governor.

However Greek he had become in some respects, King George had a very Scandinavian approach to Monarchy. Every Monday morning he held a three-hour audience at which anyone who wished could come to air their grievances. The Queen, meanwhile, busied herself with good works, especially hospitals and penal reform. It all sounds extremely modern, though there were also more traditional balls and 'Cercles Diplomatiques'. To balance this, however, there was a roller-skating rink in the stables. The King was a very accomplished roller-skater.

The Greeks seem to have been effectively ungovernable and though the King was popular with the majority of his subjects his life was threatened on a number of occasions, when he invariably reacted with admirable sang-froid. Once out driving with his daughter Marie – later the Grand Duchess George of Russia – his landau was attacked by two men with rifles. They were firing at only about twenty paces. 'I had a red velvet bow on my hat which my father thought would make a good target for them,' wrote Marie, 'so he quickly stood up, put his hand on my neck and forced me down. With his other hand he menaced them with his walking stick.'

Both horses were hit, though only slightly wounded, and one of the footmen was wounded in the leg. The King and his daughter were unscathed, and there were scenes of general rejoicing, a Te Deum in the cathedral, a royal speech from the palace balcony and so on. Next time the King went out driving he and his daughter were accompanied by two of his sons – Prince Philip's uncles, George and Nicholas. Once again there was a rifle shot – a false alarm as it turned out – and this time five revolvers emerged like lightning. The King, both sons, his daughter and the footman were all armed (though in fact the bullets from the Princess's gun had been removed by a brother who didn't trust her marksmanship). Alas, King George did finally die from an assassin's bullet, though not until shortly before the First World War.

Reading family memoirs one has an overwhelming impression of royal life in those days as a continuing European house party: of the Grand Duchess Constantine on the station platform at Pavlovsk; of the Princess of Wales somersaulting over a sofa at Fredensborg; of Grand Duke George dressing in a sheet with a broomstick to frighten his young cousins; of the Maharaja of Kapurthala giving Andrew a green and gold turban in Vienna. The world is full of Imperial yachts and royal trains and Chaliapin singing a private solo and the Sultan of Turkey presenting Turkish delight. Above all there are always, in every schloss, every shooting box, every summer palace, an inordinate number of uncles and aunts and cousins, none of them, it seems, below the rank of Grand Duke.

Prince Andrew was brought up to be a soldier. He was sent to the German-officered Athens Military Academy at fourteen and later underwent intensive private cramming from Major Panayotis Danglis, the inventor of a revolutionary gun which was light enough to be carried up and down mountains by mules and simple enough to be assembled in ninety seconds. Or so it was said. Danglis and the King imposed a harsh eighteen-month regime designed to get the Prince commissioned, come what may. The day began with a cold bath at 6 a.m. and lessons were intensive. In the spring of 1900 there was a family holiday on Corfu. While everyone else was out and about Prince Andrew and Major Danglis were closeted indoors studying artillery, fortifications, military technology, military history, military geography and military topography. The Major also accompanied him on a summer visit to Crete where Prince George, his considerably older brother, was the High Commissioner for the Powers from 1898 to 1906.

This intensive cramming for a routine exam is surprising, but demonstrates an abiding family characteristic. They do not like to be seen pulling rank. Prince Philip and his family have always sat exams like everyone else. Fortunately the Major's ministrations proved effective and, after a three-day exam in May 1901, Andrew was commissioned into the cavalry and the Major was rewarded with the Gold Cross of the Order of the Redeemer. The Commissioning Board included Andrew's father and two of his brothers – as well as the Archbishop, who can't be presumed to have been much of an expert on military technology. The Minister for War, the Commandant of the Military Academy, the King's ADC and all the tutors were also listed as examiners.

In 1903, two years after entering the Army, Prince Andrew married Princess Alice of Battenberg, eldest daughter of Admiral of the Fleet Prince Louis of Battenberg and of Princess Victoria of Hesse, eldest sister of the Empress Alexandra and Grand Duchess Serge of Russia. Princess Alice was just eighteen and once described as 'the prettiest princess in Europe'. Her younger brother, Louis, only three at the time of her marriage, was to become Earl Mountbatten of Burma, while her sister Louise was later to marry the King of Sweden. Although Alice's title was 'Battenberg' it is more helpful and in a sense more historically accurate to think of her as a morganatic daughter of the House of Hesse.*

The Grand Dukes of Hesse were descended from Philip the Magnanimous, a sixteenth-century magnate who left his estates equally between four sons. By the nineteenth century only two of these estates survived: Hesse und bei Rhein – commonly known as Hesse-Darmstadt – and Hesse-Kassel. Hesse-Kassel was annexed by Prussia after the war with Austria but Hesse-Darmstadt continued as a semi-autonomous Grand Duchy within the Empire until 1918. Darmstadt, the capital, is just south of Frankfurt and twelve miles east of the Rhine.

Princess Alice's grandfather, Prince Alexander of Hesse, was the third son of Grand Duke Louis II of Hesse und bei Rhein. Prince Alexander was the Tsar's godson, his sister married the Tsarevich and it therefore seemed only natural that he should serve with the Russian Army. This he did, and with distinction. So much so that he had a regiment of Lancers named after him, was decorated and, most significantly, was promised the hand of the Tsar's niece in marriage. Alexander was clearly an impetuous young man and when he fell in love with one of his sister's ladies-in-waiting he decided he wanted to marry her and not the Tsar's niece. The Tsar was not amused. The

---

* A 'morganatic' marriage is simply a match between a person of 'high rank' and one of 'lower rank'. The 'low-rank' partner does not take the 'high-rank' title and nor do their children.

girl was a Pole called Julie Hauke, perfectly respectable, but hardly a suitable match for a godson who had given his name to a regiment of Russian Lancers.

Despite everyone's efforts to persuade Alexander to be sensible he resolutely went his own way. Even exile in England couldn't change his mind and in 1851 he and Julie eloped from St Petersburg and married in Breslau. Thus was the House of Mountbatten born!

The couple were plainly persona non grata in Russia. Hesse was little more forgiving but Alexander's brother, Grand Duke Louis III, agreed to allow him to go on being a royal Prince of Hesse. Julie, a Polish commoner, was made a countess with the title of Battenberg. Battenberg is a small town in the north of the Duchy, on the River Eder east of Siegen. Dictionaries are in some doubt about whether or not it gave its name to the famous cake. Its anglicised form, Mountbatten, was adopted in 1917 to satisfy patriotic British sentiment. At the same time George V adopted the name of Windsor.

Because the marriage was morganatic, any children should have been disbarred from the Hesse succession but the Grand Duke's displeasure was short-lived. In 1858 Countess Julie became a Serene Highness (only marginally less grand than all the other Hessian wives, who were Royal Highnesses) and four years later the couple were allowed back to Darmstadt. 'A new house had been born,' writes Mountbatten's official biographer, Philip Ziegler. 'Royal, after a fashion, but bearing about it a faint aura of wildness and irregularity.' He adds, a little mischievously, that when Himmler read the Gestapo file on the family he commented, 'I believe that the Battenbergs have always behaved somewhat peculiarly.' I would never have thought of Himmler as an arbiter of correct social behaviour, but the Mountbatten origins are certainly not orthodox. Prince Alexander, incidentally, joined the Austrian Army and became a Field Marshal.

Odd, then, that Prince Philip and his children should so often and so widely be thought of as Mountbattens. His father's side of the family, whether it's the Royal House of Greece, or of Denmark, or of Schleswig-Holstein-Sonderburg-Glücksburg, is surely more regal and more ancient. Besides which, patronymics derive, by definition, from the paternal line.

Alexander and Julie of Battenberg had five children of whom Louis, Princess Alice's father, was the second. The family were brought up in Hesse mainly at Heiligenberg Castle, a large comfortable, sylvan home about as far from the sea as anywhere in Europe. It was curious therefore that young Louis should have conceived a passionate desire to become a sailor. Hessians, like his father, were famous as soldiers but there was no naval tradition in the family. Moreover, in the 1860s the German Navy scarcely existed. If the young Battenberg was to join a navy it would be the British Navy. There were strong links between the Dukes of Hesse and the British Royal Family and these were further strengthened in 1862 when the future Grand Duke Louis IV married Queen Victoria's daughter Alice. Nevertheless for a son of Hesse to join the British Navy, egged on by another of Victoria's children, Alfred, Duke of Edinburgh and himself a Royal Navy captain, was unorthodox to the point of perversity. Alfred, just to complicate matters, had been the Greeks' preferred choice as King.

Louis's early career in the Royal Navy seems to have been dogged by the sort of coddling favouritism that, years later, his grandson Prince Philip was so vehemently anxious to avoid. His first ship, for instance, was a frigate on which the Prince and Princess of Wales were cruising the Mediterranean. His royal connections and his unashamed Germanness alienated him from his colleagues – even when in later life he dropped his German titles, anglicised his name and became the first Marquess of Milford Haven, he never lost his German accent. His thorough-going professionalism only added to his unpopularity although it ensured that eventually he went to the very top. As First Sea Lord he had to sign the signal from the Admiralty to All Ships which ordered, 'Commence hostilities against Germany'. For a man of whom his sister once wrote, 'He was perhaps by nature the most German of us all, and was unspeakably attached to his native land', it must have been an agonising moment.

In 1883 he married Princess Victoria of Hesse. She was his first cousin once removed, which meant that his father-in-law, the Grand Duke, was his first cousin. As his bride was also a granddaughter, and a much favoured one, of Queen Victoria, Prince Louis was pulling off a considerable double coup. On the one hand he was legitimising his own morganatic Hesse status and on the other he was becoming a member, however distant, of the British Royal Family. Princess Victoria was a clever catch, particularly as her father strongly disapproved. Queen Victoria, on the other hand, was delighted for her namesake because she had met someone 'kind, good and clever whom she knows thoroughly well'. The old Queen was not to be argued with. Prince Louis was, the Duke points out, a friend of King Edward VII, and a personal ADC to him, to Queen Victoria, and to King George V.

Two years later their eldest child, Princess Alice, was born at

Windsor Castle with Queen Victoria assisting during a long and difficult labour. Prince Philip's mother, known as Princess Alice or later Princess Andrew, was christened Victoria Alice Elisabeth Julia Marie. She was beautiful, indomitable and profoundly deaf from birth. This handicap was not discovered until her grandmother Princess Julie, always a champion of hers, remonstrated when, as usual, Alice was being chided for 'not listening'.

'It's not that she's not listening,' said Princess Julie, 'I don't think she can hear. I think she's deaf.' Nowadays the problem might well have been cured, but in the late nineteenth century medical science did not have the answers and Alice remained deaf for the rest of her life, teaching herself to lip-read in at least four different languages. (How proficient she was at this depends on who you talk to!)

The combination of Royal Navy and Hessian royalty meant that hers was an itinerant childhood. 'Navy brats' are used to camp-following, trekking around the seven seas from one of their father's postings to another. Countless royal castles and palaces were available for holidays in Hesse and the Scottish Highlands, but there was no place quite like home. Princess Alice's favourite substitute was Malta where her father was 'spectacularly successful' with the Mediterranean Fleet. When, after her marriage, she moved to Athens, the blinding brightness of the Eastern Mediterranean sun beating off pale yellow stone and rock reminded her of Valletta and helped her come to love it.

The Darmstadt wedding was, in the words of Andrew's Aunt Marie,

a great family meeting . . . The Emperor and Empress came, as well as the Princess of Wales and her daughter Victoria. My parents were there, of course; so were several of my brothers and my mother's only sister, the Grand Duchess Vera, widow of Prince Eugene of Württemberg.

Vera was short, stumpy, very plain and so short-sighted that she had to wear pince-nez. This last is a family characteristic. Prince Andrew is nearly always photographed in a monocle or spectacles. His son Prince Philip used to wear contact lenses for polo and does sometimes wear glasses. Basil Boothroyd has a footnote in his biography describing how if the Duke is at the wheel of a car there is always a lurch a little way down The Mall as he puts on his specs. He does not wish to be spotted wearing them by the crowds outside the palace. When I mentioned this to Jim Orr who was his private secretary for thirteen years he said, 'Good heavens! I *never* saw him wearing glasses.'

Despite her appearance, the Grand Duchess Vera was much loved but mercilessly teased. In the afternoon everyone gathered outside the schloss to throw rice at the departing couple. Andrew's brothers Prince Constantine and Prince George, however, emptied their packets of rice all over Aunt Vera and then found a gentleman's hat which they pulled down over her head, causing her glasses to fall off. They ran away so quickly that when she got the hat off she boxed the ear of the man nearest to her by mistake. This turned out to be Prince Louis of Battenberg's ADC, Admiral Mark Kerr. The admiral took the blow in the best Senior Service spirit, laughed it off and said simply, 'I quite understand, Ma'am.' The Tsar threw a satin slipper at Princess Alice who caught it deftly and hit him over the head with it.

The ceremony itself was conducted in duplicate. Princess Marie says the couple were first married in the Russian Orthodox Church, and then married again in the 'Protestant Church of the Schloss' by the same German clergyman who had married Andrew's brother, Constantine, in Athens in 1889. The Russian Church, built for the Tsar because he had married into the House of Hesse, was designed by the architect Louis de Benois, grandfather of the author and actor, Peter Ustinov. 'I look like him,' Ustinov told me, adding that on one occasion his grandfather returned from Darmstadt seeming more than usually depressed. When Ustinov's mother asked why, the architect replied: 'The Grand Duke of Hesse is deaf in one ear and does not understand with the other.'

3

# 'The Seed Sown'

'The seed sown by the Greek soldier will one
day burst forth into a great and flourishing tree'
*Towards Disaster*
PRINCE ANDREW OF GREECE

P rince Philip's father was passionate about his military career.
He had been immersed in soldiering since first becoming an
army cadet at fourteen and, as his wife later commented, 'He
took his duties very seriously, as he loved his profession and
wished to earn his promotion like any other officer'. The same was
later true of Prince Philip. He too was thwarted in his ambitions
though less cruelly than his father. Much as one might wish otherwise, it is not easy to combine a conventional career with being a
member of a Royal Family, even now.

At the time of his wedding in 1903 Prince Andrew was a twenty-
two-year-old cavalry subaltern of two years standing. In 1905 he was
posted to the garrison town of Larissa on the old Turkish frontier,
and, after a year there as a squadron commander, he joined his regiment. For the following three years he was mainly engaged in training
peasant conscripts from the mountains – no easy task since most of
them had never seen, let alone ridden, a horse in their lives. Somehow
he managed to combine this with completing the full Staff College
course. It all sounds like the beginnings of a dedicated army career.

Politics, however, soon interfered. In 1909 a league of disaffected
officers organised a revolution, one of the lesser aims of which was to
prevent the King's sons from holding army commands. To help his
father come to terms with the revolutionary officers Andrew resigned

his commission voluntarily. So did his brothers Nicholas and Christopher, while his brother George also resigned from the Navy.

From 1909 to 1912 Prince Andrew was effectively unemployed. Spending these years in compulsory idleness caused him 'great grief'. In 1912, however, the Balkan Confederacy, including Greece, declared war on the Turks and Andrew asked to be reinstated in the Army. In view of the emergency, military considerations overcame political ones and he was duly made a major on the staff of his eldest brother, Crown Prince Constantine, the C-in-C.

The Turkish campaigns ended in defeat for the enemy and in the general euphoria Prince Andrew was promoted to Colonel and given command of the 3rd Cavalry. He remained with them for four years, 'aloof from all politics', until, in 1916, he was withdrawn from Salonica by Constantine, now King of Greece, and sent on a diplomatic mission to Paris and London. Shortly after his return to the regiment, however, politics once again intervened. King Constantine was overthrown by the Great Powers and went into exile in Switzerland. Lloyd George described him as 'surly and suspicious' and too sympathetic to the Germans. Prince Andrew naïvely hoped that he would be allowed to stay in Greece but he and two thousand other officers were dismissed from the Army for being loyal to the King and a month later he and his family followed Constantine into Swiss exile.

There he remained with his family until June 1920 when he was able to move on to Rome. He had wanted to go to either France or England but neither country would have him. After all, they had connived at Constantine's removal and the substitution of his second son, Alexander, who died tragically as a result of a monkey bite in September 1920.

In December 1920, however, there was a plebiscite in Greece. Constantine was reinstated by a vote of 1,010,788 to 10,887 and Prince Andrew suddenly found himself back in his homeland and promoted to the rank of Major-General. The previous regime had already begun a new war against the Turks and Andrew eagerly applied for active service. It was six months before his request was granted but in June 1921 he was given the command of the 12th Division in Asia Minor under the overall leadership of Lieutenant-General Papulas who, on any analysis, seems to have been one of the least competent and shiftiest military commanders in history.

The 12th Division itself was a disastrous formation. Prince Andrew had hoped to be given command of the Cavalry Brigade or of another, better equipped and more professional division. The troops he was allocated would, in his estimation, 'melt before the enemy like snow in the sun'. Early on in the campaign, after a hard day's march his men camped in a Turkish village where 'the conduct of the men . . . and the indifference of the majority of the officers unfortunately surpass belief'. He tried to check the excesses of what sounds like a serious atrocity but, in the end, was able only to observe that 'unhappily it was only too evident that the army had contracted habits that were foreign to its nature before 1917'.

Prince Andrew's own account is obviously highly personal. 'Not for a moment did I imagine . . . due to the ill will and incapacity of the Major-General commanding the brigade . . . the ridiculous optimism of GHQ . . . the characteristic incapacity of their leaders.' If he failed to conceal this assessment of his fellow officers it is hardly surprising that they seem to have been unwilling to communicate with him except on the most official terms. On one occasion some officers were so reluctant to meet him that they hid behind a hut until he was gone. To say that the Army was politicised is an understatement. It was riddled with intrigue and dissent and was chronically over-officered. The overall impression of Ruritanian incompetence is unfairly heightened by the names of some of those concerned. How can one take seriously a captain named Skylakakis? Or a major-general named Stratigos?

At the same time the conduct of the campaign does seem to have been woeful. Eventually, in June 1921, Prince Andrew wrote to the C-in-C to complain about his undisciplined 'riff-raff'. Even when some of his artillery finally succeeded in engaging its guns it fired on its own comrades; there were not enough men; their supplies were deficient, communications non-existent. And so on.

Papulas's reply was conciliatory but unpromising. He would send more guns as soon as they arrived. There was no wireless apparatus but this, too, he would send as soon as he was provided with any. Most dismal of all, 'I have ordered boots and other supplies, which are being sent to us; you will be supplied from these at the first opportunity.' He ended with the tantalising, 'I hope very soon to give you the command of an Army Corps.'

That appointment was made in early August by which time Prince Andrew 'realised that all military prudence had vanished. Then I understood the true meaning of the Greek proverb, "Those that the Gods wish to destroy they first make mad".' Scarcely a happy augury for the Prince's new command.

The Greeks were by now well into hostile barren Turkish desert which yielded little or nothing in supplies or comfort. The Turks were, admittedly, retreating but their retreat was more tactical than enforced. The Greek intelligence was largely contradictory and the interpretation put on the Turkish performance by Papulas and his staff was probably awry and certainly variable. Papulas's mood shot from extreme optimism to high dudgeon within hours. At one moment the capture of Ankara seemed imminent, at the next a hasty retreat to Athens the only conceivable course of action. Prince Andrew, almost wholly unconsulted, sulked in his tent, and muttered about Papulas's 'ignorance of the science of war'.

Matters between the Commander-in-Chief and the Commander of his second Army Corps finally came to a head at five in the morning on 9 September when the C-in-C sent an order which the Prince considered 'a cry of ill-concealed panic'. Prince Andrew's Corps was told to make an 'immediate violent attack' towards the north. The Prince replied at 8 a.m.: 'Attack by 2nd Corps in the direction indicated impossible.' He proposed a quite different plan involving the immediate reinforcement of another threatened Corps but no immediate attack, violent or otherwise. 'My preliminary orders relative to this were issued 7 a.m. and movement of transport in above direction was commenced.'

Whatever Prince Andrew's view of Papulas's competence, this was an injudicious response. The Prince's defence is disingenuous. 'No doubt,' he said, 'the above message was not in accordance with ordinary practice, but I think that, beyond that, it does not constitute an infraction of orders, nor does it show any lack of fighting spirit. There is, however, a breach of formality, and this lies in the fact that in the message the correct phrase "subject to approval" was omitted, but the omission of this phrase cannot possibly form the basis of an accusation for disobedience and abandoning one's position.'

Papulas thought otherwise. 'Astonished,' he replied, 'at plan of abandoning your positions. I order corps to remain in its position. Only person competent to judge and decide is myself as Commander-in-Chief. Cancel all orders of transfer movements.'

Prince Andrew stayed put and told his Commanders to be ready to launch an immediate and violent attack to the north but next morning he was astonished to find that HQ had sacked his Chief of Staff. The Prince was outraged. Not only by what he saw as the cowardly dismissal of a junior officer when, if anyone was to be fired, it should have been himself – but also because his views on the conduct of battle were 'not taken into the slightest consideration'. Under these circumstances, he told the C-in-C, 'It is absolutely impossible for me to continue in command of corps. Please order my immediate relief.'

This time Papulas replied with a personal and confidential telegram. 'Important reasons do not permit nor do I contemplate replacing you.' There was no need to spell these reasons out. The Prince's brother was overall Commander-in-Chief of the Army. Nevertheless the Prince ('unreasonably perhaps' in his own words) insisted, whereupon Papulas replied formally, 'I desire, and situation demands, you should remain in your place.'

Before he could respond to this, the enemy attacked and the whole Greek force was engaged in fierce though essentially indecisive battle. Subsequently, however, any attempt to capture Ankara was abandoned and the Greeks began to pull back.

Some days later rumours began spreading that this retreat was due to the 'supposed unwillingness' of the 2nd Army Corps to attack. The Prince complained and a weary Papulas responded that he had always accepted that 'all the corps have carried out their duties with exemplary heroism'. He added, 'The 2nd Army Corps has so many heroic exploits to its credit that its officers need not be disturbed at the propagation of senseless criticism of the corps' action.'

Despite this, relations between the Prince and the C-in-C were impossible, at least as far as the Prince was concerned. He disagreed totally and continually with the Supreme Command and they, 'even though they never had the courage to tell me so straight out', had lost confidence in him. Even though he knew that some 'who could not know the true facts' would accuse him of desertion, he felt he could no longer continue 'in the stifling atmosphere of Asia Minor'. Accordingly he asked for three months' leave and on 30 September this request was granted.

After two months' absence Prince Andrew returned to Smyrna as a member of the Supreme Army Council under his old adversary General Papulas. Four months later he was transferred to the command of the 5th Army Corps of Epirus and the Ionian Islands. In other words it looked, somewhat surprisingly, as if his military career was going to continue onwards and upwards despite its rude interruption.

Once again, however, events beyond his control intervened. In August the following year Mustafa Kemal launched an attack on a dangerously extended two-hundred-mile Greek front. General Papulas had been replaced by a General Hadjianestis. Hadjianestis was much preferred by Prince Andrew but by no means everyone else. In the ensuing campaign the Turks swept all before them. Smyrna was sacked with enormous loss of life and the Greeks were expelled from their toehold on the edge of Asia Minor after an occupation which had lasted 2,500 years. There were over a million Greek refugees.

The Royalists attributed this catastrophe to treason by colonels or, in the words of Princess Alice, 'treachery in its own ranks'. Worse still, 'the instigators of this frightful debacle' capitalised on the events by hurrying to Athens and setting up their own military government. The King was overthrown and sent into exile again, while the eight politicians and soldiers judged responsible for the defeat were imprisoned and put on trial. These included Hadjianestis who, along with five others, was executed by firing squad on 28 November 1922.

Throughout Prince Andrew's military campaign, his wife and family spent most of their time on Corfu where Prince Philip was born. Their villa, Mon Repos, was built for the British Government in 1824, a beautiful home set among olives, lemons, oranges, cypress and magnolia.

The new military government originally told Prince Andrew that provided he resigned his commission he could continue to live at Mon Repos. Not for the first time he seems to have been naïve. Colonel Plastiras, the soi-disant 'Leader of the Revolution', had been an officer in Prince Andrew's own 2nd Army Corps and Andrew had reported him to the C-in-C for openly formenting revolution. Years later, in 1944, Plastiras surfaced again at a 'Conference of Great Parties' convened by Winston Churchill. Sir John Colville wrote that his 'fierce mien and waxed moustaches were the cynosure of our eyes', and added that 'the Prime Minister would insist on referring to him as General Plaster-arse.'

A month after he had been assured of his safety, Prince Andrew was arrested and brought to Athens where he was tried in the Chamber of Deputies by a jury of junior officers who, according to Prince Philip's mother, 'had previously decided that he must be shot'.

Of course, the pretext for his trial was the acrimonious disagreement with his Commanding Officer in Asia Minor the previous year. He was accordingly found guilty of disobedience to orders and abandoning his post in the face of the enemy.

Princess Alice, in Athens, had been appealing on Andrew's behalf to leaders around the world. Most tellingly, her younger brother Louis Mountbatten managed to obtain an audience with King George V and with the British Prime Minister, Bonar Law. Lord Curzon, the Foreign Secretary, sent for Commander Gerald Talbot, previously

Naval Attaché in Athens and currently doing cloak-and-dagger work in Geneva.

Princess Alice wrote, 'The way in which Sir Gerald, for he was afterwards knighted by the King for his services, accomplished this miracle is for him one day to relate. Suffice it to say, that he successfully got the author [Prince Andrew] out of the clutches of the military dictators and brought him and his family away from Greece on the day after the trial in a British man-of-war.' She and her husband, she added, 'owe a deep debt of gratitude to HM the King for the promptitude and efficacy of his action'.

Prince Andrew never forgave and never forgot. In his apologia he wrote:

I cannot bring this sad account to a close without emphasising the monstrosity of this crime. For the first time after many centuries, since the time of the Byzantine rulers, a Greek King and a Greek army trod the immense plains of Asia Minor. Full of eagerness, faith and self-sacrifice, the Greek soldier threw himself into the age-old struggle of his race – the struggle of civilisation against Asiatic barbarism.

The glitter of Greek bayonets was seen once more on the fields of Kiutahia and Eski-Shehr, on the Twin Mountains, on the shores of the Sakharia and in the Axylos desert. Gordium, Justianopolis, once more heard the shouts of Greek victory, the echoes reaching as far as Angora. These achievements were realised at the cost of much pure and honourable blood, shed by the Greek soldier with heroic abnegation, because he knew that his sacrifice was made for the grandeur of Hellas . . .

And so Prince Andrew took his family into exile. It was the end of his life as a professional soldier.

# 4

# 'From His Childhood Onward . . .'

'From his childhood onward this boy [the future Edward VIII]
will be surrounded by sycophants and flatterers by the score'
KEIR HARDIE
HOUSE OF COMMONS 28 JUNE 1894

After their sudden and dramatic departure from Corfu, their
next permanent home was in France. Throughout the 1920s
Prince Andrew, Princess Alice and their children lived in
St Cloud on the outskirts of Paris. The house was a lodge
in the large garden of a bigger mansion belonging to Prince Andrew's
brother George. Prince George had married a rich heiress, Princess
Marie Bonaparte. Princess Marie was the granddaughter of a Monsieur
Blanc who founded the casino at Monte Carlo. She was also a bona
fide member of the Bonaparte family as Napoleon's brother, Lucien,
was her great-grandfather but in the straitened circumstances of their
exile the Greek princes were more in need of money than of breeding.
Prince Philip's parents were not well-off but at least he had a rich
uncle with a house to spare.

Perhaps one can exaggerate the oddity of this situation. An infant
prince of multinational extraction suddenly finds himself thrown out
of the country of his birth. He travels across Europe to stay briefly
at Kensington Palace with his maternal grandmother, the Dowager
Marchioness of Milford Haven, then moves to an apartment near the

Bois de Boulogne (also belonging to Uncle George and Aunt Marie) before ending up at the house in St Cloud. He is very much the baby of the family for his father is thirty-nine years older than him and his mother thirty-six. His sisters Margarita and Theodora are sixteen and fifteen years older so that they seem more like aunts than siblings. Even Cecile and Sophie, born in 1911 and 1914, are his seniors by ten and seven years. Look at the pictures taken to mark his parents' silver wedding in 1928. There is father, very much the boulevardier, all tall slim monocled elegance arm in arm with his four striking daughters. They look as if they are going to soft-shoe-shuffle along the promenade to the strains of 'You're the cream in my coffee' or 'Button up your overcoat'. And now look at mother and son, she elegant but slightly severe and he faintly wistful, a small boy in a sailor suit. He looks the archetypal baby brother.

Today the Duke is dismissive about the effect of exile on himself. 'I was barely a year old when the family went into exile,' he points out, 'so I don't think I suffered the same disorientation.' His cousin Alexandra, who later married King Peter of Yugoslavia, believed that Paris was so full of 'cousins and uncles, so many arrivals and departures of the Hesse family and Mountbattens' that Philip would not have been aware that his father was under formal sentence of banishment. Nevertheless, something of the disorientation of the others must have communicated itself to him, however subtly and silently. To be up-rooted from your home and dumped in a strange country to live, in effect, off the charity of your relations can hardly be other than un-settling, even if you are less than two years old.

And they *were* poor. It was a relative poverty, of course. They were not starving; all five children went to private schools; Prince Andrew even managed to go on employing a valet, though in reality he was more of a general factotum, and not very well paid. Prince Andrew was entitled to a pension, but his son suspects that this was not paid. They were funded by various relations including the Mountbattens, but there was none of the resentment that one might expect because of these disparities in wealth. Prince Philip remembers a happy extended family with his Uncle George's two daughters and his Uncle Nich-olas's three. One of these, Marina, later became Duchess of Kent.

Philip's cousin, Queen Alexandra of Yugoslavia, much the same age as him and a regular companion in youth and childhood, describes visits to their royal relations in Romania. 'Even now,' she wrote in her 1959 biography of the Prince, 'I can see our nannies all cheerfully sitting down to tea with bowls of caviare.' Even though she insists that Romanian caviare in those days was cheaper than jam, it is still a compelling image of untrammelled wealth and extravagance. Aunty 'Missy', otherwise known as Queen Helen of Romania, 'donned full dress for dinner every evening with tiara and diamonds'. Prince Philip thinks these descriptions fanciful.

It was never like that at St Cloud. The girls dressed, some of the time at least, in hand-me-downs from Princess Alice's rich relations – Edwina Mountbatten even had extra seams let into her clothes so that they could be let out for the larger Greek princesses. Philip himself was, according to his cousin Alexandra, 'trained to save and economise better than other children, so much so that he even acquired a reputation for being mean'.

'We never had any money,' says Princess Sophie. 'The Greek royals never used their position to hoard money.'

Alas, Philip's father was in no position to earn it either. His whole life had been dedicated to Greece and to serving his country as an army officer. He knew nothing else and so every day he would take the train in to the centre of Paris and meet other exiles to talk politics and plot, in a hopeful but hopeless way, the chances of a return to the country he loved. The one real task he allowed himself was the writing of his autobiographical *Towards Disaster*, published by John Murray in 1930, and translated from Greek into English by Princess Alice. Even this was a minor disaster. It was too obviously self-serving to convince and Murray printed only 2,002 copies. The book sold very slowly although the terms of the contract were unusually generous. When I asked the latest generation of Murray why this should have been so, he replied, rather sadly, 'John Murray was a bit of a snob.'

One should not fall into the trap of over-dramatising the tragedy of Philip's position. His father was far from being as melancholy as his situation might suggest. 'He had such unbelievable charm,' says Princess Sophie. 'I think Charles has inherited that a bit. He had a tremendous sense of humour.' He and Philip 'used to laugh together like mad'. And wittingly or not, he passed on gifts and attributes. He was, for instance, a talented painter, though Philip never realised this until, in adult life, he too became an enthusiastic artist. And he had a way with animals which must have communicated itself to his son. 'He *loved* animals,' says Princess Sophie, 'and they loved him. If he went to the zoo he could scratch the parrots under their beaks and monkeys behind their ears.'

Their mother, meanwhile, busied herself with a boutique in the Faubourg St Honoré, called 'Hellas', which sold traditional Greek products from embroidery to honey, not so much to mitigate her own family's parlous circumstances as to help out other Greek expatriates whose situation was even worse than hers. Princess Alice was an eccentric character but she remained, despite everything, resolutely unbowed and, to the end of her life, extremely formidable. Strong men trembled before her. 'My Uncle Dickie was terrified of her,' says Princess Sophie. Since Uncle Dickie always appeared to be one of the least easily terrified men of the century this struck me as an astonishing revelation. 'Remember,' explains the Princess, 'that she was fifteen years older than him. He would always ask me to speak to her on his behalf. "Oh, Dickie, you old fool", she used to say to him.' And he would quail. Because she later became a nun, people have thought of her as an extreme puritan but she was more complex than that. Even after taking orders she was keen on strong coffee and strong cigarettes. And she had a will of iron.

For Philip it was very much a female-dominated family. Indeed, not until his own sons grew up did he experience a family life which was anything other than a matriarchal sorority. His sisters, convinced that their parents were spoiling their baby brother, were sometimes hard on him. Since the parents did not really spoil him, the sisters' fierceness was founded in affection. All the same, he was surrounded, from the first, by adoring women. In those early days it was not just relations either. There were governesses, ladies-in-waiting, and above all the divine Nanny, whom everybody so adored. Sadly, she developed arthritis despite trying every conceivable remedy including Christian Science, and had to retire to South Africa. Her grave in Simonstown bears the legend: 'In loving gratitude from Prince and Princess Andrew of Greece and their five children'. A poignant coda to a saga which so often seems touched by loneliness and exile.

Philip's first school was officially called the MacJannet Country Day and Boarding School though it was universally known as The Elms, after the building in which it was housed. Donald MacJannet was a graduate of Tufts University in Massachusetts and he and his wife ran a smart pre-preparatory establishment for the children of rich Americans in Paris. If one had planned an exercise in disorientation technique, one could hardly have done better. After a while he used to bicycle there on a machine he apparently bought with his own pocket money augmented by the pound note which the King of Sweden, married to his Aunt Louise, sent him every year at Christmas.

School reports and diagnoses are intrinsically untrustworthy documents but MacJannet described him as 'rugged, boisterous . . . but always remarkably polite'. He added that he was 'full of energy' and 'got along well with other children'. The sub-text is interesting. It sounds as if the headmaster is saying that his pupil had immaculate manners but was a bit of a handful. The same hidden meaning is implicit in a letter Princess Alice wrote to MacJannet in September 1929. Evidently there had been some confusion about whether Prince Philip, now eight years old, would be returning to The Elms for the autumn term.

Princess Alice continues, 'I am hoping that you have the intention of forming a "cub" company as Philip is too young to be a "scout" and his character and clever fingers well fit him to be a "cub", and the training would have such an excellent influence on him, in turning his great vitality to good use. I should be infinitely grateful if you could manage it as soon as possible.' I feel I can detect a hint of maternal desperation. 'Alice, Princess of Greece', as she signed herself, was now in her mid-forties, and on the verge of a serious breakdown. Her four girls were still unmarried even though the two eldest were now in their early twenties. Her husband showed no prospect of settling down and there was very little money coming in. A tearaway nine-year-old son was the last straw.

His cousin Alexandra remembers Philip on holidays wandering off on solitary expeditions and returning 'without explanation with torn clothes, cuts and bruises'. At the seaside it was 'always Philip who ventured out of his depth or who rounded-up other boys encountered on the beach and organised intensive castle-building brigades'. He was an insatiable climber of trees. On one occasion, staying with Queen Sophie of Greece and her sister, the Landgravine of Hesse, Philip, she recalled, released all the pigs from their sties and beat them up to the lawn where the adults were taking an elegant tea. The stampeding pigs wrought a delicious havoc among the cucumber sandwiches. The Duke, however, says he *never* stayed at Queen Sophie's, and only once with the Landgravine of Hesse. And he has absolutely no recollection of anything to do with pigs.

Mr MacJannet's fears were therefore well founded. It was high time the boy was sent away to school. Princess Sophie says that their father's own memories of his strict and rather odd Greek military education played an important part in what to do with Philip. He said, 'I don't want him treated the way I was so I want him to be educated in England.'

The school chosen was Cheam, the oldest preparatory school in England. A 'preparatory' school is one which prepares its pupils for entry to one or other of the English 'public' schools. The 'public' schools would be described anywhere else but England as 'private' schools and are still, as they were in the 1930s, expensive and exclusive. Admittance to them was achieved not just by paying fees but also by passing an exam known as the Common Entrance. In those days this would have been heavy on Latin, Greek (Ancient), English Literature, Arithmetic and French, with a strong emphasis in all subjects on learning by rote. Cheam was conservative and conventional, muscular and Christian. Discipline was strict and when Philip later returned as a famous old boy he introduced his former headmaster, the Revd Harold Taylor, as the man who had caned him as a child and who, by inference, had helped to make a man of him. In later life the Duke remains an advocate of corporal punishment as an educational aid though he has a much less favourable view of the Classics and would prefer to see science take its place in the curriculum. In this, as in other matters, he has lived to see his own unorthodox views become accepted as conventional wisdom. For better or for worse, the classicists are on the run.

Most prep schools were founded in the nineteenth century or even later. Cheam, however, was established in the early seventeenth century and had been in the Surrey town of that name since being forced to flee from London during the Great Plague.* Now a nondescript London suburb, Cheam used to be a country market town. Its reputation was irretrievably wrecked by the comedian Tony Hancock who used it to symbolise all that was inadequate about suburbia. For more than two hundred years, however, the school remained there on a thirteen-acre site where it educated two Indian viceroys, two Speakers of the House of Commons, the Commander-in-Chief of the Gallipoli landings; Lord Randolph Churchill and a cousin of the diarist Samuel Pepys. These are the school's most honoured sons – a rather dim roster after three hundred years of educating the privileged, but Cheam, recalls the Duke, was never particularly 'grand'. The only other titled boy in his day was his cousin David.

The school was sometimes referred to as 'Old Tabor's' after a Victorian headmaster named Tabor who was in the habit of addressing his pupils on a carefully graded scale of respect: 'my darling child' for peers, 'my dear child' for the sons of peers and 'my child' for commoners. Obsequiousness on this level had died out by the twentieth century and, indeed, the Duke thinks the school of his day was re-

---

* It has now moved to rural Berkshire.

markably unsnobbish. The connection with his family had begun some twenty years earlier when his grandfather, Prince Louis of Battenberg, had been so impressed by a brace of ex-Cheam midshipmen that he decided to send his son George there. George, in turn, sent his son David to Cheam, and he, Prince Philip's cousin and two years his senior, became his closest schoolfriend and, later, as Marquess of Milford Haven, best man at his wedding.

'I used to get excited letters in a large schoolboy hand,' recalled Philip's cousin Alexandra. He wrote about the school diving competition which he won and about the high jump in which he came equal first. He also won the under-twelve hurdles. One of his teachers remembers him as 'very charming and very mischievous', adding, 'I remember him once flicking an ink pellet at me in class. He was a good shot.' He learned cricket and finished the 1932 season with an average of twelve and the report, 'An improved cricketer all round. Very lively in the field.' Academically he did not shine. In his letters to his cousin there was never 'a word about the harder core of school subjects'. When he won the Form III French prize Alexandra laughed and asked what the handicap was. 'When he sheepishly confessed that there had been none, I asked him jolly well why not after all the years he had lived in Paris.' There was an evaluation system at Cheam based on performance in work and games and expressed in 'gains' and 'losses'. In the Lent term of 1931 Philip had no gains at all and in the Michaelmas term he had forty-four losses. It does sound as if the time-honoured remark in his school reports, 'Could do better if he tried', was a fair comment on his performance at this ancient English institution.

His attendance at Cheam moved him into the English sphere of influence in more ways than one. His uncle, George Milford Haven, had a house called Lynden Manor at Holyport, a pretty village between Windsor and Maidenhead, some twenty miles from London, and during his Cheam years this became Philip's home from home. George Milford Haven 'assumed the role of a surrogate father' and was one of the major figures in this adolescent exile. During this period Uncle Dickie was serving in the Mediterranean and simply not in a position to exert a dominating influence in Prince Philip's life. George Milford Haven was an altogether less bombastic presence than his younger brother but that did not prevent him from becoming a father figure. In many ways, too, Philip's cousin David became the brother he had never had.

Sadly there were negative as well as positive reasons for his being moved from continental Europe to England. In 1931 Princess Alice had what her daughter Sophie now describes as 'this sort of break-down'. Prince Andrew was away from home more and more and this cannot have helped. Modern medicine would almost certainly have alleviated her problems but even the most exclusive Swiss sanatoriums seemed powerless to help her. 'And then,' continues Sophie, 'we all disappeared and the house in St Cloud was closed down.'

It was not just father's absence and mother's illness which precipi-tated this sudden family collapse. 'We four sisters all got married between December 1930 and August 1931,' says Princess Sophie, 'and Philip was nine and ten at the time.' All four married members of the German aristocracy. Sophie herself, though only sixteen, was the first. She married Prince Christopher of Hesse, popularly known as 'Cri', who was later shot down and killed while flying with the Luftwaffe over Italy. The second youngest, Cecile, was the next. Her groom was George Donatus, heir to the Duchy of Hesse-Darmstadt. The Hessians made a habit of diminutive sobriquets and he was known to family and friends as 'Don'. Margarita married Prince Godfrey of Hohenlohe-Langenburg and, finally, Theodora married Berthold, the Margrave of Baden.

The ten-year-old Prince Philip was already an unusually inter-national and multilingual child. 'My mother,' says Princess Sophie, 'always spoke to us in English so that was always our first language; later we had a French governess; and then we all married Germans. Philip had a smattering of all four languages.' The fourth language she is referring to is Greek. Princess Sophie laughingly says that her brother's efforts in this language qualify only as 'kitchen Greek', though he can carry on conversations. So, if language is a defining influence on nationality, then Greece is one of the less important coun-tries in the Prince's make-up. His only conscious memories of Greece are the funeral of King Constantine, Queen Olga and Queen Sophie in 1936;* Queen Frederica's wedding; and two holidays there with his mother.

Perhaps one should enter a caveat here. His cousin Prince Michael of Greece has recently offered an interesting interpretation of what 'Greekness' means, at least to a member of the Greek royal house.

'The Greek royal family,' he writes, 'is the fruit of an unlikely union, a union between the descendants of Vikings with those of

---

* All three died in exile but were finally buried in one ceremony in Athens after one of the periodic restorations of the Greek Monarchy.

Antiquity and Byzantium. Yet, as frequently occurs in such odd alli-
ances, the result has been, and still remains, a happy one. Although
we did not start in Greece we belong to Greece. Unless one speaks
with racial bias, Greekness does not imply membership of an ethnic
group. On the contrary, it is always used to mean (and I like to think,
still does mean) partaking in a certain spiritual outlook, religion and
language; sharing a common body of knowledge and appreciation of
a way of life.'

An interesting point of view. Prince Philip remains very much part
of the Greek royal house and perhaps that does mean that he has a
Greekness of the sort Prince Michael has conjured up. But if one *is*
talking in a more conventional and narrow way, he himself is adamant: 'I certainly never felt "nostalgic" about Greece,' he replied
when I put it to him. 'A grandfather assassinated and a father con-
demned to death does not endear me to the perpetrators.'

Even before 1931 he must have had a very disturbed sense of nationality but the only real family home of his own had been in France.
Now, quite without warning, he had a series of new German homes
– the castles of his four sisters and brothers-in-law – and English
equivalents with his Uncle George Milford Haven, his grandmother,
the Dowager Duchess at Kensington Palace, and – though this came
later – with his Uncle Dickie, Lord Mountbatten.

# 'Eccentric Perhaps'

'Eccentric perhaps, innovator certainly,
great beyond doubt'
*Foreword to 'An Appreciation of Kurt Hahn'*
PRINCE PHILIP
BUCKINGHAM PALACE 1975

The Duke is, characteristically, inclined to minimise the eccentricity of the school which played the most significant part in his education but, at least to those who did not go there, Gordonstoun has always seemed highly unusual. Although loosely categorised as one of Britain's 'public' schools it has, since its foundation in 1934, been markedly different to those essentially orthodox and regimented institutions with their traditional emphasis on team games, corporal punishment (now, mercifully, a thing of the past), social snobbery and generally conservative, not to say Conservative, outlook on life.

For a start, Gordonstoun was not founded by monks or city businessmen or muscular Christian Victorians. Its principal founder was Kurt Hahn, a German Jew, forced to flee from the Nazis not only because of his Jewishness but because of his profound and outspoken opposition to Hitler and all his works. Hahn had been secretary and friend to Prince Max of Baden, whose son Berthold married the Duke's sister, Theodora ('Dolla'). Prince Max himself was the last Imperial Chancellor of Germany and arranged for the Kaiser's abdication. He later took to philanthropy and became head of the German Red Cross.

Hahn first met Prince Max during the war while acting as an expert on the British press, interpreting and commentating on its opinions and news reporting, first for the German Foreign Office and later for the Supreme Command. Before the war he had spent four years reading Greats at Christ Church, Oxford, though he left the university without taking his final degree. This period was interrupted by major brain surgery which led to a silver plate being implanted in his skull. As a result of this Hahn had a lifelong aversion to sunlight, affecting a flowing black cape and wide-brimmed hat which enhanced a reputation for eccentricity founded on an other-worldliness which, though the Duke disagrees, I cannot help feeling he deliberately fostered.

One friend and former pupil remembers taking Hahn for a drive in his car and being warned, as they set off, that he was not to be alarmed if his passenger covered his head with a green cloth. Hahn stories are as numerous and legendary as Spoonerisms. Once in London he hailed a taxi and told him to drive to 'Hopeman 266'. This was his Morayshire telephone number. At breakfast once the school watched agog as he poured coffee into his cup until it overflowed on to his morning's correspondence, all the while protesting, 'No more . . . thank you . . . that's quite enough.' I remember him arriving at my parents' house many years later, swaddled in black, with protective glasses that seemed more like goggles. He was an extraordinary sight scuttling indoors to escape the sun's rays like an old crow pursued by hawks.

In 1919 Hahn accompanied the banker Carl Joseph Melchior to the peace negotiations at Versailles and then went back to Prince Max who had retired to the Baden family home, Schloss Salem, a former Cistercian monastery on the shores of Lake Constanz. There the two of them decided to found a school modelled on a combination of Plato and their own highly personalised idea of what the traditional English public school was all about. Prince Max once said of his creation, 'I am proud of the fact that there is nothing original here. We have cribbed from everywhere, from the public schools, from Goethe, from Plato, from the Boy Scouts.' Asked if he should not aspire to something less derivative Prince Max's response was, 'In education, as in medicine, you must harvest the wisdom of a thousand years. If you ever come to a surgeon and he wants to extract your appendix in the most original manner possible, I would strongly advise you to go to another surgeon.' In fact, even though the individual components were nothing new, the mix was highly individual. It *was* an odd notion. Nevertheless the school survives to this day (though it is leaving Salem when the present lease expires) and it has spawned a number of well-known offspring.

After the disintegration of his family in 1930 and 1931 Philip spent holidays with his sister and brother-in-law at Salem and it was there that he first met Hahn. 'Even then,' he recalls, 'Hahn was an almost legendary character. Small boys do not normally have much time to be impressed by other boys' masters, but there was an air about Hahn which commanded instant wariness and respect. Apart from that, his famous mannerisms – the stooping gait, the ball of handkerchief in the mouth, the large-brimmed hat and the flashing quizzical eye – all helped to signal the presence of an exceptional being.'

It seemed only logical that once he had finished his time at Cheam, the young Philip should be removed from conventional English education and sent to Salem where he could be kept under the watchful eye of his sister and her new Baden relations. Moreover his mother, after dispiriting experiences in a series of Swiss sanitoriums, was now herself installed at Salem dressed in the nun's habit which she wore until the end of her life (even on the Buckingham Palace balcony) and devoting herself to God and good works. It seemed only right that she and her little boy should be together.

Hahn had already left Salem by the time Prince Philip arrived there as a pupil; and in fact his first two terms were at a school annexe by the lake. He did not stay long. This was not the fault of the school nor of his new relations, of whom he became extremely fond. The trouble was that Philip quickly demonstrated an irreverence for the increasingly powerful Nazis which matched the contempt in which they were held by Hahn. Philip was particularly entertained by the 'Heil Hitler' salute. At Cheam when a boy raised his arm in this manner it did not signify salutation but simply meant that the boy wanted to ask permission to go to the lavatory. The spectacle of grown men in military uniform apparently asking, en masse, 'Please, sir, may I be excused?' struck Philip as extraordinarily funny and he made no attempt to conceal his amusement. The Nazis did not like being laughed at.

He attributes the brevity of his stay at Salem entirely to the fact that 'the Nazis were moving in'. Critics of the Duke are still, incidentally, adept at suggesting that he was some sort of crypto-Nazi himself. One of his latest biographers has written, 'Philip may well have heard the name of Hitler, who was much discussed and admired among some in the House of Hesse, which welcomed the advent of National Socialism.' Talk about guilt by association and innuendo. At Salem there was no such welcome or admiration. 'As none of that family was at all enthusiastic about them [the Nazis] it was thought best that I should move out!!' Prince Philip wrote in November 1990

– the double exclamation marks are his. He added, 'It was certainly a great relief to me.'

It is worth remembering that although Philip's sisters had all married Germans he did not feel German himself. Even now he says that he really feels 'international', though his German was rather better than another English pupil's at Salem. This boy's command of the language was so inadequate on first arriving that when Philip showed him around the school he said, in the vegetable garden, 'So, this is where we become tomatoes.' He was quite unaware that 'bekommen' means 'to get'. At least Philip could manage that.

Philip's anti-Nazi attitudes went well beyond derisory prep-school humour. When a Jewish fellow-pupil had his head shaved by anti-Semites Philip lent him his Cheam school cap to hide the indignity. Hahn himself had baited the Nazis in an even more dangerous manner. In 1932 five Nazis kicked a young Communist to death in front of his mother and were promptly rewarded with a telegram of congratulation from the Führer. An incensed Hahn retaliated by circulating every Salem old boy with an ultimatum: Salem or the Nazi Party. You could not, argued Hahn, swear allegiance to the two ideals. It was an either/or.

Hitler became Chancellor of Germany in 1933, some fifteen years after Prince Max had held the same position. In March that year Hahn was arrested. There is some dispute about the true facts surrounding his imprisonment. One school of thought suggests that it was not what it seemed but was actually a protective measure by well-wishers who had learned of a plot to kill him during a hockey match that afternoon. He was released soon afterwards, thanks to the personal intervention of Ramsay MacDonald and others, but it was obviously only a matter of time before the Nazis locked him up again. So Hahn fled to Britain, ending up in a remote corner of Scotland which he had first come to love some twenty years earlier before the outbreak of the Great War.

His destiny was already inextricably linked with Morayshire because it was a local landowner, Captain Sir Mansfield Smith-Cumming, who had persuaded the pioneering neuro-surgeon Sir Victor Horsley to perform the operation on Hahn's head which probably saved and certainly prolonged his life. The Smith-Cumming family owned a mansion between Elgin, the county town of Morayshire, and the forbidding waters of the Moray Firth. This house, Gordonstoun, was still inhabited by the elderly Lady May Gordon-Cumming, but the family were prepared to let and, ultimately, to sell it. The estate consisted of a great house, rather slab-like and forbidding on one front, more gracious and welcoming on the other, and a curious set of farm buildings known as 'The Round Square'. This had been constructed by Sir Robert Gordon, the third baronet. Sir Robert sold his soul to the devil who told him that he would come and collect his dues in a corner. The frightened man's solution was to build a courtyard with no corners at all. This curved building still houses a boys' house (the school has been co-educational since 1970) and the school library but it could not save Sir Robert, who was found dead in 1704 with 'the devil's teeth marks' in his neck. His ghost is still reputed to haunt the place. Apart from these two buildings there were three hundred acres largely composed of what had once been 'The Bog of Plewlands'.

In 1934 Hahn, encouraged by numerous friends such as his local Oxford contemporaries, Willie Calder, later Professor of Greek at Edinburgh, and Evan Barron, owner of the *Inverness Courier*, took Gordonstoun on a full repairing lease and set about establishing a new Salem in Scotland. 'It was,' says Prince Philip, looking back on the experiment a lifetime later, 'a bit like re-inventing the wheel.' Salem had been, in part, an effort to introduce the English public school to Germany. Now Hahn was bringing it back home.

Today Gordonstoun looks, at least superficially, very like its supposedly more conventional rivals. One's first impression on a grey, cloud-scudding November day is of serried ranks of rugger posts, of modern buildings, and of girls and boys in uniform grey-blue sweaters with dark grey skirts or long trousers. Most of this represents a radical departure from the days of Hahn. He was not, for instance, tremendously enamoured of traditional team games and at one stage positively forbad boys to play cricket. 'We have dethroned games,' he once remarked with pride. He was a passionate hockey player, but felt that the day-in, day-out cricket and rugby of traditional public schools was just too much. The rugger posts might, therefore, have disturbed him, at least in their modern quantity. The new, for the most part utilitarian, buildings would also have surprised him for the school that he founded with just two pupils has grown to almost five hundred children and been the beneficiary of numerous grants from such diverse sources as Prince Philip and the Bernard Sunley Foundation, which helped to finance the Technology Centre and the school sailing ship. The girls are new since Hahn's day but he was never completely opposed to the idea of co-education. I suspect he would frown on the long trousers. In the 1930s all boys wore shorts. Some still do, but only if they have been handed down from Old Gordonstonian fathers.

The present headmaster, Mark Pyper, only took over in the autumn of 1990 and comes from Sevenoaks, a much more 'ordinary' school in the overpopulated prosperous south-east of England. Until his appointment he had never seen Gordonstoun and was a stranger to Scotland. Still feeling his way, he told me that while the school, in his estimation, remained true to Hahn's values it no longer necessarily espoused his methods. He identified these Hahnian aims as 'independence and discipline' together with the less obvious ones of 'care and compassion'. 'They are all,' he said, 'in equal focus but within a modern educational context.'

When I visited Gordonstoun my host was the second master, David Byatt, a keeper of the Hahnian grail who had known the school's founder all his life. Down in the village of Hopeman we inspected the school's sailing craft moored in the austere harbour which juts out into the Moray Firth. I asked, innocently, if the school taught navigation. 'No,' he said, 'we teach them about themselves. If they learn about the sea, well and good. But that is not the point.'

Prince Philip himself, recalling his sailing experiences at Gordonstoun, once said, 'I was wet, cold, miserable, probably sick, and often scared stiff, but I would not have missed the experience for anything. In any case the discomfort was far outweighed by the moments of intense happiness and excitement. Poets and authors down the centuries have tried to describe those moments but their descriptions, however brilliant, will never compare with one's own experience.'

Hahn, no sailor himself, regarded the Moray Firth as one of his most significant teaching aids. 'My best schoolmaster is the Moray Firth,' he once said. Even now the school's glossy brochure begins its statement of intent with the ringing sentence: 'The school aims to produce balanced men and women who know the value of working hard but who have tried their hands at boats as well as books.'

Hahn himself was an immensely bookish man who had not only studied at Oxford but at the universities of Berlin, Heidelberg, Freiburg, and Göttingen. He had an intense and wayward personal enthusiasm for tennis and hockey but he was no sort of athlete, nor seaman, nor mountaineer. His interest in the outdoor life was essentially vicarious and perhaps all the more intense for being so. There is a very real sense in which he seemed to be living much of his life through his more physically gifted and active pupils and protégés.

'Young people today,' he pronounced, 'are surrounded by a sick civilisation; they are in danger of being affected by a fivefold decay:

The decay of fitness,
The decay of initiative and enterprise,
The decay of care and skill,
The decay of self-discipline,
The decay of compassion.'

His school was designed to eliminate this fivefold decay and Prince Philip was to prove one of its star pupils. From the very beginning Hahn was able to enlist the support of the great and the good. One of his earliest supporters was the headmaster of Eton, Claude Elliott. William Temple, later Archbishop of Canterbury, said that, 'I regard it as really important to our national welfare that Gordonstoun should continue and that Dr Hahn should have the opportunity to make his great contribution to our educational system and through it to the nation's life.' Hahn was always highly regarded by men whose opinions counted.

Yet despite such Establishment approval Hahn and his school were never in the mainstream, never orthodox, never wholly accepted by the complacent core of British education. The school's geographical location, far out on the Celtic fringe, and Hahn's own utterly un-English personality and background made this almost inevitable. He was one of nature's outsiders. One candidate for a teaching post protested in mid-interview that he was completely unsuited for the job and had never in his entire life been a schoolmaster. 'That does not matter,' said Hahn, 'I do not like schoolmasters.'

The comment is entirely typical of Hahn and is also precisely the sort of reaction one would expect from the Duke. For both men, conventional wisdom is not something to be received but to be questioned. It is entirely possible, of course, that this restless questioning which is an essential – arguably dominant – part of the Duke's personality has always been there and comes with the genes. But Hahn's attitudes must have had some effect.

Jim Orr, later the Duke's private secretary, was one of the earliest recruits at Gordonstoun, joining as a seventeen-year-old dropout from Harrow and becoming head of school or 'Guardian' in the Platonic idiom which Hahn adopted. 'We must not forget those pioneer days,' he says. 'We were penniless. We were under grave suspicion with the local population – "There are Nazis under every bed and machine gunners in the trees. The Germans are familiar with every inch of the coast as Gordonstoun is full of spies" – The English boys were not excluded from these misguided fears.'

Orr remembers the boy Philip for his friendliness, his sense of fun, for his 'white, white hair' and for the fact that he never 'swanked about his relatives'. As at Cheam, he was a boy with no surname. He was plain 'Philip' or, more formally, 'Philip of Greece'. The Scots pronounced the first 'i' like an 'a' and the second like a 'u', so he was universally hailed as 'Fallup'. Of the twenty-seven boys at Gordonstoun when he arrived in the autumn of 1934, a number were German exiles. There was a boy called Reggie with only one leg. Characteristically Hahn made him play games and he turned into a first-rate goalkeeper. There was another boy – later killed during the war – with a glass eye and even one, Sandy Kennedy, who had polio and had to be carried everywhere on a stretcher. He used to be set down under a tree by the west door where everyone had to pass him at least once a day, exchanging a greeting or stopping for a chat. Hahn made him a 'colour-bearer candidate' – the most junior sort of prefect. The founding headmaster loved waifs and strays, the down-and-out, the underprivileged. 'He hated success,' says Orr, 'but he loved an idiot, like myself, for whom he had to battle a bit. "You look for faults, Jim," he once told me. "I look for pure gold and I usually find it."'

Prince Philip's contemporaries think that Hahn was quite hard on the young rootless royal. 'Philip was a little bit cheeky with Hahn,' according to one, 'but Hahn brought him down with a bump.' The same schoolfriend says that Philip could be sulky at times and that Hahn's verdict on him was that his best was first class but that his second-best was very inferior. Robert Varvill, whose father was the school bursar, recalls sharing the part of 'a gentleman' with Philip in the annual Shakespeare. It was *Hamlet* that year, says Varvill, and the two boys rebelled and said they would not act ' You will,' said Hahn. 'You will each play half a gentleman.'

Philip was not a theatrical; he was not noticeably keen on work. One man who sailed with him a great deal said, 'He's a good seaman, but not *particularly* gifted.' He seems to have fitted in better than most and was more self-assured. The photographs show a thin, lanky lad but one of his friends remembers him as 'slightly podgy'. Hahn had his own little kitchenette, curtained off from the rest of the school and under the rule of the cook, Fraülein Berger. Privileged boys would sometimes sneak in and help themselves to a snack. Philip was among them and to this day he remains, despite that enviably taut figure, a considerable 'foody' of wayward taste.

Much later Hahn put together an assessment of Philip for public consumption. The words which stand out are 'spirit . . . joy . . .

sadness . . . laughter . . . merriness . . . intelligence . . . reckless-
ness . . . wildness.' Hahn found him 'often naughty, never nasty' and
detected a 'determination not to exert himself more than was necessary
to avoid trouble'. He sounds like a bit of a Jack-the-lad.

For about eight months of the year Philip was at school but the
holidays were more of a problem. The dispersal of his family meant
that he had no one single and obvious home to go to. And as the years
passed Germany became less and less appealing from a political point
of view. 'He was impossible under the Nazis,' says his sister Sophie.
Nevertheless he did stay with his German relations frequently and he
now thinks that his sisters and brothers-in-law were among the more
important influences in his life. 'To begin with I saw more of my third
sister's husband (George Donatus of Hesse) as I usually spent most of
my holidays with them in Darmstadt or at Wolfsgarten,' he says. His
sister Sophie says that 'Don' was 'a great favourite with all of us, with
enormous charm and good looks and an intense sense of humour'.

His father was often at Wolfsgarten, too, for although he was now
living in Monte Carlo he was never estranged from his children.
Photographs show him relaxed and smiling in the garden, always
wearing that monocle. Prince Philip's cousin, Alexandra, remembers
his father showing her 'absurd photographs' of him 'peeking from behind a potted plant in a nativity play or looking super-tough in hockey
or rugger kit'. There is a melancholy about the idea of Prince Andrew
despite his sense of humour – 'as funny as all-get-out', remarked the
writer Alastair Forbes who heard about him from the Kents at
Coppins. He was obviously devoted to his little boy and yet effectively
abrogated any true responsibility for him. Queen Alexandra remembers that he always spoke of his son with pride.

'"What do you think now?" he would ask with a twinkle. "Philip
has been building a pigsty and has promised to send me a photograph!" Or he would say "I have had another school report" and he
would try to hide his pleasure, looking at me very hard through his
monocle, shaking his head with mock severity.'

Wolfsgarten is a beautiful country house, an old hunting lodge
built round a courtyard in the woods. It is remarkably tranquil considering how close it is today to Frankfurt International Airport. The
windows of the grandest salon in the place are a visitors' book where
house guests scratch their names with a diamond-tipped pen. The
earliest Philip signature on the Wolfsgarten glass is dated 1931, and
he has continued visiting all his life, though the latest signatures are
qualified unexpectedly with the legend, 'Herzog von Edinburg'. Un-

like the colossal Baden home at Salem or the Hesse palace in Darmstadt – flattened by Allied bombing in the war but now rebuilt as a
museum – Wolfsgarten is on a domestic scale, with tranquil gardens
and woodlands. Cecile and George Donatus quickly made it a real
family home, producing two sons and a daughter in quick succession.
Then, in 1937, there was another family tragedy.

George Donatus's younger brother, Prince Louis, was engaged to
be married to Margaret Geddes, daughter of Lord Geddes, formerly
Sir Auchinleck Geddes who had been British Ambassador in Washington. The wedding had been postponed because of the death of the
Grand Duke Ernst Ludwig, George Donatus's father. Margaret and
her fiancé went to Croydon airport to greet the Hesse family who were
flying in for the ceremony but they never arrived. Just outside Ostend
their aircraft ran into freak fog, the wingtip brushed the top of a brick
factory chimney just outside the town and the aircraft plummeted
to the ground. There were no survivors except, briefly, for Cecile's
unborn child.

It was a stunning disaster. The wretched Louis and Margaret
had to go through with their wedding in full mourning with Lord
Mountbatten as best man. Ribbentrop and Lord Geddes signed the
register and then the newly-weds endured a rough crossing ('The
first time I was addressed as "Your Royal Highness" was by the
steward outside the lavatory when I was being violently sick,' says
Princess Margaret). At Brussels their train was met by the Belgian
Royal Family, in black, on the platform. There the bodies were
put aboard and the train proceeded to Darmstadt. 'I arrived with
five coffins,' says the Princess, 'I mean, it's not normal. Everybody
was crying. Even when they were doing the Nazi salute, they were
still crying.' Today the plain red sandstone graves lie side by side
in Darmstadt near the family mausoleum – an inexact copy of the
mausoleum of Galla Placidia in Ravenna. Just to one side is a final
postscript to the tragedy: the grave of their infant daughter
Johanna. She was the only one of the family to be left behind.
Prince Louis and his wife adopted her as their own and just two
years later she died from meningitis.

His Gordonstoun friends say that one of the remarkable things
about Philip was his lack of what they call 'side'. He never swanked,
least of all about being a prince; and he seldom if ever talked about
his relations. This time, however, he was obviously deeply shocked
and his friends knew it. There are photographs of the funeral in the
Wolfsgarten archives. They are not very good ones but they show,

among a sea of German military greatcoats, a slim blond schoolboy in a dark suit. He looks desperately out of place and alone.

After this trauma he spent holidays at Salem with his sister Theodora, known in the family as Dolla. Dolla was the most 'correct' of the sisters and would, according to other members of the family, have made a brilliant Queen of England. Her husband, Berthold of Baden, became a guide and friend. 'He taught me to drive and to fish for trout with a dry fly and must have had a major influence on my character,' says Prince Philip.

'He liked all his brothers-in-law,' says his sister Sophie, 'and got on very well with them in spite of the great age differences. In his holidays he was often together with one or the other and apart from sports and games, he would have lengthy and serious talks with them. He was so interested in everything and they helped to inform him about family relationships, family codes of behaviour, as well as about painting, music, history, politics and so on. He was always very keen to learn and understand things.'

Perhaps inevitably, his English schoolfriends had a different perception of him. To them the young Philip seemed something of an orphan, cast adrift. 'He always had difficulty finding somewhere for the holidays,' one of them recalls. His memory is of Kurt Hahn sitting down with senior boys at Gordonstoun and talking long and hard about where to send Prince Philip once term was over. The Duke insists that Hahn himself was never in any way involved with his holiday plans. He used to arrange expeditions at the end of terms and that was all. It is interesting, however, that his contemporaries at Gordonstoun should retain that kind of memory. It suggests to me that a lot of us have always misunderstood the Duke's circumstances.

In Britain he often stayed with the Wernher family at their Georgian farmhouse in Leicestershire. Sir Harold Wernher was the president of Electrolux and was a Major-General during the war, when he was responsible for the Mulberry harbours. The Wernhers were very rich. Harold's father, Sir Julius, like Prince Philip's brother-in-law, George Donatus, came from Darmstadt. The son of a railway engineer, he had made a fortune from South African gold and diamonds but the relationship with Prince Philip came through Harold's wife, Lady Zia. When I asked their daughter Myra, still a close family friend and a Trustee of the Duke of Edinburgh's Award Scheme, precisely what their relationship was she replied with a matter-of-fact brevity: 'We're sort of cousins. We have the same great-great-grandfather on the Russian side. That was Czar Nicholas the First.' It

*Left and below:* Mother and son. The signed upper picture shows Princess Alice with Prince Philip in 1925 when he was four. This was his mother's favourite photograph. The sailor suit was worn for his parents' silver wedding celebrations in St Cloud three years later.

*Opposite above:* The only known picture of Prince Andrew, Princess Alice and all five children. The photograph, taken at their silver wedding celebrations in 1928, comes from Princess Margaret of Hesse und bei Rhein's private archive at Wolfsgarten where, unfortunately, it has suffered some damage.

*Opposite below:* Prince Philip, second from right, with assorted relations.

St Cloud 7. X. 1903 – 1928

The firing squad in a Robin Hood play at his pre-preparatory school, The Elms at St Cloud. Left to right, Prince Jacques de Bourbon, Prince Philip, Theodore Culbert – son of an American diplomat – and Princess Anne de Bourbon, now the wife of King Michael of Romania.

Messing about in a boat at Hopeman Harbour on the Moray Firth near Gordonstoun.

Clearing the bar in a Gordonstoun high jump.

In the part of Donalbain, son of King Duncan of
Scotland, in the Gordonstoun production of *Macbeth*.

The first proper meeting, in July 1939, between Prince Philip, (in uniform near the back of the picture) and Princess Elizabeth (looking over the railing on the extreme left). The occasion was the visit of King George VI and Queen Elizabeth to the Royal Naval College at Dartmouth where he was a cadet.

Lieutenant-Commander The Duke of Edinburgh taking prayers aboard HMS *Magpie* in the summer of 1951.

Prince Philip's stag party at the Dorchester Hotel on the night before his wedding in 1947. The upper picture is the official Fleet Street photograph. In the lower one, the tables were turned and Prince Philip and his friends photographed the press – before making sure these were the last pictures taken that night.

Sporting a 'full set' of naval whiskers. Princess Elizabeth kept this photograph on her dressing-table during the war.

is extraordinary how polyglot the British can be. Myra Wernher is now married to Major David Butter, Lord Lieutenant for Perth and Kinross. It seems an impossibly long way from the Winter Palace.

'I have been thinking further about this "influence" business,' Prince Philip wrote after I first raised the question, 'and you can certainly add Harold Wernher to the list.'

'He could always have a good discussion with my father,' says Myra. And they did. Often. But holidays with the Wernhers were also fun and games. They rode. They fooled around. Myra remembers one occasion on which she, Philip, her sister Gina and her brother Alex, all hid behind the curtains to spring a surprise on Berry the butler. Before long Berry entered the room and began talking to himself as they knew he would. But, inevitably, he began discussing Prince Philip. This was altogether too embarrassing and the discomfited four had to emerge from behind the curtains before Berry could say anything too disastrous. Alex, like David Milford Haven, became a close friend. In 1942 he was killed in action. 'Philip wrote a letter to my mother after my brother was killed,' says Myra. 'It's so moving, I don't mind telling you I still can't read it.'

Robert Varvill's father, the school bursar, bullied by Hahn out of retirement from Rhodesian railways to take the job, lived in Hopeman, the fishing village a few miles from Gordonstoun. Prince Philip stayed with them and honed his sailing skills on trips in the converted Brixham trawler, the *Diligent*. On such voyages, as in the school schooner, *Prince Louis*, named after his grandfather, or in the two 25-foot cutters also based in Hopeman harbour, Philip took turn and turn about with everyone else. He actually helped build the cutters with a local Hopeman boat-builder. If he was the youngest on board, as often happened, he had to take on the job of ship's cook. Not that he seemed to mind. He had a heavy hand on the butter when it came to the scrambling of eggs.

Throughout these years, however, it was his Uncle George who acted *in loco parentis* though Prince Philip himself says, 'I suppose that my grandmother (Milford Haven) had a greater influence on my character than either of her sons.' But in 1938, less than a year after the death of Cecile and her family, George Milford Haven died of cancer. He was just forty-six years old and Prince Philip could have been forgiven for wondering if there would ever be permanence of any kind in his rootless and shifting existence.

# 'The Floating Bulwark'

'The royal navy of England hath ever been its
greatest defence and ornament; it is its ancient
and natural strength, the floating
bulwark of the island'

SIR WILLIAM BLACKSTONE

The Duke says now that the Royal Air Force would have been
his ideal first choice and you can see why. He has learned to
love flying and, in addition to the hours put in on the various aircraft of the Queen's Flight, he has piloted everything
from Concorde to a single-seat racer. He would have been nineteen
during the Battle of Britain and one of nature's fighter pilots. It is
not too fanciful to imagine him high in the skies over Biggin Hill
engaged in a dogfight duel with the Luftwaffe. In 1970 he told Basil
Boothroyd that, left to his own devices, 'I'd have gone into the Air
Force without a doubt.' He has said the same thing to Air Vice-
Marshal Sir John Severne, a former equerry and one-time Captain of
the Queen's Flight. To have been master of his destiny, in full control
of his own Spitfire or Hurricane, pitting his wits against the elements
and the enemy would have been, for a man like him, bliss. But it was
not to be.

Later he denied that those long, dangerous Gordonstoun hours on
the Moray Firth had anything to do with opting for the Navy. When
an official British Information Services handout offered the opinion
that, 'In choosing a naval career he was following the tradition of the
Mountbatten side of his family', he rewrote it. The official document
continued:

Prince Louis of Battenberg was an Admiral of the Fleet and First Sea Lord; his son, the second Marquess, served in the Royal Navy, like Prince Philip's cousin, the third Marquess, and his uncle, Admiral Lord Mountbatten of Burma.

All this was true, but it was not the truth that he perceived himself, much less that he wanted the rest of us to believe. His own version went:

In choosing a career in one of the services he was following the tradition of both sides of his family. Both his grandfathers served at sea. His father was a career officer in the Greek Army, and both his father's and his mother's brothers served in the Navy.

It was Lord Mountbatten who persuaded his nephew to join the Navy. 'Perhaps the most important contribution that Mountbatten made to his nephew's upbringing was to persuade him not to go into the Air Force but to stick to family tradition and join the Navy.' Kurt Hahn, as adroit a string-puller in his way as Mountbatten, confided in one of his pupils, 'The best thing I ever did for Prince Philip was to prevent Lord Mountbatten getting him into the Navy through the Royal back door.' This sounds bizarre. Even Mountbatten could not have 'fudged' Prince Philip into the Navy; and even if it were possible, Prince Philip would not have allowed it. From his very earliest days the Duke has been averse to stunts and string-pulling. He has also always been his own man, anxious to learn and be advised but, in the end, taking his own decisions in his own way. Mountbatten persuaded; Prince Philip decided.

I am not seeking to diminish the Mountbatten influence, simply to try to put it into perspective. In the course of my conversations with the Duke's family and friends I frequently found myself stumbling across Lord Mountbatten. The responses were often ambiguous. The Wernhers' daughter, Myra, who adored him, said she never thought he influenced his nephew 'here' and pointed a finger at her cranium. The Queen Mother, smiling as beatifically as ever, told me that 'we always took Dickie with a pinch of salt'. Others were less affectionate. Lord Hunt, the leader of the victorious Everest expedition and first director of the Duke of Edinburgh's Award Scheme, recalled a transatlantic flight in 1966 when he sat next to Mountbatten. Mountbatten never drew breath throughout the entire thirteen-hour flight. And what did he talk about? Mountbatten. Of course!

The Duke himself wrote to me, 'Mountbatten certainly had an influence on the course of my life, but not so much on my ideas and attitudes. I suspect he tried too hard to make himself a son out of me.'

Mountbatten came surprisingly late into his nephew's life. In March 1938, for example, he recorded, in his diary, 'Philip was here all last week doing his entrance exams for the Navy. He had his meals with us and he really is killingly funny. I like him very much.' That sounds to me like the remark of a man who is just beginning to know someone. It does not sound like the considered judgement of a surrogate father on a boy he has nurtured all his life.

In any event Prince Philip joined the Navy, excelled in it, came to love it and was sad to leave it prematurely. It is one of the very few regrets to which he is prepared to admit. So many people talk about the frustrations of his life, the constant wish to have been able to pursue some other career and get to the top of it. He himself does not see his life like this.

'As far as I am concerned,' he says, 'there has never been an "if only", except perhaps that I regret not having been able to continue a career in the Navy, although I never imagined that I would reach such dizzy heights as my uncle or Lewin.'

'Lewin' is Admiral of the Fleet Lord Lewin, the most distinguished sailor of his generation and Chief of the Defence Staff during the Falklands campaign. He has known the Duke practically all his adult life, served with him as a midshipman on HMS *Valiant* early in the war, and in the Mediterranean ten years later. He was Commander of the Royal Yacht from 1957 to 1958 and has renewed his friendship more recently as a Trustee of the National Maritime Museum. This last is another of the Duke's many hats. Lord Lewin is unequivocal in his judgement. If the Duke had stayed on in the Navy he would have been First Sea Lord, not Lewin.

The question is hypothetical, but there is no doubt that in the Royal Navy the Duke found his métier. Another witness enters his life in the Navy. Michael Parker, a young Australian, came to England to seek his naval fortune because his father, a captain in the Australian Navy, was at one and the same time a help and a hindrance to his career at home. Parker, as ebullient and extrovert at seventy as ever he can have been at twenty, is unequivocal about his and the Duke's prowess. 'We were good,' he says. 'We were bloody good.'

It had to be worked at, though. Philip did not take his naval exams direct from Gordonstoun, but went to live with a Mr and Mrs Mercer in Cheltenham. Mr Mercer specialised in preparing candidates for naval exams. The Prince worked assiduously, was short of cash, and had no distractions except for what his cousin Alexandra referred to, a touch cryptically, as 'radio or record sessions with the daughter of the house'. When he took the exam he passed sixteenth out of thirty-four successful candidates: perfectly adequate but not at first glance the stuff of which First Sea Lords are made.

There is a slight misapprehension about Prince Philip's Dartmouth. Lord Lewin puts it succinctly. 'PP wasn't at Dartmouth as most people understand it. He wasn't a thirteen-year-old entry, he entered at eighteen from Gordonstoun and if the war hadn't been approaching would have gone to a Training Cruiser. Instead his term went to some huts in a remote corner of the college for a few months' initial training!'

The traditional naval training for officers at the Royal Naval College, Dartmouth, and its predecessor, Osborne on the Isle of Wight, began at the age of thirteen, when most preparatory-school boys went to their more conventional public schools. This was regarded by an influential strand of Royal Naval thinkers as the 'correct' way of training officers. In 1912, Winston Churchill, never one to let conventional wisdom interfere with common sense, instituted a 'Special Entry' for boys who had been to landlubberish public schools and wanted to become naval officers at the comparatively late age of eighteen or so. Churchill's scheme allowed much greater flexibility and in time of war this was essential. Both world wars would have been over and done before the old Dartmouth system could have trained up a significant increase in the number of naval officers. But with the speedy Special Entry system you could expand at will.

The two schemes coexisted, a little uneasily, until the whole system was reformed in 1954 and everyone – in effect – came in on Special Entry. Until then 'Darts' and 'Specials' operated, in Lord Lewin's phrase, 'a mutual unadmiration society'. The 'huts' were known as 'the Sandquay barracks' and were, says Prince Philip, 'quite substantial buildings'. The usual form was for eighteen-year-old public schoolboys on Special Entry to begin with a three-month 'stationary' training course on the cruiser HMS *Frobisher*. When Prince Philip's time came, however, Britain was preparing for war and HMS *Frobisher* was re-arming. Hence the huts at Dartmouth. The 'Specials' were older than the most of the 'Darts' and that was one reason why they were hidden away in their shabby huts away from the main campus. It was feared they might prove a bad influence.

Prince Philip did well at Dartmouth. Indeed, in one sense his entrance performance was better than one might think at first glance. Although his written work was poor, he scored 380 out of 400 marks in the interview. Lord Lewin remarks that only two people in his own entire entry scored the maximum 400 (one was Lewin!). And as the Duke's earlier biographer, Basil Boothroyd, has pointed out, his written English was, in some respects, still poor. It had plenty of colour and dash but his spelling, as revealed in the midshipman's log that all young officers were required to keep for a year, is distinctly wayward. He was quite unable to spell 'buoy', nearly always putting the 'o' before the 'u'. Boothroyd also spotted too many 's's in 'mistake', no 'x' in except and 'Italien' for 'Italian'.

By the time Philip reached Dartmouth the British Royal Family, in the present Queen Mother's phrase, 'knew all about him'. This was hardly surprising. He was, after all, part of the family even if in its extended European sense. George V's efforts at extricating his parents from their terrible predicament in 1922 were motivated largely by the desire to help kith and kin and since then Philip had been present at a number of royal clan gatherings.

It was not until his time at Dartmouth, however, that he first publicly met his future bride and her parents. In the light of what happened later this day has assumed a symbolic significance. It was in July 1939 and one of those historic occasions whose details are fogged with romance, repetition and retrospection. At the time it seemed, at least to those not intimately involved, as routine as any other royal visit. It would not have looked extraordinary on the day's Court Circular.

HMY *Victoria and Albert*. His Majesty the King and Her Majesty the Queen, Her Royal Highness Princess Elizabeth, and Her Royal Highness Princess Margaret visited the Royal Naval College, Dartmouth. Captain Lord Louis Mountbatten RN was in attendance.

Uncle Dickie had been busy on the River Tyne fitting out the destroyer HMS *Kelly*, but was in attendance as the King's ADC for this short ceremonial cruise in the Royal Yacht. Perhaps he did sense the potential in introducing his handsome eighteen-year-old nephew to the thirteen-year-old heiress to the throne. It would be odd if someone as obsessed with his own dynastic fortunes and connections did not allow a thought of match-making to cross his mind but his official biographer is coy, though suggestive, on the subject. Ziegler makes no mention of the Dartmouth meeting that I can find but when it comes to the formal engagement in 1947 he writes: 'Whether or not their betrothal owed anything to the machinations of Mountbatten, it gave him great satisfaction, on grounds personal as well as dynastic.' Quite so.

It should be added that a prime source for this story is poor Miss Crawford, the royal governess who later turned her hand to royal memoirs of the most treacly kind. 'Crawfie' has entered the national vocabulary as a sort of Mills & Boon version of Boswell. To her we owe the remarks attributed to Princess Elizabeth when Prince Philip took the sisters to the tennis court and entertained them by jumping over the net. 'How good he is!' the future Queen of England is reported to have said. 'How high he can jump!' Hello birds, hello sky, as ffotherington-Thomas used to remark.

What seems incontrovertible is that when the Royal Yacht sailed into the Dart Estuary and to the Naval College, it was discovered that a number of cadets had gone down with one of the infectious diseases popular in such establishments. It might have been mumps or it might have been chicken-pox. Under these circumstances the royal parents decided that their little girls had better not be exposed to infection by attending morning chapel. Cousin Alexandra tells us that it was her Aunt Elizabeth and Uncle Dickie who put their heads together and got Philip out of the morning service and up to the Captain's House where the sisters were eating ginger biscuits and drinking lemonade. She suggests that he, an eighteen-year-old man-of-the-world, was resentful at having to squire a thirteen-year-old girl and her nine-year-old sister, no matter how regal. Nevertheless he carried off the chore or privilege to general satisfaction.

The real set piece, the linchpin of the romantic story, came that evening when the *Victoria and Albert*, all white and gilt, set sail escorted by large numbers of Dartmouth cadets in boats of every description. Prince Philip, typically, was alone in a rowing boat. One by one the other cadets fell away until only this single handsome, athletic, flaxen-haired oarsman was left. Far out into the open sea sailed the yacht. Far out into the open sea rowed the Prince. In the stern of the yacht the two old sea dogs, King and Captain, watched the young Prince bobbing along in their wake. And 'Lilibet' watched too. Eventually he was ordered to go back. For a time he did a Nelson and turned a blind eye, but ultimately even he recognised that the time had come and with a dip first of one oar and then of the other, he headed for home, leaving his future bride-to-be peering back wistfully through a huge pair of naval binoculars.

Prince Philip says the whole story is much exaggerated. The boats followed the yacht for only about two hundred yards, turned round and went home. And that was that.

It *is* too good to be true and yet there is no dispute about the basics.

'There's a fair consensus,' writes Boothroyd, in his breezy, matter-of-fact way, 'that this was the day that romance first struck.'

It all sounds so simple and uncomplicated and inexorable. Philip was obviously a very attractive young man and as attracted to young women as they to him. In an earlier interlude in Venice his cousin, Alexandra, writes about a holiday romance and adds that, before he started to take an interest in one particular girl, 'Blondes, brunettes, and redhead charmers, Philip gallantly and I think quite impartially squired them all.' Robert Varvill, by now in London digs, still saw his old schoolfriend from time to time and even went to the Mountbatten flat in Brook Street. He remembered the extravagance of telephones in the bathrooms and also an exotic American girlfriend who came and went with surprising suddenness. Others have linked his name with the Wernher daughters and with Hélène, the daughter of the Foufounis family, old friends of his mother with whom he had holidayed at the Normandy resort of Berck-Plage.

Prince Philip has always been a victim of gossip and the earliest sailors' gossip in his life concerned him and Princess Elizabeth.

# 7

# 'On the Seas and Oceans'

'We shall go on to the end, we shall fight in France, we
shall fight on the seas and oceans, we shall fight with growing
confidence and growing strength in the air, we shall
defend our island, whatever the cost may be, we shall
fight on the beaches, we shall fight on the landing grounds,
we shall fight in the fields and in the streets,
we shall fight in the hills; we shall
never surrender'
WINSTON CHURCHILL
4 JUNE 1940

Lieutenant Prince Philip of Greece, RN had a good war. 'He
was a very gallant officer,' said Lord Charteris, who himself
served through World War Two, went on to become private
secretary to the Edinburghs in 1950 and was later the Queen's
private secretary in the 1970s.

Serving in the Royal Navy as a very young officer provided less
opportunity for individual initiative than piloting one's own Spitfire
or Hurricane in the Royal Air Force, which is what he would most
like to have done. Peter Townsend, the ill-starred Battle of Britain
ace who became the King's equerry, was only a few years older than
Prince Philip and yet he was not only mentioned in despatches, as was
Prince Philip, he was also awarded a Distinguished Flying Cross and
bar and a Distinguished Service Order. It is difficult to think of circumstances in which a sailor of the same age could distinguish himself
quite like that. Life on board ship tended to be more of a team game.

The Duke himself put his war record in a sensible perspective in

1948 when he was presented with the Freedom of the City of London. 'In every kind of human activity there are those who lead and there are those who follow . . . I would like to accept the Freedom of this City, not only for myself, but for all those millions who followed during the Second World War. Our only distinction is that we did what we were told to do, to the very best of our ability, and kept on doing it.'

His own war record was similar to hundreds of thousands of others. 'Together,' he said, 'they represent the endeavours of the followers during the last great war, and so the greater part of our war effort.' He acknowledged that without the leadership of an older generation the efforts of the 'followers' would have been fruitless. However, he added, 'The time will come when members of our generation will have to take their place.'

This was widely welcomed as a felicitously turned sentiment and, better still, a modest one. It was also the truth.

His first posting in January 1940 was to an elderly battleship, HMS *Ramillies*. This was a reasonably conventional assignment because midshipmen tended to go to large cruisers or battleships where there were enough good officers to ensure that they were given sensible training and not allowed too much responsibility too early. *Ramillies* was based in Colombo, Ceylon, and was working as an escort ship, shepherding Australian transports to the Mediterranean. Philip joined *Ramillies* on 20 February 1940 and left on 20 April for the County-class cruiser, HMS *Kent*. This *was* unorthodox. 'Why,' asked Lord Lewin, sitting by his rural poolside fifty years later, 'did he transfer so early from *Ramillies?*' Then, frowning, he muses, 'Were they trying to keep him away from the war?'

'Of course they were,' responds the Duke. Greece was not yet at war and it would have been embarrassing to have had a Greek prince killed by enemy action while serving in a British man-of-war. It was, as far as he was concerned, a matter of the utmost simplicity. Once Greece was in the war he could be posted to somewhere likely to see action. Until then he had to be sheltered. This was not something he relished but he had to put up with it.

He certainly changed ship more than was usual. Four months on *Ramillies* were followed by brief spells on HMS *Kent*, on a shore station in Ceylon, and on HMS *Shropshire* before the Italians invaded Greece in the autumn of 1940 and he was free to join the battleship HMS *Valiant* in the eastern Mediterranean.

The early part of his service is scrupulously documented because all midshipmen were required to keep a detailed log. This was, in effect, a piece of course work, to be examined sporadically by senior officers and submitted as part of the seamanship section of the exam which would enable him to be promoted to sub-lieutenant. It was a bound foolscap volume with 150 pages and the object of the exercise was laid out with firm nautical precision in an official Admiralty directive:

Midshipmen are to record in their own language all matters of interest or importance in the work that is carried out, on their stations, in their Fleet, or in their Ship. The objects of keeping the Journal are to train Midshipmen in (a) the power of observation, (b) the power of expression, (c) the habit of orderliness.

Boothroyd, the Duke's 1970 biographer, draws our attention to his copious maps and plans and sketches of everything from a three-colour Suez Canal to something called the Weymouth Cooke Sextant Range-finder. He also has fun with the technical annotations of arcane nautical objects such as 'Cringles, thimbles, shackles, rams, yokes, thrust-blocks and cable-holders'. This visual interest and expertise, particularly in things technical, is revealing and has lasted into later life, but more significant is the way in which those three lessons of the logbook all sunk in. Unfortunately he no longer keeps a log or diary, not surprisingly because that side of his character manifests itself in his copious letter-writing but 'the power of observation', 'the power of expression' and, above all, 'the habit of orderliness' are still apparent in almost everything he does.

*Ramillies* was a spartan experience. Originally commissioned in 1917, she was over twenty years old and felt like it. She was so uncomfortable that no one ever turned in properly because she was darkened at night and 'every scuttle is shut with deadlights'. The midshipmen preferred to sleep in the gun room where they crashed out on armchairs, sofas or even a table.

There were occasional diversions. From *Ramillies*, in port at Sydney, he drove four hundred miles inland to a sheep station; from *Kent* in the Solomon Islands he and three friends went on a fishing expedition with explosive charges and came back with fifty or sixty dynamited fish. Fremantle, Colombo, Bombay, Aden, Mombasa, Alexandria were all on the itinerary, but the Duke says they were not nearly as exotic as they may sound now or as they may have become.

Durban, South Africa, however was a favourite and merits a head-line on several separate occasions in his logbook, embellished with the familiar ducal exclamation marks ranging on a scale of one to three.

More often, however, the long watches on board ship were dark and dull. In June 1940 *Kent*'s 1st Lieutenant wrote in his log off Bombay,

It rained most of the Morning Watch. Luckily had Prince Philip as the snotty and he makes the best cup of cocoa of the lot.

The lessons learned in the galley of the *Diligent* and *Prince Louis* were paying dividends.

Enemy action, however, proved elusive. Another entry in the Duke's logbook reads:

We have something to look forward to, there is an enemy raider in the Indian Ocean and there is just a chance that our tracks will cross.

No such luck, though as if to compensate for this period of phoney war *Kent* did run into a gratifyingly heavy storm causing a roll of more than twenty degrees.

Seas were breaking over the fo'c'sle almost continuously. On one occasion a particularly heavy sea completely smothered the bridge and platform, and even the crow's nest felt the spray from it. Steaming with the sea on the beam and at twenty-one knots the rolling was greatly emphasised, and a lot of innocent fun was had in the mess, watching the Goanese stewards diligently laying the table, and then the plates, knives, forks, spoons, butter dishes, toast racks and marmalade landing in a heap on the deck.

He has always been a stoic foul weather sailor – unlike the Queen – as those who have crewed his sailing boats will testify. One man told me that in a race down the Solent they finished with the Duke's mainsail stained with seaweed *above* the yacht's number. The 'innocent fun' in the mess is harmless enough though I doubt whether I would have seen the joke if I had been one of *Kent*'s Goanese stewards.

On 28 October 1940 Italy finally invaded Greece, which greatly eased Prince Philip's position. Now Mussolini's invasion put him formally into the allied camp in theory as well as fact. On 2 January he joined the battleship HMS *Valiant* where one of the senior group of four midshipmen (out of a total of twenty-four) was the future Admiral of the Fleet and First Sea Lord.

'He was unusual,' recalls Terence Lewin, 'in that he came on his own. Normally we were transferred in groups but here was an experienced midshipman on his own and that was odd.' No reputation preceded him. 'We just knew that he was Royal and we assumed that he would be effete and favoured.' Wrong. Lewin and his fellow midshipmen realised their mistake almost from the first. 'He slotted in splendidly,' he says. 'He could more than hold his own, gave as good as he got, and had no airs and graces.' As far as doing the job was concerned he was definitely above-average.

The logbook entries, expressed with a certain terse economy, nevertheless give an impression of real relish. *Valiant* was 'a super ship', in Lewin's words, and had only recently finished a comprehensive three-year modernisation. She was one of the first three ships to be equipped with proper radar and she had a formidable array of anti-aircraft guns and pom-poms. And, at last, there was a serious prospect of action.

In Athens in January 1941, on leave from Alexandria, where *Valiant* was based, he was reunited with his mother who had settled there for the duration. His cousin Alexandra recalls a 'gay, debonair, confident' young man 'bounding up the hundred steps' to her house 'ready for gramophone records and fun, and dancing with a whole new group of friends'. The Duke has no recollection of the hundred steps and is dubious about the gramophone records and the dancing friends. He does, however, remember that his mother was living in a small house in a quiet street with no steps!

Almost immediately afterwards his log records that,

. . . the Battle fleet put to sea and shortly afterwards we were told we were going to bombard Bardia on the Libyan coast. We arrived off the coast on Thursday morning at dawn. In the dark the flashes of the guns could be seen a long way out to sea. We went to action stations at 0730, and at 0810 the bombardment commenced . . . the whole operation was a very spectacular affair . . .

A few days later, off Sicily,

At dawn action stations on Friday gun flashes were sighted on the starboard bow. We increased speed to investigate, and by the time we were within five miles it was almost daylight. *Bonaventure* signalled that *Southampton* and herself were engaging two enemy destroyers. We could just see one of these destroyers blowing up in a cloud of smoke and spray. The other escaped. Shortly after this the destroyer *Gallant* hit a mine and her bow was blown off, and floated away on the swell . . . At noon two torpedo bombers attacked us, but a quick alteration of course foiled their attempt, and their fish passed down the port side. Shortly after this sixteen German dive-bombers attacked the *Illustrious*. She was hit aft and amidships and fires broke out. Then the bombers concentrated on us and five bombs dropped fairly close . . .

Boothroyd's comment on this is that, 'The record is matter of fact.' But I think he does it less than justice. Certainly it contains facts but the writing also has pace and economy and to me at least it conveys a vivid sense of action and excitement plus a very definite sense that Prince Philip was enjoying himself. He likes to test himself and it is difficult to imagine him showing fear – at least in the face of any physical threat.

His most exciting, and distinguished, moment came a few weeks later, on 28 March, at the Battle of Cape Matapan. Lewin had been transferred from *Valiant* by now, but is convinced that Prince Philip thoroughly deserved the 'mention in despatches' which he received for his part in the battle and possibly more than a mention. Biographer Boothroyd thought that 'when it comes to decorating princes, those responsible may be sensitive to suspicions of favouritism.'

The Commander of the British Mediterranean Fleet, Admiral Sir Andrew Cunningham, had received intelligence reports that the Italian Navy was about to attack British convoys bound for the Greek port of Piraeus. Cunningham immediately sent four cruisers and four destroyers to a position just south of Crete where they were to be joined by five more destroyers at dawn on the twenty-eighth. On the evening of the twenty-seventh Cunningham himself in his flagship HMS *Warspite*, a veteran of the Battle of Jutland, set sail from Alexandria accompanied by *Valiant*, another battleship, *Barham*, an aircraft carrier, *Formidable*, and nine destroyers.

Early next morning Cunningham's aeroplanes found the Italian fleet, consisting of a battleship, eight cruisers and fourteen destroyers. The smaller subsidiary British force attacked and the Italians, with no air cover, turned round and started to head back towards Italy. At three fifteen that afternoon a British aircraft hit the Italian battleship with one of its torpedoes, slowing it down dramatically. A later attack completely halted one of the Italian cruisers, *Pola*. The Italian Commander thought Cunningham's force was further away than it actually was and detached a couple of his cruisers to guard *Pola* while continuing to limp home with his damaged battleship.

At 2100 hours Admiral Cunningham was leading his battleships – including *Valiant* – towards the three darkened Italian cruisers and their escorting destroyers when Prince Philip's log takes up the story:

My orders were that if any ship illuminated a target I was to switch on and illuminate it for the rest of the fleet, so when this ship was lit up by a rather dim light from what I thought was the flagship I switched on our midship light which picked out the enemy cruiser and lit her up as if it were broad daylight. She was only seen complete in the light for a few seconds as the flagship had already opened fire, and as her first broadside landed and hit she was blotted out from just abaft the bridge to right astern. We fired our first broadside about seven seconds after the flagship with very much the same effect. The broadside only consisted of 'A' and 'B' turrets as the after turrets would not bear.

By now all the secondary armament of both ships had opened fire and the noise was considerable. The Captain and the Gunnery Officer now began shouting from the bridge for the searchlights to train left. The idea that there might have been another ship, with the one we were firing at, never entered my head, so it was some few moments before I was persuaded to relinquish the blazing target and search for another one I had no reason to believe was there. However, training to the left, the light picked up another cruiser, ahead of the first one by some 3 or 4 cables. As the enemy was so close the light did not illuminate the whole ship but only about ¾ of it, so I trained left over the whole ship until the bridge structure was in the centre of the beam. The effect was rather like flashing a strong torch on a small model about 5 yards away . . . she was illuminated in an undamaged condition for the period of about 5 seconds when our second broadside left the ship, and almost at once she was completely blotted out from stem to stern . . .

When that broadside was fired, owing to the noise of the secondary armament, I did not hear the 'ting-ting' from the DCT, the result was that the glasses were rammed into my eyes, and flash almost blinding me. Luckily the searchlight was not affected so that when I was able to see something again the light was still on target. Four more broadsides were fired at the enemy, and more than 70% of the shells must have hit. The only correction given by the control officer was 'left ten,' as he thought we were hitting a bit far aft.

When the enemy had completely vanished in clouds of smoke and steam we ceased firing and switched the light off.

Both Italian cruisers, *Zara* and *Fiume*, were destroyed and two of the destroyers were also sunk. Later that night the original target, *Pola*, was also sunk by British destroyers. The crippled Italian battleship however managed to escape, much to Admiral Cunningham's chagrin. Incidentally, Cape Matapan's precise location seems to cause problems for some writers. It is actually the southernmost point of the Peloponnese between the gulfs of Lakonia and Messinia.

Unfortunately this was the last British success in the Eastern Mediterranean. Assisted though it was by Prince Philip's canny illuminations, the crucial factor in the victorious engagement off Crete was that the British had air superiority. The Italians had no aircraft at Cape Matapan. In May, however, when the Battle of Crete was properly joined, German air dominance was total. Mountbatten's *Kelly*, for instance, was sunk early one morning by wave after wave of unopposed Junkers dive-bombers and the same happened to many other ships in the Fleet.

The log again; this time for 22 May, the day before his uncle's disaster:

As we came in sight of the straits we saw *Naiad* and *Carlisle* being attacked by bombers. We went right in to within 10 miles of Crete and then the bombing started in earnest. Stukas came over but avoided the big ships and went for the crippled cruisers and destroyer screens. *Greyhound* was hit right aft by a large bomb, her stern blew up and she sank about twenty minutes later. *Gloucester* and *Fiji* were sent in to help them. Three Me. 109s attacked *Warspite* as dive-bombers and she was hit just where her starboard forrard mounting was . . . When we had got about 15 miles from the land 16 Stukas came out and attacked the two cruisers. *Gloucester* was badly hit and sank some hours later. The fleet had then some more attention, and we were bombed from a high level by a large number of small bombs dropped in sticks of 12 or more. One Dornier came straight for us from the port beam and dropped 12 bombs when he was almost overhead. We turned to port and ceased firing, when suddenly the bombs came whistling down, landing very close all down the port side.

Once again the Duke's prose is short on frills. But if the facts speak for themselves there is no need for embroidery. One of the first rules of journalism.

Soon afterwards in Egypt he encountered his uncle Lord Louis Mountbatten after his destroyer, *Kelly*, was lost along with three cruisers and five other destroyers in the Battle of Crete. As a bedraggled Mountbatten came ashore only twenty-four hours after the tragedy, still covered in fuel oil, almost the first thing he saw was 'the cheery grinning face of our nephew Philip'. According to Mountbatten, Prince Philip roared with laughter at his blackened uncle. 'You look like a nigger minstrel!' he said.

A few days after these baptisms of fire Prince Philip was on his way back to England for the sub-lieutenant's exam at Portsmouth. This was divided into five sections – gunnery, torpedoes, navigation, signals and seamanship – and each result was graded one, two or three. 'Was he a "five-one"?' Lord Lewin wanted to know. 'If so, he was a true professional.' The answer is 'not quite'. He was a 'four-one' with just one subject graded 'two'. Lewin was, naturally, a 'five-one'!

As a sub-lieutenant Prince Philip was posted to the destroyer HMS *Wallace* in June 1942. There he first met a man who was to become one of his closest friends. This was Mike Parker, later his equerry and private secretary. After a few months, in October at the specific request of his Commanding Officer, Prince Philip became First Lieutenant of *Wallace* and in direct rivalry to Parker, just a year his senior, who held the same position – second in command – of HMS *Lauderdale*. Prince Philip was barely twenty-one and one of the youngest first lieutenants in the Navy.

'We were highly competitive,' says Parker, 'we both wanted to show that we had *the* most efficient, cleanest and best ship and ship's company in the Navy. And instead of pushing us apart it drew us together.' Not that close, however. The Duke says that he only got to know Parker really well in 1944 en route to the Far East.

In Parker's estimation it was not just the driving ambition and desire for excellence that drew the two men together. 'I was an orphan,' says Parker, 'because I came from Australia.' Parker remembers once in port when all the other officers had gone off on leave, he looked across at *Wallace* and saw Prince Philip standing alone on deck. 'You're a poor bloody orphan just like me,' he thought. It was not just the parental deprivation which united them either. They were bound together by poverty. Relative poverty anyway. 'He was better off than I was,' says Parker, 'but compared with many people he didn't have a brass razoo!

'The fact that he was a Prince didn't register with me. I gave him deference when it was official but if it was not official then "relax" was the order of the day.' Even now Parker phones the Duke direct and when he writes him a letter it begins 'Dear Philip' and ends 'Yours ever, Mike'.

The new posting was a stark contrast to the exotic, if inactive Far Eastern days on *Ramillies* and *Kent*. *Lauderdale* and *Wallace* were on convoy duty up and down the east coast of Britain from Rosyth on the north shore of the Forth to Sheerness at the mouth of the Thames Estuary. This stretch of coastline was known as 'E-Boat Alley' because it was swarming with 'E-boats', the snappy German *Schnellboote* capable of a top speed of thirty-nine knots and armed with twin torpedo tubes. It was a tough but hardly a romantic assignment and it must have been a relief to be posted, the following year, 1944, to a brand-new destroyer bound – though they were not told it at the time – for action against the Japanese in the Pacific.

This was HMS *Whelp*. Michael Parker, fortuitously, was posted to her sister ship, HMS *Wessex*, and the two sailed together in the 27th Destroyer Flotilla under Admiral Sir James Somerville. They were almost too late. On 2 September 1945 *Whelp* escorted USS *Missouri* – the same battleship that was pounding Saddam Hussein's army of occupation from the Gulf in 1991 – into Tokyo Bay. There the Japanese signed the formal instrument of surrender. Ten days later in Singapore the Duke's uncle Lord Mountbatten took delivery of the Japanese generals' ceremonial swords in Singapore and HMS *Whelp* was ordered to collect a cargo of newly released prisoners-of-war before heading home to Blighty.

In Portsmouth the destroyer's decommissioning was presided over by her First Lieutenant, Philip, Prince of Greece, RN

It was 1946, and the end of the war was an anticlimax. His next two postings were to Pwllheli in north Wales and Corsham in Wiltshire. But there were compensations.

# 'An Infinite Debt'

'The sum which two married people owe to one another
defies calculation. It is an infinite debt, which can
only be discharged through all eternity'
*Elective Affinities*
GOETHE

Towards the end of the war in 1945 when HMS *Whelp*, with Prince Philip, and HMS *Wessex*, with Michael Parker, were in the Far East much of their time was spent in Australia and the two First Lieutenants took leave together. Mike Parker, unlike some, is never mealy-mouthed when it comes to talking about sex. Before Australia there had been runs ashore in North Africa. 'Of course we had fun in North Africa,' he says, 'but never anything outrageous. We'd drink together and then we'd go and have a bloody good meal. People are always asking, "Did you go to the local estaminets and screw everything in sight?" And the answer is "No! It never came into the picture. There was so much else to do."'

Prince Philip's cousin, Alexandra of Yugoslavia, in her biography paints an extravagant picture of those Australian leaves and does so in a style worthy of Dame Barbara Cartland. 'Philip,' she writes, 'with a golden beard, hit feminine hearts, first in Melbourne and then in Sydney, with terrific impact.' Mike Parker puts it slightly differently. 'There were always armfuls of girls,' he says, drily.

Obviously there were some terrific parties and lots of pranks on those Australian holidays. At least once Prince Philip managed to swap identity with his friend, who had also acquired a full set of whiskers though not as gloriously golden. For years 'society' had been speculating about Lieutenant Prince Philip and the young Princess Elizabeth. He did not like it. He did not like being talked about behind his back at all. On leave with Parker he went to some lengths to avoid being compromised and gossiped about. 'You know,' says Parker, pondering the past, 'he always seemed to have one eye over his shoulder. Could it possibly have been "her"?' Even he, Prince Philip's closest male friend, was not privy to that kind of secret. 'He never said anything to me, and I never said anything to him.' But when he did finally tell Parker, two years later in 1947, that he was engaged to be married, 'I wasn't surprised,' says Parker with nice understatement.

The war had almost orphaned Philip. His immediate family were all abroad. His surviving sisters were all in Germany; one brother-in-law killed in action and two wounded. His father stuck in Monte Carlo, under the rule of Vichy France and therefore effectively in enemy hands, died of a heart attack in 1944; his mother had stayed on in Athens after the rest of the Greek Royal Family had fled following the German invasion. She was a stubborn and very brave woman, devoted to the young orphans she looked after in the King's former house. For the most part the Germans left her alone. Prince Philip had, of course, seen her in January 1941 on leave from *Valiant*, but subsequently he was as cut off from her as he was from his father and sisters. The only communication possible was via his aunt Louise married to the Crown Prince of neutral Sweden.

During those gruelling months on E-Boat Alley he had on occasion managed to go further afield than Rosyth in Scotland and stayed with his English relations; sometimes at Coppins, the home of his cousin Princess Marina, Duchess of Kent, near Iver in Buckinghamshire and conveniently close to Windsor Castle. Almost fifty years on even the Duke is unsure of *exactly* how often he visited his royal relations. He was certainly with them for at least one Christmas and definitely attended the Castle production of *Aladdin* in 1943.

Marion Crawford, the former royal governess, and his cousin Queen Alexandra of Yugoslavia both describe the occasion. This is singularly bad luck on the Duke, because they are both manifestly unreliable sources. There are several stories in Queen Alexandra's book of which Prince Philip has, to put it kindly, 'no recollection'; and Miss Crawford's version of events is always highly coloured. She also, as Robert Lacey points out in his biography of the Queen, managed to describe the bearing of the guardsmen at a Queen's Birthday Parade in 1955 which never in fact took place and the enthusiasm at an Ascot race meeting which was postponed until after her account appeared.

Clearly Crawfie and Alexandra are economical with the truth, but that is not to say that they ignore it altogether. These two writers exaggerate, they gush and they make mistakes – Queen Alexandra, for instance, moves the Milford Havens' Berkshire house at least thirty miles from its real location to a wholly mythical 'upper reaches of the Thames' – but they have been widely read and sometimes believed. The Duke plainly finds this intolerable and indeed is appalled by the whole fairy story industry which has grown up around him. One of his former equerries showed me a book called *Manifest Destiny* (not by either Crawfie or Alexandra), which was published in 1953 to celebrate the triumphs of the Mountbatten family. The equerry bought it for himself and asked his boss to inscribe it for him. The Duke indeed signed it. Above his signature on the title page he wrote, 'Manifest Bunkum!'

People who, in his view, wrote 'bunkum' about him after the event were tiresome but almost worse were those who talked 'bunkum' behind his back at the time. Sir Henry 'Chips' Channon, for instance. I mentioned to Mike Parker that allusions to Sir Henry did not seem to be going down terribly well and he chortled knowingly. 'So you've hit the Channon nerve,' he said. Channon, a rich American who married into the Guinness family and became a Member of Parliament, kept a spiky, snobbish diary, which was published in 1967 after his death. Unfortunately for all concerned, Channon happened to be in Athens in January 1941 when Prince Philip was on leave from HMS *Valiant*.

'He is to be our Prince Consort,' wrote Channon in the diary, 'and that is why he is serving in our Navy.' That afternoon Channon had been chatting with Prince Philip's aunt Helen, wife of Prince Nicholas of Greece. Unfortunately he does not give the full details of that conversation, but it sounds as if the two had been discussing Philip's marital destiny. Certainly there was no doubt or hesitation in Channon's verdict and being an inveterate gossip he told everyone he met.

He repeated his belief in the ultimate royal marriage more than once again during the war years. In February 1944, for instance, he wrote that Lord and Lady Iveagh had been to tea with the King and Queen at Buckingham Palace. On the strength of what he hears from them Channon confides to the diary, 'I do believe that a marriage may well be arranged one day between Princess Elizabeth and Prince Philip.' That autumn he visited Coppins, the Duchess of Kent's country home. 'As I signed the visitors' book I noticed "Philip" written constantly. It is at Coppins that he sees Princess Elizabeth. I think she will marry him.' The Duke, insisting that no thought of marriage to Princess Elizabeth crossed his mind until at least 1946, is infuriated by the thought of Channon spreading these rumours.

Alastair Forbes, the writer, and himself a Coppins regular, remembers Channon's chatter. 'He and Freda Dudley Ward were always going on about how "Lilibet" had fallen for him,' he recalls. 'I think everybody knew "Lilibet" had got his photograph.'

'Everybody' here is a relative term. In Forbes' usage it means, broadly, 'society' in the days when such a thing could be said to exist.

A useful corrective to this notion of 'everybody' gossiping about Prince Philip and Princess Elizabeth is the Olga Franklin story. Olga Franklin, herself of Russian extraction, later became a well-known feature writer on the *Daily Mail*, but in 1944 she was a young reporter on the *Newcastle Journal*. She is dead now but in 1980 I interviewed her about her war-time scoop in which she 'discovered' Prince Philip who was on Tyneside for the commissioning of HMS *Whelp*. Her brief was typically world-weary. 'There's some Greek prince in town,' she was told and off she went to the dockyard to find him.

Her story says almost as much about the change in newspaper style as it does about the relative obscurity of Prince Philip forty-five years ago.

### SHIPYARD STRANGER IS
### A ROYAL PRINCE

Very few workers in a North-East shipyard are aware that the tall, ash-blond first lieutenant, RN, who travels by bus to work among them each day, is a Royal Prince.

Citizens have been equally unaware that this twenty-three-year-old naval officer, Prince Philip of Greece, has been living quietly in an hotel while 'standing by' on a British destroyer.

Prince Philip, who has the looks of a typical Prince of a Hans Andersen fairy tale, will certainly have been noticed by many a girl worker at the shipyard.

Even thirty-five years later when I talked to her in semi-retirement in one of London's south-eastern suburbs, Olga Franklin was still plainly smitten by the dashing young naval officer she remembered so vividly. After a quick dash through his ancestry and war record, the article goes on,

The Prince was amused at my suggestion that he might find the northern dialect difficult to understand.

'I understand the local people perfectly,' he said, 'and I am enjoying my stay.'

This was confirmed by another naval officer.

This 'other naval officer' was actually his CO, sitting in on the interviews, of which there were no less than five, to ensure fair play. Olga Franklin's final paragraph really is astonishing evidence of the change in journalism.

This is the first time the Prince has been interviewed and reported in this country . . . and I thanked him for the good humoured and kindly way he had accepted 'exposure'.

Prince Philip himself, talking to Basil Boothroyd in 1970, described his war-time relationship with the Royal Family in determinedly un-Crawfie, un-Channon terms.

'I went to the theatre with them once, something like that. And then during the war, if I was here I'd call in and have a meal. I once or twice spent Christmas at Windsor, because I'd nowhere particular to go. I thought not all that much about it, I think. We used to correspond occasionally. You see it's difficult to visualise. I suppose if I'd just been a casual acquaintance it would all have been frightfully significant. But if you're related – I mean I knew half the people here, they were all relations – it isn't so extraordinary to be on kind of family relationship terms. You don't necessarily have to think about marriage.'

He is absolutely clear that he did not think seriously about marriage until 1946 when he went to stay at Balmoral. 'I suppose one thing led to another,' he told Boothroyd. 'It was sort of fixed up. That's really what happened.'

That doesn't sound wildly romantic, but Prince Philip is a man who, however romantic he might be in private, would rather be seen dead than seem so in public. Even after his engagement to Princess Elizabeth there were those who thought him unnaturally formal with her. This may have indicated a certain natural reserve, but it also has something to do with the fact that his was not a courtship like anybody else's. He was becoming engaged to the future Queen of England, and however much the young couple might have been in love, which they were, there were other considerations involved. She was going to be Queen of England and that set her marriage apart.

This, after all, was the reason for all those tiresome rumours. Princess Elizabeth had to marry someone 'suitable' or 'eligible' and Prince Philip was easily the most 'eligible' candidate.

'After all,' he said to Boothroyd, 'if you spend ten minutes thinking about it — and a lot of these people spent a great deal more time thinking about it — how many obviously eligible young men, other than people living in this country, were available?'

It is a fair question. As far as Princess Elizabeth herself is concerned there seems to be universal agreement that although there were young Guards officers with whom she danced and whose company she enjoyed, Prince Philip was the only real object of her affections right from the first real meeting at Dartmouth in 1939. Of course she was barely in her teens then, but by the end of the war she was nineteen, grown up and with a mind of her own.

As far as official 'eligibility' was concerned the list was non-existent to short. American fantasists advanced the name of one foreign royal and two English aristocrats. The foreigner was Prince Charles of Belgium, forty-one years old, but preferred to Prince Philip by *Time* magazine (of all sources!). The home-grown 'candidates' were the Earl of Euston, heir to the Duke of Grafton and a Grenadier Guardsman serving (from 1943 to 1946) as ADC to the Viceroy of India, and another Grenadier Guardsman, the Duke of Rutland. The latter two were eminently suitable but, quite apart from other considerations, both got married to other people in 1946. The Earl of Euston's wife, Fortune, now Duchess of Grafton, has been Mistress of the Robes to the Queen since 1967.

No doubt other candidates could have been found, but why should anyone look further than Prince Philip when he was so obviously Princess Elizabeth's first and only choice?

His candidacy was not, however, without obstacles. Despite his war service and his Cheam and Gordonstoun education he was still not a British subject. Lady Longford, in her biography of the Queen (1983) says that in 1972 Ernest Augustus of Hanover (one of his innumerable German relations) established that under the 1705 Act of Succession all descendants of the Empress Sophia were automatically British subjects. Because Prince Philip was descended from the Empress Sophia he had been a British subject since the day of his birth on Corfu. Lord Mountbatten argued that this meant that he had been Prince Philip of Great Britain and Northern Ireland all along. It is an irrelevant argument since immediately after the war Prince Philip and everyone else who mattered knew only that he was Lieutenant Prince Philip of Greece, RN. He was universally acknowledged as a foreigner no matter how well disposed, attractive and unforeign he might appear. If he wanted to stay in the Navy, which he did, he would have to take

British nationality. And if he wanted to become the husband of the future Queen he would undoubtedly have to become British. He also needed a surname.

There is a certain weariness and wariness in Prince Philip's response on this matter. 'There was much "to-ing" and "fro-ing" about my adoption of a surname and just as much argument about the "house" name,' he says. 'I think it would be better to keep my views to myself.' At the time he was angry about the fuss. 'Philip' had always been quite sufficient throughout school and in the Navy. He himself said that he did not wish to have any style or title but simply to be known as 'Lieutenant'.

But he still needed a surname. It was apparently the Labour Home Secretary, Chuter Ede, who suggested he take his mother's family name, after 'Oldcastle' was rejected. 'Oldcastle' was the anglicised form of 'Oldenberg' which was the original family name of his father. This had later been changed to Schleswig-Holstein-Sonderburg-Glücksburg which was also an unattractive idea. Double-barrelled names are one thing, quadruple quite another. And so it was Mountbatten. On 7 February 1947, Prince Philip was naturalised and from then until marriage brought new titles he was known simply as Lieutenant Philip Mountbatten, RN.

The change was posted in the *London Gazette* along with about eight hundred others, many of them those of German Jewish refugees or Poles who had fought with the British all through the war.

There was some opposition to the match from the bride's parents although this had nothing to do with Princess Elizabeth's choice, simply with the timing. She was still very young and the King and Queen felt protective. When one cousin, King George of Greece, wrote to another cousin, King George of England, to promote Prince Philip's suit, the approving reply was that the suitor was intelligent, had a sense of humour and thought about things 'in the right way'. But it was still too early.

More tiresome was the opposition of what one member of the Royal Family described to me as 'the trad. upper classes of the moustache type bristling away about "ghastly foreign fellows", especially just after the war'. Queen Elizabeth's brother, David Bowes-Lyon, was originally strongly opposed to the match and so, it seems, were men such as Lord Salisbury, Lord Eldon and Lord Stanley. They detected in Prince Philip qualities they considered un-British. He was not their idea of 'an English gentleman'. Prince Philip himself was obviously aware of a certain coolness in some quarters and when asked if there was any hostility from the more xenophobic areas of the Establishment commented succinctly: 'Inevitable; vide Albert', a phrase that recurs. It was noticeable that he was much more at ease with the more exotic friends of his cousin Marina, Duchess of Kent, who had married into the British Royal Family in 1934, than the stuffier courtiers at Buckingham Palace, Windsor and Balmoral.

There had been two significant events on the family front. On 3 December 1944 his father had died in Monte Carlo, cut off from his entire family by the fortunes of war. His daughter Sophie had tried time and time again to persuade the German authorities to allow her to visit him but to no avail. He was buried first in the Russian Orthodox Church in Nice, and in 1946 conveyed by Greek cruiser to Athens where he is buried in the gardens of the royal palace at Tatoi. After the war Prince Philip and Mike Parker went to collect his personal effects from the woman who was the companion of Prince Andrew's final years.

'We were sitting in the Hotel Paris,' recalls Parker, 'waiting for her, with a cocktail each, and in came this woman with blue glasses. I'd never seen glasses like that. And as she entered she smiled at the doorman and said "Evenin' Charles". I'll always remember that.'

Her name, says Parker, was Doris and as she and Prince Philip 'hit it off from the first', he left them to reminisce. Prince Andrew's pension had certainly never found its way to Monte Carlo and he died in straitened circumstances, leaving just a few personal possessions for his son to collect.

I remembered Princess Sophie telling me that because he was born premature and tiny, Prince Andrew spent his first few days in a cigar box being fed with a tooth-pick; and how on that ill-fated Asia Minor campaign he had acquired two geese but instead of eating them – as intended – had made pets of them. He sounded charming and funny and now all that was left were memories, a pair of hairbrushes, cuff links . . . It was all very sad.

The other family event was his sister Sophie's second wedding. The war years had been hard for her after her first husband, Prince Christopher, was killed in active service. Then she met the gentle, scholarly former cavalry officer, Prince Georg of Hanover, who was to become headmaster of Prince Philip's old school at Salem, and became engaged to marry him. Princess Sophie had not seen her young brother since he was a schoolboy at Gordonstoun seven or eight years before.

She was certainly not expecting to see him at her second wedding at Schloss Salem. The war, after all, was barely over; Germany was still a shambles, chaotic, impoverished, defeated. Prince Philip was in the British Navy, heaven knows where. In fact he was closer than she realised. Somehow he got hold of an army vehicle. 'How could he do that?' asks a still bemused Princess Sophie, 'when he was in the *Navy?*' And he drove across Europe to be at his sister's wedding. This is a characteristic more than one person has remarked on. If the Duke's presence is important he will get there no matter what. He is uncommonly loyal to relations and true friends. Sophie was amazed and delighted to see him. He had grown up. He looked so like their father.

Back in England plans for his own wedding were proceeding slowly and not altogether smoothly. There was a tour of South Africa to be undertaken in 1947 and that took priority. The King had promised the South Africans a visit as a thankyou present for their war effort. Their loyalty had been in the balance in 1939 when General Smuts had defeated General Hertzog who advocated a policy of neutrality. The vote in Parliament was disturbingly close – eighty to sixty-seven – and it was obvious that the Dominion's allegiance was fragile. The plan was for the King and Queen to make it a family affair, taking both daughters with them. Princess Elizabeth would celebrate her twenty-first birthday on the ten-week trip.

By the winter of 1946–7 she and Prince Philip were unofficially engaged and their relationship was public though unacknowledged. The King and Queen remained adamant, however. The young couple must wait. In September the Palace issued a denial of newspaper rumours that there was an engagement. In the years to come the official denial of a royal engagement became almost a ritual harbinger of wedding bells. Even on this occasion it is doubtful whether anyone believed it.

The formal announcement came on 10 July 1947 and was received with widespread enthusiasm. The only dissenting newspaper was the *Daily Worker*, the official organ of Britain's Communist Party, and therefore unlikely to approve of anything to do with the Royal Family short of abdication. The general perception was that this was a true love match and not an arranged wedding. They were a wonderfully romantic-looking couple and the fairy-tale element was a perfect antidote to the austerity of these immediate post-war years.

For Prince Philip marriage obviously meant an immediate transition from the relative obscurity implicit in Olga Franklin's *Newcastle Journal* article to genuine stardom. There was no reason, however, to think that it would mean any change in his chosen career. He enjoyed the Navy, was well suited to it and never displayed the slightest sign of wanting to opt for civvy street. Despite his own modesty the genes – on both sides of the family – suggested an aptitude for high command and under normal circumstances one would have expected him to stay in the Navy and to be successful. There was no reason for marriage, even this royal marriage, to interfere with his ambitions. The King had barely turned fifty so Prince Philip's wife would be unlikely to succeed to the throne for another twenty or thirty years. Once she became Queen he would presumably have to leave the Navy – though even that was not a certainty – but given reasonable luck Prince Philip could look forward to being able to go on serving in the Navy until he was over fifty himself. So there was every chance that he could become Admiral Mountbatten on merit and in his own right.

Of course there would have to be change. After marriage the royal couple would not only be living together in a house of their own, they would also have their own household and staff. One of the Prince's first acts, even before the engagement was announced, was to invite his old friend Mike Parker down to the Petty Officers' Training School at Corsham and ask him to become equerry-in-waiting. Princess Elizabeth knew Parker by now and was keen that he should do the job, but this was very much Prince Philip's appointment and, in a sometimes hostile environment, Parker always remained his closest friend and ally at court. The arrangement suited Parker well. As Prince Philip knew, his friend was having marital problems. He had been hoping to return to Australia to join the Australian Navy but his young Scottish wife refused to accompany him. This new London-based job might just be a solution.

The two other key appointments were secretary and Comptroller. The new secretary was John 'Jock' Colville, a young diplomat who had already been private secretary to Sir Winston Churchill. He was bored with the Foreign Office and accepted the offer, which came from the King's private secretary, Sir Alan 'Tommy' Lascelles. Colville's mother, Lady Cynthia, was a lady-in-waiting to Queen Mary, so Colville was very much an Establishment man. He had, however, never previously met either Princess Elizabeth or Prince Philip.

This was a very young team and it was clearly felt that an older, wiser man should be appointed to exercise a restraining influence.

Lord Mountbatten already saw himself in this role, albeit in an unofficial capacity, and was so keen to be what his nephew described as 'the General Manager of this little show' that Prince Philip had to remonstrate with him, explaining that Princess Elizabeth might not 'take to the idea quite as docilely as I do'. It is difficult to imagine Prince Philip accepting Mountbatten's General Managership with docility; nor did he seem initially happy when it was proposed that the Comptroller of the Household should be Lieutenant-General 'Boy' Browning. Browning, formerly Mountbatten's chief of staff, came with a warm recommendation from his old commander.

'Boy would sooner die than let his boss down,' wrote Mountbatten. 'Frankly, Philip, I do not think you can do better.' Browning had commanded the Airborne troops at the Battle of Arnhem where he had distinguished himself by his heroism, and was married to the romantic novelist Daphne du Maurier, though she lived in Cornwall and rarely came to town. Prince Philip had met Browning when he was on his uncle's staff in South-East Asia. He felt that as an older, more worldly-wise figure, he could be very useful in fighting their young household's corner against the more conservative elements in and outside the palace.

The question of a home and office was more of a problem. On 1 September 1947 Sunninghill, just outside the Great Park at Windsor, the country house earmarked for them, burned down. 'Chips' Channon was asked if he would lend or loan them his house but refused. Eventually a suite was found at Buckingham Palace and a house, Windlesham Moor, in Berkshire. Not until 1949 did they move into Clarence House on the Mall which became one of their happiest homes.

The wedding itself took place in Westminster Abbey on 20 November 1947, preceded by two glittering parties at the Palace during one of which the Duchess of Kent fainted and the Duke of Devonshire was molested by a drunken Maharaja. More than 2,500 presents were received and displayed at St James's Palace where Chips Channon noted with pleasure that his 'faux Fabergé silver box was prominently displayed though he 'was struck by how ghastly some of the presents were'. A woman in New York sent a turkey on the grounds that the English were known to be starving and Mahatma Gandhi sent a piece of cloth handwoven by himself. This was the idea of the Viceroy, Lord Mountbatten, and precipitated an altercation between Queen Mary and Prince Philip, who stood up for the Mahatma. Hundreds of women sent nylon stockings.

On the night before the wedding Prince Philip held a stag-night at the Dorchester Hotel. The guests included Mike Parker, his best man David, Marquess of Milford Haven, and his uncle, Lord Mountbatten, who after much soul-searching had taken a brief leave from his duties in India. Every one of the guests was in Royal Naval evening dress. The press were invited in for a formal photo session and chat; then the royal party offered to take their photos too as a souvenir of the occasion. The press, in thick belted overcoats reminiscent of the Crazy Gang, sat on the edge of the sofa and smiled. When the cameras had flashed Mike Parker called out a command and the camera bulbs were thrown against the wall. There is some dispute about this gesture, but Parker says that it was done to prevent any photographer sneaking extra pictures after the official photo-call. If so, it was a sign of things to come!

Generally speaking, the verdict on the wedding itself endorsed that of Winston Churchill, who starred at the Abbey with an inimitable cameo role, arriving late to a standing salute from the full congregation including a magnificent assembly of European Monarchs. Churchill described the marriage as 'A flash of colour on the hard road we have to travel'. Others were less generous. Chips Channon said that 'many people' thought it had been 'mishandled'.

'First,' he wrote, 'the ridiculous fuss of Prince Philip changing his name and nationality – then the original intention of keeping the Wedding private . . . and someone in the Government apparently advised simplicity, misjudging the English people's love of pageantry and a show.'

This meanness of spirit may have something to do with the fact that Channon himself was not 'commanded but had to make do with a pass to the "parliamentary enclosure"'. Other politicians also apparently felt snubbed – he mentions an 'affronted' R. A. Butler, one of the leading members of the Conservative Opposition, wandering around in the crowd outside. Much more significant ghosts at the wedding, however, were Prince Philip's three surviving sisters and his brothers-in-law. His mother was present, but not Margarita, Theodora or Sophie. All through his engagement the German element in his family had been conspicuously played down while the Mountbatten connection had been emphasised. After all, his name on the wedding programme was plain Lieutenant Philip Mountbatten, RN. There was no mention of his being a Prince of Greece.

On the morning of the wedding, however, he changed his title again. The King created him Baron Greenwich of Greenwich, Earl of

Merioneth and Duke of Edinburgh. It was not until 1957 that he became a Prince once more – a special reward from his wife after ten years of marriage. Titles have never meant quite as much to him as they did to his uncle Dickie and plain Philip is perhaps what he prefers, but for more than forty years he has been the Duke of Edinburgh, and it is as Duke of Edinburgh that he is best known. Although he was to return to active service in the Navy he would never again be plain Lieutenant Philip. His status was changed for ever, and so, though it took a little time for everyone to realise it, had his life.

# Part Two

# 1947–1957
# THE DUKE

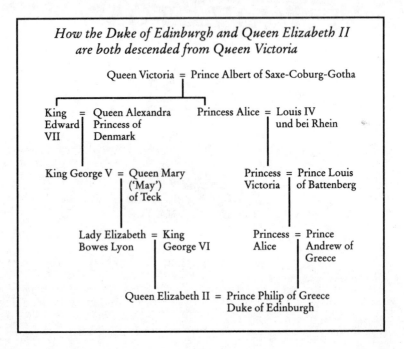

*How the Duke of Edinburgh and Queen Elizabeth II
are both descended from Queen Victoria*

Queen Victoria = Prince Albert of Saxe-Coburg-Gotha

King = Queen Alexandra    Princess Alice = Louis IV
Edward  Princess of                  und bei Rhein
VII      Denmark

King George V = Queen Mary      Princess = Prince Louis
           ('May')        Victoria  of Battenberg
           of Teck

Lady Elizabeth = King       Princess = Prince
Bowes Lyon    George VI     Alice    Andrew of
                                 Greece

Queen Elizabeth II = Prince Philip of Greece
Duke of Edinburgh

# 'When a Man Marries'

'Have you not heard,
When a man marries, dies, or turns Hindoo,
His best friends hear no more of him?'
*Letter to Maria Gisborne, 1820*
P. B. SHELLEY

In his wedding address the Archbishop of York, Dr Cyril Garbett, said that the service for Princess Elizabeth and the Duke of Edinburgh was 'in all essentials the same as it would be for any cottager who might be married this afternoon in some small country church in a remote village in the dales'. However, the Archbishop knew perfectly well that even if in the sight of God this was a wedding like any other it was far from being an ordinary wedding in the sight of the man in the street. The Edinburghs, as they were often known, were not like the rest of us. The biggest single difference was that for most couples a wedding is a relatively private affair. But the Duke's wedding, like so much of his life from now on, was a private matter with a public dimension. The wedding was observed and for the first time in his life he found his every movement and gesture, every item of his clothing, every glance and word subject to scrutiny. It was all written down and used in evidence. The Duke says that actually this sort of unwelcome scrutiny had begun months earlier when rumours of his engagement first spread beyond 'society'.

There is nothing like a royal wedding for enpurpling the prose. Alongside the official picture by the Duke's friend, the society photographer Baron, in the Pitkin Pictorial souvenir of the great event there is an 'eye-witness account'. The day was 'great', the bride 'radiant', the cheers of the 'waiting multitudes' were 'loyal and affectionate', and the whole article is proof positive that from now on, while the Duke of Edinburgh might strive mightily to be his own man, there would always be a chorus of men and women from the media to watch over him.

Collie Knox, the author of this flowery piece, reveals that

By the miracle of radio, 200,000,000 people throughout the British Empire and the world heard the response 'I will' softly spoken by the bridal pair as the Archbishop of Canterbury pronounced them man and wife. By the wonder of television the processions to and from the Abbey had been seen in thousands of homes.

The point is well made. Press reporting of royalty had long been a fact of life but radio and, far more dramatically, television was to play a vital role in transforming the image of Monarchy. By the next decade the TV cameras would be inside Westminster Abbey for the Coronation service. By the end of the sixties the Royal Family would be starring in a TV documentary when the cameras filmed their private life even on holiday at Sandringham and Balmoral. In 1947 it was radio which claimed the two hundred millions and television which was still restricted to 20,000 homes around London.

Another revealing reference is the throwaway allusion to 'the Empire'. On his death-bed King George V is supposed to have uttered the final words, 'How is the Empire?' By 1947 it was still looking in good shape but some cracks were beginning to appear. The Indian sub-continent, after the final Viceregal administration of Lord Mountbatten, had ceased to be a part of the Empire and been translated into a member of the Commonwealth. The Commonwealth was an altogether more egalitarian organisation which still kept King or Queen as its head while in no sense deferring to the hegemony of the United Kingdom itself. The Commonwealth meant very little to the average citizen of the United Kingdom but for the whole of her reign it would mean a great deal to Princess Elizabeth and her husband.

Of Prince Philip himself, Collie Knox wrote:

The Bridegroom in naval uniform, wearing five rows of medal ribbons and the star of his newly bestowed Order of the Garter, looked extraordinarily composed. Dignity and a becoming self assurance sat easily upon him, as from time to time he exchanged a whispered word with his Groomsman.*
He has a natural poise, has Prince Philip, allied to good looks and a supple

---

* Synonym for 'best man'. It is popular usage at royal weddings.

figure. To my mind there still comes the recollection of a long talk I was privileged to have with him some five weeks before the Wedding when his realistic outlook towards life, his patent interest in everything and everybody – and his marked sense of humour – so strongly impressed me . . . That day in the Abbey, waiting for the approach of his Bride, he bore himself reliantly and well. Not by a single movement of nervousness, did he betray his inward feelings.

If five rows of medal ribbons seems an unusually large haul for a young lieutenant, the most striking feature of that paragraph is the level of intrusion. From now on, wherever he went and whatever he did, people would stare and speculate and gossip, often in print. There would always be men such as Collie Knox watching him in the hope that in some way he *would* 'betray his inward feelings'. It was something the Duke was going to have to learn to live with.

Not every reporter got quite as close as Collie Knox. The *Daily Telegraph*, for instance, preserved a more decorous distance.

All the way back to the Palace crowds were trying to surge forwards in an effort to get a closer view of the Princess. As the last car in the procession passed they spread across the streets and surged down the Mall like a gigantic wave.

With police, troops and public wedged there in a solid mass, the cry went up: 'We want the Princess.'

For an hour the crowd kept up an intermittent chanting of 'we want the bride' and 'we want Philip'.

Then exactly on the stroke of 1.30 a storm of cheering went up as the windows of the red and gold draped balcony were opened and the Princess and the Duke stepped into view. They stood smiling and waving to the rapturous crowd, which shouted and waved flags and handkerchiefs.

The cheering increased as the King and Queen and the bridesmaids joined the couple and stood acknowledging the tumultuous reception. For five minutes the royal party remained on view.

The honeymoon began at the Mountbatten house, Broadlands, in Hampshire and then, after four days, transferred to Birkhall on the Balmoral estate in Scotland for a further three weeks. When they returned they were both obviously happy though one close observer thought the Duke a shade querulous.

Perhaps it was just that the honeymoon was over, but there was also an unanswered question mark hovering over his life and work. He had not had a sea posting since decommissioning *Whelp* at Portsmouth in 1946 and in January 1948 he was due to start work at the

Admiralty. Even after six years of war no young naval officer likes to spend too long ashore. You join the Navy to see the sea.

In war there was always a tendency for the young and able to win accelerated promotion and to be given responsibility at an early age. In a peacetime Navy the pace inevitably slows and 'Buggin's turn' becomes the order of the day.

Besides, the Duke was now a member of the Royal Family and that was, in some ways, a sobering prospect. Immediately after the wedding his father-in-law, the King, had written to Elizabeth to affirm his love for her, to express his regret for having made her wait so long before getting engaged ('I was so anxious for you to come to South Africa as you knew'), and to remind her of her duty.

Our family, us four, the 'Royal Family' must remain together with additions of course at suitable moments!! [The Royal Family's fondness for the exclamation mark is an interesting field for literary study!!] I have watched you grow up all these years with pride under the skilful direction of Mummy, who as you know is the most marvellous person in the world in my eyes, & I can, I know, always count on you, & now Philip, to help us in our work . . . I can see that you are sublimely happy with Philip which is right but don't forget us is the wish of your ever loving & devoted papa.

There is something slightly daunting in that letter. At least if I were a son-in-law reading it I would find it a touch forbidding. The core of the family, mother, father and the two daughters, was extremely close. The King had been pitched into a job he did not want and for which he was in many ways ill-prepared, through the Abdication of his brother. This would have made any team of wife and daughters even more than usually protective, but the bonds were further cemented by the experience of being the Royal Family under fire, leading the nation from the heart of blitzed London. They were a very tight-knit family with a highly developed sense of their role. Philip was a newcomer and, like any other new son-in-law, something of an outsider and even something of a threat. Jock Colville, remarking on French adulation of Princess Elizabeth during the Edinburghs' visit to Paris in 1948, wrote that 'Princes who do their duty are respected; beautiful Princesses have an in-built advantage over their male counter-parts.' This depends on your point of view. A female writer might hold the opposite opinion.

There was never any hostility towards their new son-in-law from the King and Queen. 'The King,' says Mike Parker, the Duke's equerry, 'was bliss. He literally taught me.' The King also used t take Parker out shooting and generally tutored him, realising that he was completely unused to life at the Palace and to the 'right' way of doing things. On his very first day at the Palace Parker was shown into the King's presence and found him scrutinising a set of naval plans. They were the blueprints for the Royal Yacht *Britannia* and the King couldn't see how the large bureaucracy of the Palace could be fitted into such a relatively small vessel. He gave it to Parker as a problem to solve. After all he knew ships at first hand. He and the Duke had quite a say in the design of the yacht, and the Duke enlisted Sir Hugh Casson to add his own inimitable touches as well. Sir Hugh vividly remembers earmarking furniture and paintings from the previous Royal Yacht *Victoria and Albert* in Portsmouth. He has regularly advised on design and décor and recalls a later occasion choosing the paintings for a guest wing at Windsor Castle in the presence of Sir Anthony Blunt, Keeper of the Royal Pictures. The Duke and Sir Hugh went entirely for modern art. Sir Anthony, later to be revealed as a Soviet secret agent, believed there was no serious painting after Poussin. He remained silent throughout. 'He was obviously unsympathetic to all our proposals,' says Sir Hugh.

Not everyone, however, was quite as welcoming as the King. 'I felt,' says Parker, 'that Philip didn't have many friends and helpers.' There were people who were in a position to give a helping hand and who, it seemed to Parker, were reticent about doing so. He, as an Australian, always took people as they came, on merit. Some of the British Establishment were, in his view, hidebound and prejudiced. There were those among the upper classes who affected to find the Duke 'teutonic', and there was also the business of all his German relations. 'We had just been through a war,' says Parker, 'and Germans were Germans.'

Picking up the threads of family life in the aftermath of war was often fraught and confused. On 23 April 1947, for instance, the Duke's old friend and mentor, Sir Harold Wernher, wrote to Lieutenant-General Dick McCreery on a 'matter of some urgency'. This concerned the Duke's three surviving sisters, or as Wernher described them, Dickie Mountbatten's 'three nieces living in Germany'.

Evidently Prince Andrew had put some valuables into a Paris safe deposit before the war. Princess Alice wanted to see them but the French bank would not allow her access without the written consent of her three daughters who had joint power of attorney. Theodora of Baden had already signed but there was no reply from Sophie of

Hanover or Margarita of Hohenlohe-Langenburg, even though the Duchess of Kent had sent telegrams.

The job of getting the signatures was given to Peter Linklater, a young captain with the Scots Guards, who was assigned the Army Commander's personal plane and pilot and told to obtain them by the end of the week.

His first port of call was to Prince Louis of Hesse, at Wolfsgarten. Linklater, now living in Lewes, remembers a grand piano covered with photographs of European royalty and an exchange of pleasantries concerning 'Cousin Dickie's new job in India'.

Prince Louis told Linklater that Princess Sophie was staying with her husband Prince George of Hanover, Duke of Brunswick, and that Princess Margarita was with relations in the American zone. Colonel Andrew Horsbrugh-Porter, who had played polo before the war with both Sir Harold Wernher and General McCreery, volunteered to get Margarita's signature and Linklater flew to Hanover to obtain Sophie's.

The castle in which she was staying, remembers Linklater, 'had a small guard of British soldiery, perhaps explained by the fact that the owner was the Duke of Brunswick, whose alternative title used to be the Duke of Cumberland. I recall a portrait of the so-called Butcher of Culloden hanging in the castle as an honoured ancestor. This produced something of a frisson in a Scot; however I found Princess Sophie charming so bore no malice.'

That evening he and Horsbrugh-Porter rendezvoused in Frankfurt. Horsbrugh-Porter had found Margarita, 'living in very uncomfortable and straitened circumstances' but he had her signature. They immediately took off for Paris, arriving at Buk Airport in the early morning, spending some happy hours carousing in Montmartre before a shave and coffee at the Hotel Bristol and safe delivery to the Military Attaché at the British Embassy who was Christopher Soames of the Coldstream Guards, son-in-law of Winston Churchill.

'Quite an interesting anecdote about post-war relationships with our late foes,' comments Linklater, 'and if you wish to ask Philip what actually happened I would be rather intrigued.'

I relayed the story to the Duke who knew nothing about it and expressed some scepticism. Princess Sophie did not remember either, but remarked, 'At that time we didn't have proper postal communications even inside Germany.'

*

The precise nature of the Duke's job was elusive. 'I do not have a "job",' he wrote back when I asked him about this. 'In fact the more I do, the more it costs me. I never set about planning my career. I had two general ideas. I felt that I could use my position to attract attention to certain aspects of life in this country and that this might help to recognise the good things and expose the bad things. I also believed that I might be able to start various initiatives.'

In part therefore his role was reactive – he had to wait for people to invite him to do things; in part he could create initiatives. This second was obviously more difficult and he had to proceed with caution. In any case at this stage in his life he was fully employed by the Navy and after a day at the Admiralty 'there was often only time for a quick wash and brush-up before haring off to open an exhibition, chair a committee, present a cup, dine with some men.' The words are Basil Boothroyd's and Boothroyd makes a telling further point when he adds that sometimes he and his wife were together, sometimes not. The separation of duties became much more pronounced after the Accession but even in these early days they could not always be in the same place at the same time. Besides, a naval officer has to spend long periods away from home as part of his job. Even in London in the latter half of 1948 the Duke was having to spend the whole week at Greenwich where he was on the Royal Naval Staff Course. He came 'home' to the Palace at weekends.

One of his first important positions was the presidency of the National Playing Fields Association, a charity in which he continues to maintain a genuine day-to-day interest, keeping even its hyperactive chairman, Gyles Brandreth, permanently on the hop. He took this on in 1949. The same year he became Chancellor of the University of Wales, due in part to the fact that the King had made him Earl of Merioneth, which in those days was one of the Welsh counties.

It is a peculiarity of royalty that its members are so often being invited to fulfil functions for which they are at first glance ill-suited or unqualified. As he himself put it at his installation at the Welsh University, 'My generation, although reasonably well-schooled, is probably the worst educated of this age. The war cut short any chance there was of acquiring a higher education.' He belonged, he told his audience, to 'this lost generation trying to make up for what it missed between 1939 and 1945'. The paradox is that he has gone on to be virtually a professional university chancellor, adding, in turn, Edinburgh, Salford and Cambridge to his portfolio, though all for varying lengths of time. His old friend and mentor, Lord Zuckerman, a true academic's academic, admires his intellect greatly, pointing out that he has the prime intellectual quality of genuine curiosity. Perhaps the experience of studying at a university might have dulled it, but his stimulating love of questioning everyone and everything, particularly if they are 'experts', has made him a surprisingly popular chancellor in academic circles.

The most celebrated event of those early years of marriage was the birth of a son and heir. Princess Elizabeth became pregnant three months after her wedding, 'an achievement', writes a somewhat breathless Lady Longford in her book about the Queen, 'that was to be paralleled many years later by her daughter-in-law'. There are echoes here of the signal the Duke sent to Mike Parker when Parker's first child was born: 'It takes a man to have a son!'

The King's first grandson was born just before a quarter past nine on the evening of 14 November 1948. Commander Richard Colville, press secretary to the King, strode across the gravel and pinned up a note in his own handwriting. It read:

The Princess Elizabeth, Duchess of Edinburgh, was safely delivered of a Prince at 9.14 p.m. Her Royal Highness and her son are both doing well.

A huge and noisy crowd had been waiting outside the Palace railings since daybreak. The King, the Queen and Queen Mary were all waiting in an anteroom while the Duke, not one of the world's great waiters, played squash with Mike Parker. He and Parker were evenly matched. Jock Colville, who also played them, was not quite so good. Hurrying from the squash court, the Duke was able to present the proud mother with carnations and open champagne to toast the new arrival. Mike Parker repeatedly failed to quieten the boisterous crowd but finally asked the first sensible-looking person he could find to explain that mother and child were trying to sleep. The man who managed to quieten the crowd was David Niven who had starred, the previous year, in a celluloid version of *Bonnie Prince Charlie*.

This was a neat coincidence because the new arrival was named Charles Philip Arthur George. Only five days before his birth it had been pointed out that because his father, the Duke, was not a royal prince, the new baby would not be a prince either. 'Letters Patent under the Great Seal' were duly issued by the King so that any child of the Edinburghs would be a prince or princess despite their father's lack of rank. Otherwise he would have taken the courtesy title of 'Earl of Merioneth'. The question of names and titles rumbled on tiresomely for years.

If the Duke's wedding served as a reminder that he had become public property, the arrival of his firstborn served to confirm it. This was a matter for public, as well as private, celebration; for the Monarchy it meant that the succession was apparently secure for another generation. Given a reasonable life expectation, the probability now was that the infant Prince would still be King of England well into the twenty-first century. *The Times*, forgetting about Edward VII's wife, Queen Alexandra, said that the Prince was the first heir to the throne to have Danish blood since the death of Harthacanut in 1042 and the *Daily Express*, claiming, as always, to speak for the nation, said: 'Congratulations Princess Elizabeth! The British people join in your happiness. They are delighted that it is a boy. They hope that the Prince will grow up strong and vigorous to share their struggles and achievements in the exciting years ahead.' In the United States the birth was rated the tenth most important news story of the year – behind the election of President Truman and the death of the baseball player Babe Ruth.

In a sense the birth also made the Duke seem more peripheral. He was the son-in-law of the King, the husband of the future Queen, the father of the future King. In this sense, therefore, he existed primarily in relation to others. He was, already, an impressive figure with obvious charisma and strong views on a variety of subjects, but he only commanded a national stage because of his relationships with the others. He was a personality by marriage but he still had to prove himself a personality in his own right.

That year, 1948, an idea was mooted that the Duke should spend a month working as a coal-miner. He rejected this as a 'stunt' and 'playing to the gallery' but he was much more amenable to the idea that he should spend the whole of the following year working for two months at a time in a variety of different industries, studying their organisation and problems but carefully eschewing the dreaded 'stunts'. Unfortunately nothing came of it.

At the beginning of 1949 the Edinburghs finally moved into Clarence House just off the Mall. This was their first real permanent home, even though they had been renting Windlesham Moor, a country house in Berkshire. A bridge, 'Browning's Bridge', named after 'Boy', connected the house with the offices at St James's Palace next door. The atmosphere everywhere was light, bright, fresh, and full of energy and enthusiasm. Looking back on those years, Mike Parker repeatedly uses the word 'fun' to describe the sense of drive and electricity. Apart from General Browning it was a very young set-up.

Parker, Colville and the Duke himself were all still in their late twenties and all full of dash.

The contrast with the failing health of the King was all too marked. Shortly before Prince Charles's birth, George VI was suffering severe pains in his legs and when arterio-sclerosis was diagnosed it was thought at first that he might have to have his right leg amputated. This did not happen but the proposed royal tour of Australia and New Zealand had to be postponed and the King had major surgery on his leg in March 1949. In his Christmas broadcast at the end of that year he reviewed the state of the nation in grim terms. Progress had been made, he conceded, 'but none of us can be satisfied till we are standing upright and supporting our own weight, and we have a long way to go before we do that'. He was ostensibly talking about the economy, but it sounded as if he was talking about himself.

His elder daughter heard that broadcast in Malta where her husband, Lieutenant Mountbatten, Duke of Edinburgh, was serving with the Mediterranean Fleet. He was First Lieutenant or 'Jimmy', in naval argot, on board HMS *Chequers* which was the leader of the 1st Destroyer Flotilla. This was a return to the active service he enjoyed and he took full advantage of it, helped by the fact that his Commanding Officer, Captain Michael Townsend, was a born leader and wartime destroyer hero with a DSO and DSC to his name. Also on board was his old shipmate Terry Lewin who was serving as the flotilla's gunnery officer. The tradition is that the lead ship in a flotilla is unpopular with the others. It carries too much brass – 'too many bloody staff officers', in Lewin's phrase. The Duke was not helped by being the youngest of all the First Lieutenants. Nor was the presence of his uncle, Lord Mountbatten, an unmitigated blessing. Mountbatten had stepped down from being Viceroy of India and was now commanding the 1st Cruiser Squadron. Throughout most of his life Mountbatten excited fierce admiration or extreme dislike, and although he was by no means the most senior officer in the Mediterranean Fleet he was unquestionably its best-known personality. When he met his nephew in Malta Mountbatten explained to the press that he was meeting the Duke as 'an uncle not an admiral'. Even so . . .

'If your flotilla leader is popular,' explains Lewin, 'then you've made it. I would claim that *Chequers* was extremely popular. All the other "Jimmies" were pretty experienced but he won them round. They admired him because he was good.'

There were happy days ashore as well. Mike Parker commuted regularly between Clarence House and Malta, enabling the Duke to keep in touch with such new interests as the National Playing Fields Association. At first the Mountbattens had the Duke and Princess Elizabeth to stay at their home, the Villa Guardamangia, and later when Mountbatten was posted home as Fourth Sea Lord the Edinburghs took on the lease. There were parties and polo, swimming and dancing, even shopping and trips to the hairdresser. Of course there were moments when protocol intervened and the Governor gave them a ball or local dignitaries wanted to make a fuss of the Duke, not understanding – as the Duke did – that it was his captain's duty to make the house calls while the Duke was supposed to be keeping the ship clean. However, their life at this time was more like many other people's than before or since.

In July 1950, a few weeks before the birth of a second child, Princess Anne, he was promoted Lieutenant-Commander and appointed to his first command, the frigate HMS *Magpie*. There was a minor hiccup before this when something went wrong in what should, for him, have been a routine 'Command' examination. Unaccountably he failed in Torpedo and ASDIC.* Other biographers make a minor meal of this episode with a picture of Mike Parker summoned by a furious Commander-in-Chief, Admiral Sir Arthur John Power, who wanted to overrule the examiner. On hearing this the Duke exploded, saying, 'If they try to fix it, I quit the Navy for good.' Whereupon he resat the exam and 'went through like a breeze'. Contemporaries, however, say that the exam was almost entirely oral, and that the Torpedo and ASDIC examiner was a 'funny little chap' who played polo and probably fell foul of the Duke on the field of play. Not a big deal, though if he had been given a command without passing, other officers would have had a 'jolly legitimate gripe'. Whether or not the story is significant, it yet again makes a crucial point. What seems to the Duke to be important or significant or unusual in his life does not always strike outside observers in the same way. And vice versa.

His command of *Magpie* was a success. He was tough, hard, mucked in with everybody, and if he had a fault it was a tendency to intolerance. It is not just his enemies who have commented on this last trait.

It seems he had every justification for being critical of *Magpie* when he took over. One of his younger officers told me that under the Duke's predecessor – 'an absolute swine' – *Magpie* was 'the most miser-

---

* ASDIC is another name for an echo-sounder. It derives from Anti-Submarine Detection Investigation Committee.

able bloody ship I've ever seen'. For her new Commander the only way to go was up. 'All we wanted,' said his junior, 'was someone who was fair and reasonable and didn't bump into things.'

Lieutenant-Commander the Duke of Edinburgh never bumped into another ship but he did acquire a reputation for shouting at the bumboats who got in the way in Sliema Creek when *Magpie* was trying to manoeuvre herself in or out. Almost immediately after his arrival on board, the ship bloomed and her complement of eight officers and a hundred and fifty men suddenly began to take a pride in serving on what detractors referred to as 'Edinburgh's Private Yacht'. Determined to turn her into one of the smartest ships afloat, the Duke managed to tune his crew to such a pitch that in the annual Fleet regatta *Magpie* rowed away with six out of the ten trophies. He himself stroked an officers' crew and did rather better than when similarly employed in a *Chequers* crew which also had Lord Lewin in the bow. They came thirteenth. 'That boat was like lead,' says Lewin.

The crew of *Magpie* called their captain 'Dukey' and they enjoyed a heady mixture of naval routine and ceremonial visits. In his years with the Mediterranean Fleet the Duke opened the State Legislature in Gibraltar, dined with King ibn Saud in Jedda and with King Abdullah in Amman. He debated with students in Venice and took his wife, who travelled aboard the Commander-in-Chief's Despatch Vessel, HMS *Surprise*, to see his relations in Greece. His mother was still living in Athens and his cousin Paul was King. This was the occasion of the celebrated exchange of signals:

*Surprise* to *Magpie*: 'Princess full of beans.'
*Magpie* to *Surprise*: 'Can't you give her something better for breakfast?'

The Duke has always enjoyed this sort of joke even though his biographer Boothroyd, *Punch* staff writer and, like the Duke, a member of the famous *Punch* table, the magazine's equivalent of the Thursday Club, observed with professional superiority, 'Not topline wit'. On another occasion, overflying HMS *Vigo* the Duke, responding to *Vigo*'s somewhat caustic bon voyage, and echoing a radio catchphrase of the time, signalled back, '*Vigo* – vi come back'. It is bad luck on the Duke that this sort of line sounds cracking when it is delivered spontaneously and from the hip, but can lose, as it were, in translation.

In Athens that summer King Paul of Greece 'found with astonishment' that the captain was not only running the ship, but was also helping prepare the forthcoming Festival of Britain and planning a complex foreign tour from his cramped cabin under the bridge. Everything was being drafted in pencil personally by the Duke. 'Uncle Palo,' writes Alexandra of Yugoslavia, 'imagined I think that he would find a qualified commander acting as nominal First Lieutenant under Philip – but nothing of the kind.'

This image of the Duke burning both ends of the candle is not only characteristic, it is also a reminder that the *Magpie* idyll could not last for ever. In May 1951 the King succumbed to an attack of bronchitis which proved so difficult to shake off that his doctors feared he might have cancer. Princess Elizabeth's place in the tiny Family Firm was at home at her father's side. The Duke's place was at his wife's. And so he left active service for the last time in July 1951.

'As far as I am concerned,' he wrote to me in November 1990, 'there has never been an "if only", except perhaps that I regret not having been able to continue a career in the Navy.'

In the autumn the King and Queen were to have gone on a coast-to-coast tour of Canada followed by a lightning visit to President Truman in Washington. The King was not well enough and it was decided that the Edinburghs would go instead. Then, a few days before the scheduled departure aboard the transatlantic liner, *Empress of Britain*, the King's doctors discovered that he had a malignant tumour on the left lung. On 23 September, in a two-hour operation at Buckingham Palace, the lung was removed. 'The King pretty bad,' recorded Harold Nicolson in his diary the following day. 'Nobody can talk about anything else – and the election is forgotten. What a strange thing is monarchy.'

It was obviously impossible for Princess Elizabeth and the Duke to leave Britain under these circumstances, but if they flew they could stay on long enough to be sure that the operation was a success. The problem was that royalty did not fly. After a personal interview with the Duke, the new Prime Minister, Winston Churchill, was persuaded, although at first he was violently opposed, but eventually he too succumbed. Much later Mike Parker had an even worse row with Churchill on the subject of helicopters, Royal Family, for the use of. The old man was fiercely protective of Princess Elizabeth and he thought these reckless young men with their flying machines were placing her in needless jeopardy.

In the event the King staged a recovery and the tour went ahead, with the Edinburghs flying from London Airport to Montreal in a Boeing Stratocruiser piloted by one of the British Overseas Airways Corporation's most experienced pilots, O. P. Jones. The whole long Canadian exercise was a triumph and so was the brief American after-

math, even though this had its curiosities. The Duke had never previously experienced American security and was not amused by the
profusion of armed guards, all seemingly under different authorities.
At the Trumans', President Harry insisted on taking his guests to the
top floor of Blair House – the White House was out of commission
due to a refurbishment programme – in order to meet his exceedingly
old and very deaf mother-in-law. The President's mother-in-law had
evidently heard that Winston Churchill had just been returned as
Britain's Prime Minister. She beamed at Princess Elizabeth. 'I'm so
glad,' she exclaimed, 'that your father's been re-elected.'

Still the King was not well. His Christmas broadcast, prerecorded
in short bursts, was rather glum, thanking God for his grace, his
doctors, surgeons, and nurses for their skill, and his people for their
support in helping him to 'come through my illness', but not sounding wholly convinced.

At the end of January 1952 the Edinburghs set off to tour East
Africa, Australia and New Zealand. In London the night before their
departure, they and the rest of the family went to the Drury Lane
Theatre for a performance of *South Pacific*. At the airport next day the
King and Churchill drank champagne and bade the young tourists
goodbye. In the photographs the King looks dreadful, but Mike
Parker and Lord Charteris, both of whom were on the trip, say that
the cameras lied and that he looked better than he had for an age. If
they had realised how ill he really was they would never have made
the tour. Churchill thought the King was 'gay and even jaunty'.

Less than a week later, on 5 February, the King enjoyed a day's shooting at Sandringham. It was a clear, light blue day and the King was in
good form. His last shot of the day cut down a hare, killing it outright.
That evening he sent messages of congratulation to his keepers, planned
the following day's shoot, dined with the Queen, Princess Margaret and
their friends, and retired to bed at ten thirty. A watchman saw him
fiddling with the window latch at midnight, but next morning, when
his valet arrived at seven thirty with the morning tea, the King was dead
of a coronary thrombosis. He was fifty-six.

The Edinburghs had arrived in Kenya, where they had spent the
night at Treetops, now a large and moderately sophisticated game
park hotel from which you can watch wild animals at the salt lick
below. In those days it was little more than a tree house up a fig tree,
a precarious three-bedroom hide reached by rickety ladders. After a
night watching elephants and a troop of baboons who had stolen the
Treetops lavatory rolls and were throwing them over the branches like

so many football hooligans, the Edinburghs went fishing for trout in the Sagana River in the Aberdare game reserve and then returned to Sagana Lodge, a wedding present from the Kenyan people, for a siesta.

It was Mike Parker who broke the news. Unfortunately this was the one place on the entire tour where the communications were hopeless. The first he knew about the King's death was a call from Martin Charteris who was staying at Lord Baden-Powell's final home, the Outspan Hotel, Nyeri. Charteris had the news from a newspaper reporter, but it was still garbled and uncertain. Parker twiddled the dials of his radio, found London and the BBC, and confirmed what had happened. The Duke was asleep so Parker woke him and gave him the news.

'I never felt so sorry for anyone in all my life,' said Parker. 'He looked as if you'd dropped half the world on him.' More recently Parker told me that he remembers the Duke saying nothing at all, just breathing in and out, twice very deeply, as if in shock. When Charteris arrived later he found the Queen, as she had now become, very composed, and writing telegrams. The Duke was slumped in an armchair, arms akimbo, a newspaper spread in front of his face. He did not put it down, nor did he speak. Parker managed to get the whole party out of the place and on to a Dakota for Entebbe Airport within the hour. Charteris and the Queen dealt with different sorts of formality concerning the Accession.

Everyone but the Duke had much to do.

At London Airport at dusk on 7 February Queen Elizabeth II, a tiny figure all in black, came down the steps from the BOAC plane. Standing to attention on the tarmac was the bare-headed, black-coated figure of her Prime Minister, Sir Winston Churchill.

The Duke of Edinburgh waited in the aircraft until his wife was back on English soil. Only then did he emerge to join her. It was a symbolic moment.

# 'Of Crown, of Queen'

'Thus was I, sleeping, by a brother's hand,
Of life, of crown, of queen, at once dispatch'd'
*Hamlet*
SHAKESPEARE

On 5 May 1952 the first meeting of the Coronation Commission took place with the Duke of Edinburgh in the chair.

'My Lords and Gentlemen,' he began. 'First, as Chairman, welcome to the first meeting of the Coronation Commission. There is a tremendous amount of work to be done, so the sooner we get down to it the better.'

The Duke has never been a man for small talk and this demand for action the day before yesterday is very much what we have come to expect from him. The verve, attack and, above all, the optimism is entirely in character, and the ultimate success of the Coronation owed much to his brisk chairmanship of the Commission.

Its first meeting came just three months after the despair of Sagana Lodge. It is what one expects from the Duke in particular, but also from royal dynasties in general: out of tragedy, hope; from ashes, the Phoenix; life must go on; the King is dead, long live the Queen. The seventy-seven-year-old Prime Minister, Sir Winston Churchill, summed up his tribute to the King with the words: 'I whose youth was passed in the august, unchallenged and tranquil glories of the

Victorian Era, may well feel a thrill in invoking once more the prayer and the anthem, "God Save the Queen".' Before long, people began to talk and write about a new Elizabethan Age. The signs were propitious – the Korean War was more or less successfully concluded, a little local difficulty with the Persians over oil was resolved, and before the Queen was crowned the last vestiges of food rationing were removed. You no longer needed a coupon for sugar.

All this euphoria centred on the undeniably romantic figure of the Queen herself. Although her husband was chairing the Coronation Commission and amassing a considerable portfolio of other duties and responsibilities, there was no escaping the fact that this was the Queen's show and that her husband, while still the husband she had promised to love, honour and obey in Westminster Abbey less than five years earlier, was now her subject. Indeed in the Coronation service, once more in Westminster Abbey, he was required to say to his wife, 'I Philip, Duke of Edinburgh, do become your liegeman of life and limb and of earthly worship; and faith and truth I will bear unto you, to live and die against all manner of folks.' There is nothing whatever to suggest that he himself ever had any problem with reconciling the apparent conflict between the role of husband and subject but others were quick to assume that he did. It is yet another example of the thought transference that has dogged his life. Everybody assumes that because they would feel certain things if they were in his shoes it follows that he, too, must feel them. Not necessarily so.

The Coronation was both a solemn ritual and an extravagant spectacle. The *Daily Telegraph*, as always the ultimate *news*paper, reported in a typically matter-of-fact manner:

In the Abbey Church of St Peter, Westminster, endowed richly by the first illustrious Elizabeth, Her Most Excellent Majesty Queen Elizabeth II dedicated herself yesterday to the service of her people.

Of the Duke, the *Telegraph* reported that she took his hands in hers, 'before he drew back to touch the Crown and to kiss her on the left cheek'.

The Coronation was most emphatically the Queen's day and the Duke's was a supporting role. However, he did play an important part in the most dramatic Coronation Day present of all. That very morning news arrived that the British Everest Expedition, of which he was patron, had succeeded in conquering the world's highest mountain for the first time. This was almost as much of a coup for the *Times* correspondent James Morris, now the travel writer Jan Morris, as it was for Sherpa Tenzing and Sir Edmund Hillary who actually set foot on the summit.

The previous night the climbers had brought out the rum and toasted the Duke 'who had followed our progress with such keen interest and sympathy'. Now on Coronation Day, far away in the Himalayas, the expedition heard with amazement that the news of their success had not only been in the morning's *Times* but also relayed to the Coronation crowds through loudspeakers on the route.

As the expedition leader, Brigadier John Hunt, wrote:

It all sounded like a fairy-tale. Although we were still far from grasping the full significance of the event we already knew quite as much as was good for us in one evening. Another jar of rum was called for and a second celebration took place. There would be many more to follow. The Sherpas naturally shared in the revelry. We drank a loyal toast to Her Majesty the Queen, assuming the privilege of drinking it seated upon the ground or on ration boxes, for space forbade otherwise.

Before long the newly knighted Sir John Hunt would be the first director of the Duke of Edinburgh's Award Scheme.

As if to remind the Duke of the fact that he was, in some people's eyes, his wife's junior partner the name business cropped up yet again in Coronation Year. This was thanks to the insensitivity of his uncle, Lord Mountbatten. At a private dinner party at Broadlands shortly after the Accession, Mountbatten boasted that since 7 February the Royal house was *his* house. The Queen was, in effect, Mrs Mountbatten and the House of Mountbatten ruled. Not the House of Windsor. Prince Ernest Augustus of Hanover, who had been at the Broadlands dinner, reported the comments to Queen Mary who, according to Jock Colville, was 'greatly disturbed' and asked him to come and see her. Colville had left royal service and was now well placed working again as private secretary to Winston Churchill, the new Prime Minister. Colville told 'the poor old lady, who had spent a sleepless night' that it was most unlikely that the Cabinet would agree to this. Nor did they, but when it was proposed that a proclamation should be issued saying that Windsor should definitely be the 'house name' the Duke wrote what Colville described as 'an ably but strongly worded memorandum' of protest. He suggested that 'the House of Edinburgh' would be appropriate. This annoyed Churchill (not the only time the Duke irritated the old man) and with the full backing of the Cabinet the Prime Minister told the Queen that the ruling house was the House of Windsor. The Duke said that in that

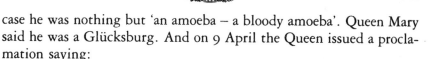

case he was nothing but 'an amoeba – a bloody amoeba'. Queen Mary said he was a Glücksburg. And on 9 April the Queen issued a proclamation saying:

The Queen today declared in Council her Will and Pleasure that She and Her Children shall be styled and known as the House and Family of Windsor, and that Her descendants other than female descendants who marry and their descendants shall bear the name of Windsor.

If it all seems a lot of fuss about nothing, it was still a lot of fuss, and it was not yet finished. If only Mountbatten had kept his counsel.

There were at least two other disputes between the Duke and the Prime Minister. The first concerned Clarence House. The young family was very happy there. It was a convenient size, very private, and had recently been completely redecorated according to their taste. It would be much more convenient to stay there. If it was necessary for either the Queen or the Duke to go to the office, then Buckingham Palace was only five minutes' walk away or about thirty seconds by car. What could be simpler? Churchill would not even contemplate it. Every English Monarch had lived and worked at Buckingham Palace since Queen Victoria first moved there in 1837. It was not going to change now.

The other disagreement concerned helicopters. In the run-up to the Coronation large numbers of Commonwealth and Colonial troops due to be on parade that day were scattered in barracks all over the kingdom. It was felt the Duke ought to visit them all and the logistics were complicated. Using ground transport it was practically impossible and so he and Mike Parker decided that a helicopter borrowed from the Royal Navy was the only answer. Returning from one such engagement and landing in the Palace garden, Parker spotted an unfamiliar figure with a briefcase and bowler hat.

'You're in trouble,' he was told, as the messenger asked him to be good enough to accompany him.

Their destination was 10 Downing Street. When they arrived, Parker was shown into the Prime Minister's office where the great man was going through a theatrical performance of shuffling his papers and affecting not to notice the young Australian.

Eventually he looked up and glared over his spectacles.

'Is it your intention to destroy the entire Royal Family in the shortest possible time?'

Or words to that effect. Almost forty years on Parker tells the story with a degree of theatricality himself.

He stood his ground while the Prime Minister fulminated away about what scandalous risks were being taken and how improperly Parker was behaving. When he had had his say Parker replied that, with respect, he understood that Mr Churchill had an arduous engagement outside London the following day and that it would take many hours of tiring driving to accomplish the mission. 'I am authorised to say,' he concluded, 'that the Commanding Officer of the Royal Navy Helicopter Squadron would be honoured to put one of his machines at your disposal.'

For some seconds Churchill stared at Parker as if he were a very low form of life. Then he said one word, drawing each syllable out to its maximum length so that it seemed to go on and on in a manner which can only be described as Churchillian.

'HELICOPTERS!' It was a little like Lady Bracknell in *The Importance of Being Earnest*, saying, 'A HANDBAG!'

In the event, Churchill succumbed to the appeal of the helicopter and that particular dispute was resolved, but he continued to be, from time to time, ruder to the Duke than anyone else ever dared. Meanwhile the Duke remained ill at ease with much of the old Establishment. For a number of reasons this was inevitable. Once again, 'Vide Albert,' the Duke suggested to me, but as Lady Longford, biographer of Queen Victoria as well as of Queen Elizabeth II, has argued, the differences between Albert and Philip were considerably greater than the similarities. When Albert married Victoria she was already 'mistress of her own house' and he had to establish himself as master. The Duke, however, had already enjoyed nearly five years of marriage and was well set in the dominant husband and father role within his family.

In terms of public function, however, the situation was reversed. Queen Victoria was not supported by the full-scale bureaucracy inherited by Queen Elizabeth, with the result that Albert assumed those functions himself and acted as secretary and adviser. In 1952 Elizabeth took over what was in effect a department of state. Buckingham Palace was stuffed with courtier bureaucrats and they all reported to the Queen. Her private secretary was in no way bound to defer to the Duke nor even to let him know how he was advising her. The same went for a whole battery of other officials from the Lord Chamberlain, the Master of the Horse and her press secretary to such deceptively lowly figures as the formidable 'Bobo' MacDonald, the Queen's dresser. When the Queen's men felt that the Duke was becoming involved with matters that were not his concern, there were rows. 'He wrote wonderful speeches for himself,' said one old Palace hand, drily, 'but less good for the Queen.'

Before the Accession the Edinburghs had shared their staff but now the Queen inherited her father's as well as taking Martin Charteris, who had succeeded Jock Colville in 1950. The Duke kept on 'Boy' Browning as comptroller and treasurer and Mike Parker as private secretary. Mike Parker's position as the Duke's friend and confidant was unassailable but Browning's position was more equivocal. Was he a restraining influence on the young Duke and his brash Australian friend? Or was he an invaluable ally in fending off the more difficult and conservative elements at court? After all, Browning was a man of considerable standing and, as a senior army officer, had been the superior of many of the younger Guards officers whose influence Parker and the Duke thought pernicious. The relationship was complex. In the end, which came in 1957, Browning had a nervous breakdown. Some people thought he simply could not stand the pace of the Duke's household but there were personal reasons too. His relationship with his wife, Daphne du Maurier, was distant. 'Boy' was attractive to ladies and his choices were sometimes injudicious. This caused severe strains.

In Boy Browning's case there was no public scandal, but some time later Parker had to endure a particularly unpleasant divorce from his wife Eileen and this led to his departure. It was ironic because his joining the Duke's household in 1947 was, in part, an effort to save his already shaky marriage. It went disastrously wrong.

Parker had a reputation for exuberance and rakishness, some of which attached itself to the Duke and much of which derived from their membership of an organisation called the Thursday Club. This was a lunch club which met on Thursdays for the express purpose of bringing the weekend closer. Not everyone liked it much. 'No dancing girls,' said one of the starchier courtiers of the day, 'but quite lewd talk. Quite lewd.' Members met in an upstairs room at Wheeler's restaurant in Old Compton Street, Soho. One recent book has even described it as a 'secret society' but in fact it was not secret enough. All sorts of odd people turned up either uninvited or invited by mistake. 'There was that ghastly little man who played the mouth organ,' said Sir Reginald Bennett, the sailor and politician. 'I don't know who let him in.' He meant Larry Adler. Bennett brought along his boss, Iain Macleod, later to become a brilliant Chancellor of the Exchequer. Macleod loved it. 'Someone from the Foreign Office brought Kim Philby one day,' said Mike Parker, 'he turned out to be the dullest man in the place.' Another regular was the society osteo-path Stephen Ward, a talented artist who drew several members of the Royal Family including the Duke. Ward achieved notoriety dur-ing the Profumo case as the man who introduced Profumo to Christine Keeler; his smart friends ditched him and he committed suicide. Both Parker and Bennett told me they thought there was something un-savoury about him and they gave him as wide a berth as they gave Larry Adler.

'We've been given the reputation for being wild,' says Parker, 'but the truth is that we enjoyed fun and going round with people who knew what was going on. The Thursday Club was a great sounding base and the idea that it was a drunken orgy was absolute rubbish. People got very merry but never drunk. As far as being wild, not guilty. As far as hanging around women, not guilty.'

The Thursday Club members included Arthur Christiansen, editor of the *Daily Express* and Frank Owen, editor of the *Daily Mail*; the actors James Robertson Justice and David Niven; Lord Glenavy, bet-ter known as Patrick Campbell, the wit and raconteur; Pip Youngman Carter, writer and artist married to the crime novelist Margery Allingham; Peter Ustinov; Monja Danischewsky, the scriptwriter of, among other films, *Whisky Galore*; Compton Mackenzie, author of the novel on which it was based; and the ubiquitous court photographer, Baron.

The story of Baron and the cuckoo clock does much to explain the wardroom boisterousness of the club. The room at Wheeler's had a cuckoo clock and on the half-hour the cuckoo emerged very briefly, delivered a quick 'cluck' and went back into its house. You would have to be very quick to snap a picture of it and the club bet Baron, a wager expressed in dollars, that he couldn't do it. The first time the club staged such a noisy diversion that Baron was shaking too much with laughter to hold the camera steady. Next time he brought his tripod but at the crucial moment Parker gave it a nudge and he failed again. On the third occasion Baron insisted that no one should stand nearer than three yards. This time Parker got hold of three 'thunder-flashes' — a sort of low-powered hand-grenade used in military train-ing. (Parker was rather given to letting off thunder-flashes though *never*, as his wife has suggested, in the Palace.) The Duke had one, Parker another and either James Robertson Justice or Arthur Chris-tiansen the third. As the hands reached half past one, all lit their thunder-flashes. One landed under the camera, one under some wine-glasses and the third in the fireplace by which the Duke was sitting.

Clearly no one had swept the chimney for an age. Down came the soot, turning the Duke into an instant Al Jolson. The police arrived in seconds, in force and highly excited. They did not see the funny side of the story.

Nor perhaps will everybody else. 'I can't understand that side of him,' said one of the Duke's admirers. 'All that footsteps on the ceiling stuff.' Perhaps it *was* rather adolescent or undergraduate or wardroom, or whatever pejorative word one uses to describe this sort of thing, but it was never, according to the participants, anything more than high-spirited and the idea that the Duke and Parker were part of some secret vice-ring is hotly denied. Much of the misunderstandings stem from a book by Parker's former wife which appeared in 1982. In it she also suggests that her husband and the Duke were in the habit of slipping out of the Palace on clandestine jaunts under the pseudonyms 'Murgatroyd and Winterbottom'. Parker thinks that perhaps during an evening charade at Windsor he and the Duke might have performed a sketch based on these two characters from the Tommy Handley radio comedy *ITMA*, but the idea that they used the identities for cover while playing hooky from the Palace is described by Parker as 'the biggest load of hogwash I've ever read in my life'. After the book was published, Parker drew it to the Duke's attention. 'I had no idea that Eileen had written a book,' he replied, 'and now that you have mentioned it I have no intention whatever of reading it.'

It is easy to understand why the Duke should not wish to read tittle-tattle about the Thursday Club or Murgatroyd and Winterbottom. Yet there are moments in these early years when he seems hopelessly caught between the desire to strike out and be different, informed, informal, in-touch and unstuffy and the equally keen desire of others to make sure that he did nothing of the kind. It was not just the old-fashioned courtiers, the landed aristocracy and the men with moustaches. Pomposity took many forms and emanated from the most unlikely sources. At the end of 1954, for instance, the Welsh gave him the freedom of Cardiff and the Town Clerk, Mr S. Tapper-Jones, all wig and gown, announced that 'His Royal Highness Philip, Duke of Edinburgh, Knight of the Most Noble Order of the Garter . . . being a person of distinction within the meaning of Section 259 of the Local Government Act, 1933, be, in accordance with the provisions of the said Act, admitted an honorary Freeman of the City of Cardiff.'

The Duke made a joke of it, of course, but even so it is an indication of what he was up against and of why he needed something informal and unpompous like the Thursday Club to preserve his sanity. A treadmill was in danger of developing. In the months after that first meeting of the Coronation Commission he opened the Braille Centenary Exhibition and the Affric Hydro-Electric Scheme at Fasnakyle Power Station in the north of Scotland and the Imperial Cricket Memorial at Marylebone Cricket Club and the Royal Yachts Exhibition in the Octagon Room at the Royal Observatory. He unveiled the extension to the Naval War Museum in Chatham and an extension to the Municipal College in Portsmouth and the Memorial Roll of Honour of the Staff of the London County Council who lost their lives in the Second World War. He opened an engineering laboratory in Cambridge and addressed a dinner to celebrate the centenary of Sir William Ramsay, the Nobel Prize-winning discoverer of argon, helium, neon, krypton and xenon. He opened the 'Model Engineer' exhibition and found evidence 'of the British desire to create – of the dexterity, concentration, self-discipline, and originality on which our past successes have been based and our future depends'. He presented medals to students at the London Master Builders' Association and prizes to cadets on HMS *Devonshire*. The cadets were told, 'Promotion is not a question of "jobs for the boys"; it is a competition of service in the interest of the Navy and the country.' Shades of Kurt Hahn's remark about 'the Royal back door'.

He visited the Military College of Science where he told them that whereas, until now, all service officers had been required to handle men, 'Modern warfare undoubtedly has added two other requirements: the ability to handle machines, and the ability to handle paper.' He toasted the British Radio Industry at the Radio Industry Council Annual Dinner where he took a stab at design and technology, saying that 'We, that is the customers, know that the things ought to work; our choice will now depend upon what they look like.' And he proposed the health of 'The Society' at the Land Agents' Society Jubilee Dinner. He thanked the Agents for 'a most excellent and enormous dinner' and then, typically, said that if this was their usual standard, 'land agents should eat half as much and then we should not have to produce twice as much food'. A week later he was given the freedom of the Mercers' Company and replied to the toast to the health of the new Freemen with another joke to the effect that 'from what you say there is only one older profession than a Mercer'. There were endless toasts. He also toasted the Chartered Insurance Institute at their annual dinner and the National Union of Manufacturers at their annual luncheon and told them that 'I believe the solution lies in our wits'.

He took the passing-out parade at Cranwell and was Field Marshal Montgomery's guest at the Alamein Reunion.

And all this before the end of Coronation Year.

The question is inevitable and obvious and he has asked it himself. 'You might just ask whether all this rushing about is to any purpose. Am I just doing it to make it look as if I'm earning my keep, or has it any national value?' One way of answering this is to actually go out with him on tour and watch, listen and try to form a judgement from personal observation. I did that later and found it instructive. Here, however, we are talking about almost forty years ago and as the various different events come surging at you off the printed page I do get a sense of action at all costs. The industry is formidable. Even the shorter speeches have been properly researched and the longer addresses — on becoming Chancellor of Edinburgh University, for instance, or his scholarly twenty-page speech to the British Association for the Advancement of Science — are serious and thoughtful. Even so I sense a danger, running through that list, that he might simply have turned into one of those men — like Sir Arthur Dickson Wright and Lord Mancroft — who became most famous for all-purpose after-dinner speaking. A sort of 'turn'.

However these years, the fifties, were those in which he was defining himself. Under those circumstances it was, perhaps, inevitable that there should be an element of hit-and-miss. Some people thought Mike Parker was a bit too much of a live wire. 'Mike was always starting hares,' said a colleague of this time, but one result of all this frantic activity was that the Duke was able to develop an interest in one or two particular areas. One old courtier quoted Jock Colville at me; 'Jock,' he said, 'said of the Queen that she was a person with wonderful *negative* judgement. That meant she was frightfully good at knowing when to say "no" though not so good at saying "yes". Philip on the other hand is good at "yes".' Not, you understand, the sort of 'yes-man' who agrees with everyone else, but the sort of 'yes-man' who will take a risk.

The trouble is that his position as the Queen's husband restricted the amount of allowable risk. Physical risk was one problem — hence the trouble with Churchill over helicopters and endless argument when in these years he learned to fly. His instructor, Caryl Gordon, was always having to turn a blind eye and steer a path between his pupil's flamboyance and official caution. Part of the reason for learning to fly, incidentally, was so that he could legitimately wear wings on his uniform. Prince Bernhard of the Netherlands, another keen royal pilot and still flying his own aeroplanes as he nears eighty, says that it was he who told him very firmly that he must not, like George V, wear wings to which he was not really entitled, but I guess the thought of doing so would never have crossed the Duke's mind.

Prince Bernhard, husband of Queen Juliana of the Netherlands, though ten years the Duke's senior, is an interesting point of comparison and none more so than in the early nineteen-fifties. In 1953, while the Duke was chairing the Coronation Commission and being busy in an essentially peripheral capacity, Bernhard got one of the two most interesting opportunities in his life. In February, Holland was devastated by severe flooding which breached the country's sea defences. A national disaster was declared and Bernhard was put in charge of dealing with the emergency. Earlier, during the war, he had a similar opportunity for the unrestricted exercise of power when he was in command of the Dutch free forces. Today, sitting dapper, buttonholed, pipe smoking in his study at Soestdijk Palace, he said that he believed one of the sadnesses in the Duke's life was that he had never had that sort of opportunity. In general, Prince Bernhard felt the British Royal Family had to tread more carefully than the Dutch. He himself, for instance, was quite free to telephone any member of the Dutch Government at any time. The Minister was not obliged to do what Bernhard wanted but there was free and frank discussion about everything – including politics. This was not possible for the Duke.

In the early fifties, at the outset of his career as consort, the Duke was obviously anxious to make something of his life and it was therefore essential that he should devote more time and trouble to some areas than others. Various demands and constraints mean that he is bound to be more of a generalist than most but if he were not to become a walking platitude it was necessary to become at least something of an expert and retain an active interest. Already he was devoting himself to the National Playing Fields Association, and under the tutelage of Sir Harold Hartley he was becoming a pioneer advocate of the marriage between science, technology and design. These have remained with him throughout his life, and there were other priorities too. The Central Office of Information has produced an official handout on the Duke and it was the very first document Brian McGrath gave me when I started out on this project. It is a bald document, but it does précis his priorities. 'In particular,' it says, 'he interests himself in scientific and technological research and development, in the encouragement of sport, the welfare of young people, and in the conservation and the state of the environment.'

It was in the fifties that he started planning two of his most innovative schemes – his Commonwealth Study Conferences, the first of which took place in Oxford in 1956, and the Duke of Edinburgh's Award Scheme which also began its first tentative operations in 1956. These are his two great inventions. His involvement with the two other organisations to which he has devoted so much – the World Wildlife Fund and the International Equestrian Federation – began later, in 1961 and 1964. In both these cases he took over from his friend and fellow Prince Consort, Prince Bernhard, so that he was not actually starting something brand-new however much the two bodies might have grown and developed under his leadership. Besides, his interest in wildlife and in horses was well established by the end of the fifties.

Ceremonial is a vital part of royalty and the Duke had been an integral part of royal ceremony ever since his dashing appearance in that be-medalled naval uniform at his wedding in 1947. Much, though not all, such ceremony is associated with the armed services. Even at a civilian state occasion such as the State Opening of Parliament, the Duke will appear in warrior's uniform. Since the early fifties he has had plenty of choice when it came to kit. At the Accession in 1952 he became Admiral of the Sea Cadet Corps, Colonel-in-Chief of the Army Cadet Force and Air Commodore-in-Chief of the Air Training Corps. In Coronation Year he rocketed to the top of all three armed services with his elevation to the rank of Admiral of the Fleet, Field Marshal and Marshal of the Royal Air Force. He also became Captain General of the Royal Marines and Colonel or Colonel-in-Chief of numerous regiments.*

The portfolio was becoming recognisable: honorary jobs of a largely ceremonial nature; one-off assignments and events on his own, usually involving some talking; a few pet schemes, enterprises and interests; leisure; and holding the Queen's hand. His support of the Queen is, and was, the first essential. Time and time again those who have been close to him emphasised how the Queen always came before everything else, how determined he was that everything he did should be for the benefit of his wife, both as a person and as Her Majesty. 'Make no mistake,' said Martin Charteris, 'he's done a wonderful job for the monarchy and he's been a superb consort to the Queen.' That has always been the bottom line but it has never prevented him from developing his own distinct identity. Being the Prince Consort in all but name is just one of his jobs. 'By the way,' I asked Charteris, who

* See Appendix.

was a long-serving private secretary to the Queen, 'that title "Prince Consort" — is it important?'

'Meaningless,' he replied.

In 1956 the Duke went on a long cruise in the Royal Yacht. This began with an invitation to open the 1956 Olympic Games in Melbourne and turned into a world tour of parts of the Empire and Commonwealth which the Royal Family does not usually reach. It was a watershed tour in a number of ways. It was also almost a serious embarrassment. For instance, they were sailing east of Trincomalee, the harbour on Ceylon's east coast, when English and French paratroopers dropped into Egypt to frustrate President Nasser's seizure of the Suez Canal, thus precipitating an international crisis. On board the Royal Yacht were the Duke and Lord Cilcennin, ex-First Lord of the Admiralty. The first they heard of the matter was when Arthur Christiansen called Mike Parker from the *Daily Express*. *Britannia*, after all, was designated a hospital ship. They naturally wondered what to do, but after only a few days, the Americans intervened, the crisis was resolved and *Britannia* sailed on.

There were many good reasons for this tour, but it did mean that the Duke was away from his family for four months including not just the Suez Crisis but also Christmas and New Year. The Queen opened Parliament with her sister instead of her husband. Prince Charles was eight and Princess Anne six. Tongues wagged. Surely their father should not have been away so long? The concept of a 'royal rift' gained currency in the popular press.

The tour was serious and arduous, enjoyable but involving hardship and sacrifice too. The Duke and Mike Parker felt that its serious side was under-reported and that the media was only interested in exploiting it in a salacious way. Unfortunately there was plenty of opportunity for this.

During his absence Eileen Parker sued her husband Mike for divorce. The Parker saga was messy and long-running. With the benefit of hindsight, Parker now says that his marriage was 'the silliest thing I've ever done in my life'. It was one of those war-time marriages.

The press had already enjoyed a field day with the love affair between Princess Margaret and Group Captain Peter Townsend. The Group Captain was divorced from his wife and the Princess was not in the direct line of succession. Nonetheless she felt obliged not to marry him and to make a public announcement to that effect. Had she renounced her rights of succession she might have been allowed a civil marriage but, 'Mindful of the Church's teaching that Christian marriage is indissoluble, and conscious of my duty to the Commonwealth, I have resolved to put these considerations before any others . . .'

There were any number of sad ironies following on from this, not the least, of course, being that when she did marry the photographer Antony Armstrong-Jones, later Lord Snowdon, that marriage ended in divorce, which in the interim had become more acceptable to public opinion and indeed the Church. Mike Parker recalls that Armstrong-Jones was working as an assistant in the studios of Baron, the royal photographer and friend of Parker and Prince Philip. It had been suggested that Baron should go on the round-the-world *Britannia* trip as official photographer but shortly before departure he went into hospital for a hip operation and died unexpectedly on the operating table. Parker wondered if one of Baron's assistants might go instead and went round to the studio to check Armstrong-Jones out. He came back with a definite thumbs-down. The young man was far too bohemian. He was highly amused when, less than three years later, it turned out that the young, bohemian photographer was to be the Duke's new brother-in-law. It was the Duke who told him!

Poor Mike Parker's divorce was grist to the press's mill. In the context of the times it was inevitable that he should resign when his divorce became public. When the yacht docked in Gibraltar on the way home he caught a flight back to London. He and his lawyer found themselves on an aeroplane in which every other seat was occupied by a lady or gentleman of the press. At London Airport he was compelled to give a press conference, but to his relief found that the Queen's press secretary, Commander Richard Colville, had motored down from the Palace, presumably to help out. Parker remembers thinking what a splendid gesture this was from a man with whom he had always enjoyed frosty relations, but just as he was about to thank him, Colville spoke.

'Hello, Parker,' he said, 'I've just come to let you know that from now on, you're on your own.' With which he turned and was gone.

Parker's troubles diverted attention from the tiresome press rumours about a 'rift' between Queen and Duke. They were further defused by two *coups de théâtre*. The first was private. At one point on the tour the Duke grew a beard, the first time since the end of the war when his golden whiskers had so captivated Australia. In Lisbon *Britannia* docked and the Duke drove to the airport where the Queen was due to arrive for a State visit. Bounding up the stairs he entered the aircraft to find that every single person aboard, from his wife to the lowliest lady-in-waiting, was sporting a large false ginger beard. Laughter all round, and of course, when the royal couple emerged from the plane seconds later, they were both still wreathed in ecstatic smiles, delighted to be back in each other's company. The perfect riposte to rumours of a 'royal rift'!

The other grander, public demonstration of mutual goodwill was that the Queen conferred on her husband the title of 'Prince'. In the past, of course, he had been Prince of Greece, but that title had gone when, before the wedding in 1947, he had taken British nationality. Many people had continued to refer to him as Prince Philip but they were, technically, incorrect. He had been only a duke.

Now he was a British prince, unassailably a pivotal figure in the Royal Family and seen to be such.

His household, however, was in a state of turmoil. Parker's resignation was 'a severe blow', and 'Boy' Browning's nervous breakdown meant that he became quite unable to take any decisions. A young equerry, David Alexander, later a Royal Marine general and commandant of the Scottish Police College, but then, in his own words, 'a very green and inexperienced young officer', was asked to take on some of Browning's duties as a stopgap.

Parker's replacement was James Orr, who had been 'Guardian' or head boy at Gordonstoun shortly before the Duke was. Orr was serving in the Kenya police, which he hated, and had fortuitously renewed his acquaintanceship with the Duke at Mombasa right at the beginning of the round-the-world tour. He was standing on the quayside as the Duke joined the ship and was invited on board for a gin and tonic.

The press enjoyed the irony of his appointment. '"HE WAS MY FAG, BUT HE'S THE MASTER NOW," SAID JIMMY WITH A WINK' ran one headline. Orr grimaces at the memory. There was no fagging at Gordonstoun, and Orr is not given to winking at newspaper reporters. He is long retired now and living in south-west London. 'They say Prince Philip doesn't suffer fools,' he added ruefully, 'but he suffered me for thirteen years.'

Orr is not only joking, he is being gratuitously modest, but he would never be another Parker. Where Parker was hail-fellow-well-met, egalitarian and, above all, a long-standing friend of both the Duke and the Queen, Orr was by nature quieter and more deferential. Loyal servant though he was, he would never be on the same sort of terms with the Duke as Parker had been. His appointment represented a sea-change and so did the replacement of 'Boy' Browning. Browning had become a broken man, but he had always been an authority figure within the Duke's household. He was so much older, more experienced and, above all, used to command. From the very first he felt that he should 'run the show'.

His replacement was Rear-Admiral Christopher Bonham-Carter. Like Orr he was an old acquaintance and had served with the Duke in the Mediterranean. The Duke liked familiar faces in his team, but whatever his rank, Bonham-Carter was no 'Boy' Browning.

# INTERVAL

# 'Prodigious Momentum'

'A very wise man plans his life, seeking in a
routine and in the reassurance offered by material
objects, as well as in the love of his wife and children,
that second wind which enables him to maintain his
prodigious momentum'

*Tour de France*
RICHARD COBB

The distinction between history and current affairs has always been blurred and the cut-off points arbitrary. When I was an undergraduate modern history appeared to finish in 1914. Today it seems to encompass everything up to and including the war in the Gulf. Most division by dates is artificial. The sixties, for instance, really began in the fifties and went on into the seventies; you can attach any number of different dates to 'the Industrial Revolution' or 'the Enlightenment' and make them plausible.

Yet such divisions are necessary even if one is attempting to explore and explain an individual life and not some impersonal movement or organisation. You have to make selections and decisions in reducing a life to printed matter; you have to categorise and simplify, sort into chapters and footnotes even something as elusive as what Richard Cobb, former Professor of Modern History at Oxford, once described as 'the apartness and integrity of the individual'.

The apartness and integrity of the Duke of Edinburgh speak for themselves, but you cannot appreciate his life without imposing some sort of pattern on it, even when the pattern may not seem obvious to others or indeed to the Duke himself. As Professor Cobb's old master, Georges Lefebvre, used to say, 'Pour faire de l'histoire, il faut savoir compter.'

Nineteen fifty-seven, the year the Duke became a Prince again, and the year that Michael Parker had to resign, seems to me to be the moment when he passes from history to current affairs. It was also, incidentally, the year that he published his first book – a collection of speeches put together by Oxford University Press, which was an odd choice of publisher as he is Chancellor of the other place. Not, of course, that he was the Cambridge Chancellor at that time. It was Sir Harold Hartley (Oxon) who chose the publisher and the Duke only became a Cambridge man subsequently.

In distinguishing between his life before 1957 and his life afterwards I am not suggesting that in 1957 he came to a full stop. James Orr, who became his private secretary that year, said of him, 'He was wonderfully brave, a real self driver. He would go on till he dropped.' The sixties and seventies and eighties were full of incident and achievement. The Queen bore him two more children. Prince Andrew was born in 1960 (ten years after Princess Anne), and Prince Edward four years after that, when the Duke was in his early forties. It was also in the sixties that he took on both the International Equestrian Foundation and the World Wildlife Fund. The Award Scheme continued to grow. His life was full of variety and interest, and he travelled widely.

All this is true, but essentially the changes have been gradual, the landmarks illusory and the mixture as before. He acquired some new interests; he grew older, mellower, more reflective. He can still give a general a public rocket at a cocktail party (he may not have considered it a 'rocket', but the general did), but there is a consensus that he is no longer quite as alarming as he used to be. 'He's always as soft as a kitten's wrist when I see him now,' said one old sparring partner fondly.

In 1957 five years had passed since the Accession and ten since his marriage. In that time he had established himself, successfully overcome much of the suspicion and resentment of 'the men with moustaches' and created the platform he wanted.

He is acutely aware that other people do not always see this. 'I suppose I am alone in thinking that I had ample opportunities to make a contribution where I was,' he told me. 'In some ways the relief from having to try to reach the top may have released energies for other things. Ambition may be a great motivator, but it can also colour judgement.'

The full range of his contributions may represent life to the recipients but they are death to his biographer. Time and again members of his loyal staff have urged me to include a chapter on the Duke and engineering or the Duke's visit to Codfish Island or the incredible amount of time he devoted to the knotty problem of defence cuts with reference to the Brigade of Guards. I have repeated, time and again, Sir Hugh Casson's remark about the 'loose-fit portrait' and more than one other person's advice that if you give the 'correct' weight to all his activities you won't see the Duke for the trees. I have tried to concentrate on examples that illuminate the man and his achievements but at times I have been distracted because he and those close to him want to emphasise what *they* think important.

I have also sometimes had to fight my way out of a bog of detail. I have found myself at Buckingham Palace arguing – with some heat and at some length – about whether the Duke had induced a famous English cricketer to hit a catch to long leg or mid-wicket; about whether the carriages of the Royal Train could properly be described as 'svelte' (me yes, Duke no); and what precisely the Duke might say to his valet if his cufflinks went missing. In the end the selections, the compressions, the omissions, the emphases, the judgements and the plain mistakes are my fault. I know that if I were writing a curriculum vitae for the Central Office of Information I would have done it differently and I am aware that, for example, the Duke of Edinburgh's Royal Regiment, the beneficiaries of the Prince Philip's Trust and the members of the Royal Commission for the 1851 Exhibition will think that I have given them less than their due. I have not paid enough attention to his husbandry of the royal estates. Or the London Federation of Boys' Clubs. I have, in other words, picked and I have chosen.

The world has changed a great deal since 1957. It was the year Anthony Eden resigned as Prime Minister and was succeeded by Harold Macmillan; the year the Common Market began with the signing of the Treaty of Rome; the year Gromyko became Russian Foreign Secretary and Molotov and Malenkov were sacked. In 1957 Eisenhower formulated the Eisenhower Doctrine, John Braine wrote *Room at the Top* and John Osborne *The Entertainer*. David Lean made *The Bridge on the River Kwai* and *West Side Story* was the hot new musical. Peter May and Colin Cowdrey put on 411 for the fourth wicket against the West Indies at Edgbaston.

Nineteen fifty-seven seems a very long time ago and it is rather astonishing to think that His Royal Highness Prince Philip, Duke of

Edinburgh, was already firing on all cylinders in a role which had never previously existed but which is now so accepted and acknowledged that it is almost as if it is one of the great offices of state.

If there wasn't a Duke of Edinburgh now, we should have to think seriously about inventing one.

# Part Three

# 1957–1991
# THE PRINCE
# AND THE DUKE

# 'The Division of Labour'

'Work . . . does not exist in a non-literate
world . . . where the whole man is involved there is
no work. Work begins with the division of labour'
*Understanding Media*
MARSHALL McLUHAN

Today the Royal Family headquarters is, as it has been since Queen Victoria moved in more than 150 years ago, Buckingham Palace, the huge, 600-room building which proved to be the downfall of John Nash, the architect. Nash was commissioned to design a new palace by King George IV, but the enterprise foundered and Nash, caught between the conflicting demands of Government and Monarchy, retired in disgrace to the Isle of Wight. It is not, in other words, a custom-built office block and the various different households tend to operate from converted bedrooms separated from each other by miles of red carpet.

Within the Family Firm, Edinburgh Enterprises is a very small unit with a very small staff.

Prince Philip's private secretary is Brian McGrath. Eton, Irish Guards and the wine trade. Before taking up the job in 1982, at the age of fifty-six, he was a director of Allied-Lyons and chairman of Victoria Wine and Grants of St James's amongst other 'Allied' companies. He is brisk, breezy and clearly as used to giving orders as receiving them. He knows his way around and has something of his boss's apparent gruffness of manner. Asked why he was selected he is inclined to reply that he was the only Irish wine merchant that the Duke could find. In fact he was personally head-hunted by his predecessor, Lord Rupert Nevill, as his assistant. Sadly, however, Nevill died just as McGrath arrived, so he was thrown in at the deep end. Prince Philip also knew his father, though he had not made the connection between McGrath *père* and *fils* until after the appointment. My own guess is that it was because of his no-nonsense approach, reluctance to be daunted by outside pressures and a familiarity with business and business leaders.

McGrath operates from his own large office overlooking the Palace gardens. It is decorated with nautical paintings and a Chevalier of 'The Queen and Royal Family on their way to St Paul's Cathedral on the occasion of the Thanksgiving for the recovery of the Prince of Wales February 27th 1872'. The room also contains a table given to Princess Elizabeth by the people of Sierra Leone in 1947. A wedding present.

'Private secretary' is a slightly misleading description. His official title is 'The Private Secretary and Treasurer to the Duke of Edinburgh' and he is more of a 'chef de cabinet' and 'head of the household' than what most of us think of as a 'secretary'.

Immediately under him is Brigadier Clive Robertson. Brigadier Clive also has his own lofty-ceilinged executive's office overlooking the Palace courtyard where the newly invested have their photographs taken after the pinning on of their insignia. McGrath is responsible for every aspect of the Duke's work, except for the minutiae of event planning. This is divided between the Brigadier and the equerry. The Brigadier sees to forward planning and then, once the six-monthly calendar has been locked in place at one of the two annual diary conferences, he hands all his files over to the equerry.

The equerry also has a room overlooking the gardens. The 1991 equerry is a naval man, Lieutenant-Commander Malcolm Sillars. This job is alternated between the three services. His predecessor was a soldier from the Royal Artillery, Major Sir Guy Acland – the sixth baronet. The equerry accompanies the Duke on his engagements and is responsible for cars, menus, timings and so on. The main office where 'the girls' sit has a faintly naval feel. It's L-shaped and cramped with the four workers sitting in line astern at their word processors. The system was computerised a few years ago and Prince Philip no longer dictates all his letters, but types them out on his own machine so that they come down to the office ready typed, topped and tailed. Then they are photographed for filing.

The girls have something of the look of superior 'Wrens'; the sort of pretty English rose faces that stare out at you from the 'engaged to be married' page of *Country Life*.

It is obviously the sort of place where you don't have to be mad, but it helps. There is a view, by no means confined to this office, that the Duke's household is the best in the Palace. It may be a touch eccentric, but it achieves results. There is a strong sense of 'Action This Day', inspired no doubt by naval tradition and emanating from the top.

The filing system, also now computerised, is extraordinarily complex and comprehensive. 'It stretches down to Australia,' says Commander Sillars laconically. Letter shelves come rolling up from the bowels of the Palace on a sort of Heath Robinson conveyor belt. I have seldom seen so much paper. Hardly surprising of course. As the Duke points out, it holds forty years of correspondence.

The administration is in the hands of Jimmy Jewell, a former Grenadier Guards man, Warrant Officer rank. Prince Philip is Colonel of the Grenadiers though he had not been appointed when Jewell joined his staff. No regimental favouritism here.

The team is completed by a temporary equerry, usually the Assistant Adjutant of the Grenadier Guards and usually a second, temporary one from the Royal Marines.

The Duke himself works above the shop. His own private suite of study, library and dressing room are on the first floor of the Palace overlooking its gardens on the north-west front which faces Constitution Hill and Green Park beyond. Despite the fact that the Palace faces on to a busy traffic roundabout where Constitution Hill joins the Mall, London's grandest and most ceremonial avenue of all, the rooms on this side of the Palace are surprisingly quiet, almost pastoral. Only the distant blare of military music sometimes disturbs the peace.

Books do furnish a room but they also reveal a personality. Unlike his critics I could perfectly well imagine him reading a book, but not just for pleasure. I felt that he would think the idea trivial. 'I think,' he agrees, 'that you would be right to say that I read more for information and instruction than for indulgence.' The use of that word 'indulgence' is revealing. It reminds one of a generation that thought reading a novel before lunch was almost a sin.

There are 8,385 books on his shelves. That was the count on 22 November 1990, and it was rising. As I suspected, they tend to be means to an end rather than ends in themselves. They reflect his interests and they are tools to enable him to master a subject. He owns 560 books on birds, 456 books on religion (ammunition with which to confront preachers after morning service!), 373 on horses and other equestrian matters, 352 on the Navy and ships. There is more poetry

(203 volumes) than fiction (a mere 170). And as I had suspected the novels suggest formative rather than mature tastes: R. M. Ballantyne, Sir Arthur Conan Doyle, C. S. Forester, Captain Marryat, Saki, Somerville and Ross, H. G. Wells. These are the authors of a classic English upper middle class upbringing. *The Cruel Sea* and *Mr Midshipman Easy* are an easily predictable pinch of salt. Françoise Sagan's *Bonjour Tristesse* is a slight surprise. He used to read detective stories when he was in the Navy but I did not notice these. I can imagine him chucking those old green Penguins overboard into the Mediterranean when he had finished with them, which would explain their absence. He has a useful collection of cookbooks too, and they are contemporary enough to suggest that this is a continuing interest. Elizabeth David is there, implying a culinary taste that goes back to the early fifties, but there is also more recent work by the Roux brothers and Antonio Carluccio's book on mushrooms. There are plenty of delicious fungi on the royal estates.

There are 194 volumes of humour – Giles annuals, Osbert Lancaster, *Parkinson's Law* for which he wrote the foreword ('You can get away with the most unpalatable truth if you can make it appear funny'). For a man who enjoys such a supposedly spiky relationship with the fourth estate he is an avid collector of cartoons which take the mickey out of him. He has 197, scattered for the most part in lavatories in the various royal houses. A typical cartoon catalogue comment is 'Gun Room Toilet, Sandringham'.

Although the style of the Duke's rooms is bookish, it is not the bookishness of the don or the bibliophile; there are no open volumes, no piles, no confusion. All is well ordered, disciplined, catalogued efficiency. These are the books of a man who might want to look something up in a hurry.

There is also something plain and masculine about these rooms though it is difficult to put your finger on it precisely. They are naturally much less feminine and chintzy, for instance, than his daughter's drawing room in another part of the Palace, though they are not without personal touches. The most obvious and significant of these are the large and very fine de Laszlo portraits on either side of the door leading from his study into the library. De Laszlo, born Philip Alexius Laszlo de Lombos, came to England in 1907 from his native Hungary and took British nationality in 1914. He was an archetypal society painter, whom the Duke much admires. Princess Alice, on the left of the doorway, is serene, beautiful, her dress rippling and elegant; Prince Andrew, in army uniform, is imperious, military and upright.

They are striking images but what is most striking about them is that they dominate the room. These are the pictures that look down on the Duke every moment of his working day as he bangs out another memo on his laptop word processor.

By contrast, the only visible image of his uncle, Lord Mountbatten, is a small doll-like figure in naval uniform, between six inches and a foot tall. He is one of a series by a Maltese named Apap – and the rest are on a shelf next door in the library. Most are British political figures from the forties and early fifties – Bevan, Bevin, Attlee, Gaitskell, Montgomery, and, of course, Churchill. There is one of his own paintings of the Bahamas and an Edward Seago of the Queen on horseback. Other pictures include a June Mendoza of Prince Edward, a Graham Sutherland design for one of the Coventry Cathedral tapestries, a Derek Foster of his yacht, *Bloodhound*, a much-loved family boat until its sale in 1969, and a portrait, by the desk in his study, of his grandfather, Prince Louis of Battenberg, the first Marquess of Milford Haven. In the library there are scale models of the Royal Yacht, *Britannia*, and of HMS *Magpie*, his sole naval command. A large number of 'objects', either presented to him over the years or accumulated in the course of travel, give the rooms a certain well-controlled sense of clutter.

Rooms like these inevitably reflect a bit of their owner's personality. I thought of the room in the Soestdijk Palace where I had interviewed Prince Bernhard. What had characterised that room for me was the extravagant display of game trophies, the array of signed photographs of the great and good, and the well stocked pipe-rack. These were missing here, though of course, they may lurk in other places I never penetrated. This, the Duke's working environment, is essentially functional – there is an octagonal table in the library for meetings too small for the Chinese Dining Room, computer space, good working surfaces. It feels shipshape, purpose-built and efficient. It is also comfortable without being luxurious and decorated with just enough souvenirs and reminders of life, family, friends to have something of the quality of a family scrapbook.

There are relatively few opportunities of seeing the team in action together because the Duke is usually accompanied only by McGrath, the Brigadier or the Commander. Just occasionally, however, they do meet for an 'O-Group'.

In 1970 when Basil Boothroyd was researching his biography of the

Duke he attended one of his regular programme meetings. 'Everybody hates it,' said Boothroyd, 'but that's understood. No point in going on about it.' Twenty years later the atmosphere has changed. Certainly there is an air of tension and challenge, but not of fear and loathing. None of the key players is the same as in 1970 apart from the Duke himself but the atmosphere and the procedure are practically identical. Without this regular, six-monthly piece of forward planning the jobs simply would not get done. It is like fitting a jigsaw together; the dates for the next six months represent the board and a series of lists of dinners, openings and 'events' of every conceivable description have to be slotted in. If pieces don't fit they obviously can't be fitted in.

Punctuality is vital throughout the Palace but nowhere more so than in the Duke's household. Kick-off was scheduled for nine thirty. So, one Tuesday morning, the day of the Oxford and Cambridge rugby match, I found myself at nine fifteen in the increasingly familiar surroundings of the waiting room inside the Privy Purse door. I was even beginning to recognise the figures in *Blind Man's Buff* by David Wilkie and *Departure Scene, Paddington Station* by William Frith.

The meeting took place in McGrath's office because it is nearer the filing system than the Duke's. Tables and extra chairs had been brought in so that the usually spacious room now had a cluttered feel. McGrath's desk facing the door was empty and waiting for the boss. To its left was a table for McGrath and the Brigadier. Then there was a small table for girl A and copious file, and another facing the Duke with a second girl and Malcolm Sillars who sat behind a globe, a *Times Atlas of the World* and sundry guides and timetables. At right angles to him the final table was laid for three: me, Jimmy Jewell and John Haslam, the assistant press secretary with special responsibility for dealing with the Duke. All of us sat with a clean pad of paper, a newly sharpened pencil and a serviceable India rubber. Everyone except the Duke had a blotter. 'Shouldn't Prince Philip have a clean blotter?' asked McGrath, looking at his own dirty blotter. Then he remembers, 'Prince Philip doesn't *have* a blotter.' He sounds exasperated, as if any fool would know that the Duke of Edinburgh wouldn't be seen dead with a blotter. The very idea! The men were all in dark suits with ties; and the atmosphere was rather like morning assembly before the headmaster arrives. No one actually said, 'I hope sir's in a good mood this morning' or 'Please God he doesn't ask me any questions about last night's homework', but I felt they might at any moment.

Dead on nine thirty he breezed in and we all stood. He was determinedly relaxed in fawn trousers, an open-neck striped shirt and one of his rather elegant cardigans, a sort of blue-grey, buttoned down the front. 'It's like the Court of Star Chamber,' he said, looking round jovially. I dare say it did look a bit like it, though my perception was different. Then he sat down and there was a sudden hiatus because he seemed unaccountably and very untypically to have arrived with the wrong pieces of paper. A mild 'damn!' and he ambled off, not too concerned, to get the right ones, reappearing moments later, waving us back into our seats as we stood. I felt like a confused member of congregation in a strange church. The others are used to it. I am not. It was very hot, despite the winter chill outside, and the Duke quite rightly detected a smell of burning paint coming from the radiator. There were a few more introductory remarks, comments, rustling of papers. It is ninety per cent logistics: 'I thought I'd come up on the second to do the ATC thing' . . . The second of what? . . . I wonder, and sense that I am not the only one. 'I was going to go to Denmark on Monday morning so it's pointless having a meeting in Holland. We either do it here that morning or in Denmark.'

This decision was assimilated and approved, there was a throat clear and then he said, 'How do we want to do this?' The question sounded rhetorical since I guessed everyone knew precisely how we wanted to do this. I am sure it had been done in identical fashion since before any of those present had first joined the Palace.

This is essentially the Brigadier's meeting. Every potential category is identified by category – EPA means 'Engagement Provisionally Accepted.' These are more than 'provisional'. It will take earthquake, wind, fire or other act of God to change them and the same applies to what Boothroyd, in his Punchy fashion, referred to as 'Joint Jaunts with the Queen'. A joint jaunt with the Queen means such jollities as the annual Maundy Thursday service, scheduled, in 1991, for Westminster Abbey, the annual Garter Service at Windsor, the State Opening of Parliament and the Birthday Parade on Horse Guards. This is the skeleton of the schedule. It can't be changed. Beyond this there are 'P'-category engagements which have priority over the third category, which will be fitted in if humanly possible, but are more expendable.

A difficult item presented itself. 'I thought the simplest decision would be to stay away another day,' he said. 'We can spend another night in the Canaries or the Azores.' He did look, at this point, like a cat who had killed a number of birds in one go and got the cream too. There was a ripple of laughter and the Brigadier seemed chuffed too. The problems involved with getting home a day early were plainly too dreadful to contemplate.

There was a pause, some furrowed brows, a drumbeat of pencil tapping. 'That's not my idea of fun, I must say . . . Belgium, well that's out . . . yes . . . oh, sorry, sorry, I'm looking at February . . .' A visit to the dentist had to be fitted in. Hardly an affair of state and yet royal teeth are as susceptible to decay as the common man's. Another 'event' zoomed into focus. 'But what's this meeting FOR?' he wanted to know. The Brigadier seemed momentarily stymied. 'What's the purpose?' asked the Duke, not letting this one go.

'It's really to plan,' ventured the Brigadier. I was reminded of the Princess Royal, a few days earlier, telling me that the one thing her father was good at was spotting flannel.

'There's nothing to plan,' said the Duke. 'It's all done. It exists. I'd like to know what it's FOR!'

This was unanswerable and we moved on. I felt rather sorry for the Brigadier who nevertheless remained steady under fire, and was not in the least put out.

A day in Cambridge suddenly showed signs of becoming dangerously overcrowded. It began with the University veterinary school but then other organisations such as the Kurt Hahn Trust were putting in bids for an hour here and an hour there. Every few minutes someone would say, 'Perhaps we could slot that into the Cambridge day', until there came a time when 'the Cambridge day' became a running gag, expanding inexorably until it was evident that if every potential Cambridge engagement were fulfilled the Duke would be there for a week at least.

And then there was the weekend of carriage-driving in Brighton. These equestian weekends are inscribed in stone. The previous day the Duke was scheduled to be in the far north with the Queen. 'Robert [Sir Robert Fellowes, private secretary to the Queen] thought you could fly down, drop the Queen at Heathrow and then go on.'

Yes, but how? A fixed-wing flight from Heathrow to Gatwick at five thirty on a Friday afternoon would throw the air traffic controllers into a terrible state. The M25 would be a different sort of nightmare. Was there an airport on the south coast? Shoreham perhaps? Shoreham only had a grass strip. What about a chopper? In the end this was referred back for further thought, but it was typical of the recurring problem: how, in effect, to get as near as possible to being in two places at the same time.

'I wonder if I might come back to Edinburgh from Sweden . . .

does the train go through Harrogate? . . . it's simply not practical to go all the way to Dartmouth and be back in time for the Economic Summit dinner.'

'It can be done, sir' – this from Malcolm Sillars. 'We could spend the afternoon on the train to Portsmouth and then the train could shove off and the luggage could go to Windsor by car.'

After a while I was beginning to feel as if a cold towel was in order as increasingly disparate series of engagements were ticked off, abandoned, slotted in, juggled, welcomed and disparaged.

'That's no good.'

'Well, sir, they said they could change it if you want to chair it.'

'I don't want to chair it.'

'What do they want me to do here? Is it a lunch? Or a reception? It says "event".' A rustling of paper and shuffling of files ensued as the cross-references were followed. 'Ah! A *huge* fund-raising event!'

Laughter.

And then, before I knew what had happened, 'Would it be possible to change the days round in the Falklands?'

The Brigadier blenched. 'We haven't had the Governor's suggestions yet. I'm rather reluctant to change it round at this stage . . .'

'Shall we call on the President of Brazil?' The World Wide Fund for Nature have suggested the President might like to accompany the Duke on a visit to its turtle project but the President might be busy. How long would it take to get from Brasilia to Salvador?

'It's a big place.' The Duke laughed.

Commander Sillars twirled his globe. 'About two hours, sir. It's a hundred and forty miles.'

'There's always the twenty-second or the nineteenth.'

'No, that's the Rose Festival and the King's Lynn Festival and all that business.'

'Could that be included in the Cambridge day?'

More laughter.

'No, I can't get back in time for the garden party. You can never go out to lunch on garden party days. You get stuck in the traffic.

'Hunstanton Golf Club? What are they offering? It just says "visit" . . . We can do the Helicopter Club after the garden party . . . Thailand? We could do that on the way back from Hong Kong . . . well there's that Friday, I could get on the train after the Industrial Society dinner . . . What does it mean here, a "meeting" of the Arthritis people? That doesn't sound right . . . the Isle of Bute's out . . . Loughborough's out . . . Islington's out . . . I'm not at all keen on this one, it's that ghastly man, what's his name . . . put that in for the autumn . . . Why does he say I MUST have seen Victoria Falls . . . I suppose I've seen it . . . I don't remember . . . Oh, wait a minute, what was that date? . . . Monday the which?'

And so on. After three hours I was, to put it mildly, confused. Everyone else, however, Duke included, seemed to take it entirely in their stride. Indeed, by the standards of such meetings this one was a breeze. No tempers frayed, indeed there were a lot of laughs. Once or twice there were ducal asides – an anecdote from the previous night's dinner party; occasionally a bluff comment from McGrath such as 'She's a good girl', apropos the newly elected President of the Irish Republic, broke any suspicion of ice. And chaotic though the exercise sounds when reduced to a few pages of print, it was all underpinned by endless letters and phone calls, logged, minuted, filed and computer-coded. When, finally, it came to the point where we all checked through the day-to-day diary it did, miraculously in my view, make a degree of sense and the beginnings of a seamless, effortless progress was starting to emerge. The Duke wrote everything down meticulously in a ring-file log – he is emphatically *not* a Filofax man, though the principle is not dissimilar. And he left smiling. After he had done so McGrath motioned to Commander Sillars to shut the door and there was precisely the same hubbub of relieved pleasure that greets the headmaster's departure after a morning assembly that has not gone too badly.

Twenty years after Boothroyd I had expected to find the energy diminished and yet, although it was obvious that there were places the Duke did not much like and people he liked even less, his appetite for work was effectively insatiable. If he could cram it in, he would. I was also struck, as always, by the uncivilian nature of the operation. Many years before, the atmosphere of Clarence House when the Duke first became a public figure was compared to the bridge of a naval warship going into battle and something of that atmosphere remained. I could not help feeling, as the Duke rattled out his queries about distances and flight times and the availability of heads of state, as the Commander twirled his globe, and the Brigadier produced his background briefs, and the girls delved into their files, that this was a task force embarking on a difficult operation against impossible odds in a hostile world. Not true, of course, because the only real enemies were the relentless invitations, the unending demands on time and effort and enthusiasm. One could not help feeling, in that meeting, that the whole world wanted the Duke to give it a piece of his mind;

to lunch, to speak, perhaps to entertain. Those demands showed no sign of diminishing and the problem was to accommodate them. A friend of mine, a manufacturer of beautiful Spanish guitars, has more orders and more wood than he can possibly cope with in his lifetime and I felt the same as I contemplated the Duke's dilemma at Buckingham Palace that morning; there will always be a lighthouse unvisited, a charity unlunched, a ship unlaunched, a building unopened, and a bridge too far.

'We'll have to scrub the twenty-eighth. Let's talk about it later.'

# 'Winds of the World'

'Winds of the World, give answer! They are
whimpering to and fro –
And what should they know of England who only
England know?'

*The English Flag*
RUDYARD KIPLING

On Wednesday 7 November 1990 Her Majesty the Queen opened Parliament. At the time few people thought this would be a parliament of high drama which just goes to show what an unpredictable business politics can be. On Wednesday 7 November, Mrs Thatcher was Prime Minister of Great Britain and clearly intent on leading her party into the next election. Nothing in her demeanour that day as she led her government from Commons to Lords to listen to the Queen's Speech suggested that she had the merest inkling of impending political demise; nor that within weeks she would be at Buckingham Palace saying goodbye to the Queen after a decade of weekly meetings. In just over two months Her Majesty's forces would be at war with Iraq in order to force Saddam Hussein out of Kuwait. Somehow this did not seem to be at the forefront of Her Majesty's speech either.

As a harbinger of real live political events, therefore, the State Opening, in which the Duke of Edinburgh plays a prominent part, was remarkably unrevealing. As Harold Wilson observed, a week in politics is a long time.

Walter Bagehot, still, over a hundred years since he wrote his book on the English constitution, the greatest expert on that subject puts this and other pieces of royal ceremonial into an intriguing context:

The characteristic merit of the English constitution is that its dignified parts are very complicated and somewhat imposing, very old and rather venerable; while its efficient part, at least when in great and critical action, is decidedly simple and rather modern. Its essence is strong with the strength of modern simplicity; its exterior is august with the Gothic grandeur of a more imposing age.

The State Opening is certainly august with Gothic grandeur. In the Royal Chamber after the doors open at 9.50 it is all wigs and breeches, boots and spurs, swords and Sam Brownes. The directive on the formal Order of Ceremonial instructs 'The Master of the Horse, the Captain of the Honourable Corps of Gentlemen at Arms and the Captain of the Yeomen of the Guard: Full Dress Uniform without Robes'. In the minutes before the ceremony officials such as these stride to and fro looking splendid and truly dignified, none more so than the Captain of the Honourable Corps of Gentlemen at Arms, the Lord Denham, magnificent with his sword and boots and frock coat.

The Lord Denham in his pomp brings home to me an essential truth about this and all such ceremonies in the United Kingdom. My reaction, irreverent no doubt, was 'That's not the Captain of the Honourable Corps of Gentlemen at Arms, that's Bertie.' The Lord Denham in real life is the government's chief whip in the House of Lords. He is also the author of *The Man who Lost his Shadow* and *Foxhunt*. Captain of the Honourable Corps of Gentlemen at Arms? Surely some mistake? And that tall gangling fellow in the striped trousers and the black tail coat carrying a long white wand. The Comptroller of Her Majesty's Household? It looks terribly like Sir George Young, the bicycling baronet who sits as Member of Parliament for the Ealing, Acton constituency in west London. The man dressed in a tabard is his cousin Theo Mathew, masquerading, according to the programme, as Windsor Herald of Arms.

Dress someone up, in other words invest them with a grand title, and disbelief is suspended. Even people one knows in an everyday context acquire dignity, mystery and grandeur. It is the King's new clothes in reverse.

At 11.27 Her Majesty enters the Royal Gallery and the Procession advances into the Chamber of the House of Lords.

Consider, for a moment, the procession. At the centre, in bold Gothic script, is 'The Queen's Most Excellent Majesty'. Beside her, on her left, holding her hand – *literally* – is the Duke. All around them are other uniformed gentlemen and ballgowned ladies. A Woman of the Bedchamber, a Mistress of the Robes, a Lady of the Bedchamber, a Gold Stick in Waiting, a Silver Stick in Waiting (some ranks behind), and a posse of heralds straight from Shakespeare – Richmond, Somerset, Lancaster, Windsor, Chester and York; to say nothing much of Maltravers Herald Extraordinary and the four Pursuivants, Rouge Dragon, Rouge Croix, Bluemantle and Portcullis.

Amid all this 'Gothic grandeur' only one person managed to remain relaxed and normal throughout: the Duke. After forty years he has obviously grown accustomed to it. Whereas everybody else, even the Queen, looked straight ahead and nervous throughout the whole performance, the Duke was smiling, glancing around him, curious, human, aware of his surroundings and almost, as near as dammit, normal.

Most important he was holding his wife's hand. This sounds a common-place observation and yet is symbolic of a vital, perhaps *the* most important role in his life. Here was this single slight woman, who for all her crown and queenliness, was still a single human being surrounded by all the pomp that the Mother of Parliaments can muster and confronted by the most powerful people in the country. And here holding her hand and giving her the obvious and manifest support that a husband is supposed to give and which only a husband can give was the Duke. Of course, it is subsidiary to the main thrust of the occasion but it is in its way a powerful affirmation of what the Duke of Edinburgh is *for*.

We, the British, can explain – with reference often to Walter Bagehot – how this kind of ceremony is merely the outward symbol of a quite different and altogether more serious inner truth. The presence of insouciant television cameramen on top of artificial platforms at the end of the Royal Gallery reminds one of a new reality about the British Monarchy and its surrounding ceremonial: that it is always on show, not just to the privileged few in the Palace of Westminster, but to the wider world beyond.

The point is that ceremonial and ritual play a part in all our lives, especially where the British Monarchy is involved. The Duke is in some ways still the least formal and stuffy of all the royals and yet he has always been steady on parade, almost as much a part of the modern majesty of Monarchy as the Queen herself.

Since he became a member of 'the firm' the pomp has remained, but the pomposity diminished. There are no longer State Balls and when there is a party at Buckingham Palace, like the multiple birth-day celebrations in December 1990, the music is by contemporary pop groups, not by an orchestra playing waltzes or even gavottes. The year 1990 was the Queen Mother's ninetieth, Princess Margaret's sixtieth and the Princess Royal's fortieth. The old custom of young 'debutantes' being introduced at court, for years the linchpin of the London season, was dispensed with largely at the Duke's instigation. An innovation, also prompted by him, has been a series of informal lunches hosted by the Duke and the Queen for a representative cross section of well known people from a variety of different walks of life. Here a nuclear physicist, there a biographer, here an Olympic athlete, there a university vice-chancellor.

Looking through the calendar for the year the fixed high and holy days begin with the Maundy Thursday service, an almsgiving which originated in 1213 when King John distributed thirteen pennies to thirteen men at Rochester Castle. It takes place just before Easter and in 1990 was held in Newcastle. In June there is the Queen's Birthday Parade mounted by the Guards Division. The Duke rides in this as Colonel of the Grenadier Guards wearing the famous blue and crimson uniform of the regiment surmounted by black bearskin. 'He's got a very fine bearskin,' remarked one Guards officer, approvingly. 'He always used to say it seemed as if it was raining,' says Jim Orr, re-calling his old boss describing the view from underneath that furry hat worn so low over the eyes. Shortly after the Trooping, the Ascot race meeting, with the royal family's formal drive in horse-drawn car-riages down the racecourse itself, has assumed something of the status of royal ceremonial though the draconian rules about eligibility for admission to the Royal Enclosure have now been relaxed. Divorcees used to be banned. Horse racing appears to be the least of the Duke's equine passions and although he is invariably in the carriage on the drive to the races he frequently seems to be missing during the racing itself. It has been alleged that on such occasions he enters the royal box, walks straight through, out the back door and into a waiting car to drive home. In fact he usually goes to the back of the box and works quietly on his papers. His wife's interest in the turf is, of course, legendary. On one occasion the Duke was asked if the Queen would like to be shown a piece of state-of-the-art technology he was inspecting. The answer was pungent and to the point. 'Certainly not,' he said. 'Unless it farts and eats grass, she's not interested.'

There are several garden parties in the garden of Buckingham Palace during the summer, and one at Holyroodhouse in Edinburgh. Lord

Cobbold, a former Lord Chamberlain, once said that they are 'the most useful thing the Queen does in her contacts with the public', though they play – as the Duke mentioned in his planning meeting – havoc with the London traffic. They are always held during the working week and more than twenty years ago a London evening newspaper asked for them to be switched to a Saturday or moved out of town. Approximately eight thousand people throng the gardens for these teas which were started by Queen Victoria. Originally 'society' affairs, they have become rather like the informal lunches in the sense that they have been democratised. An invitation to a royal garden party is a reward for public service.

The autumn ceremonials include the State Opening of Parliament and the Remembrance Day wreath-laying at the Cenotaph. Despite the presence of so many uniforms and medals this is not the glorification of war, but the remembrance of loss, suffering and sacrifice. It is a melancholy occasion, popularly known as 'Poppy Day' because of the red buttonhole flowers everyone wears in commemoration of the nation's dead. They originally symbolised the poppies which grew so rampantly in the battlefields of the Great War.

> In Flanders' fields the poppies blow
> Between the crosses, row on row
> That mark our place.

Those were the words of a Canadian Medical Officer, Colonel John Macrae, writing at the Battle of Ypres in 1915. It was in his memory that the first flowers were distributed. The Duke's poppy, and the personal wreath that he lays, are manufactured at the Royal British Legion factory in Richmond-upon-Thames and the money from their sale – millions of pounds each year – goes to help Britain's disabled ex-servicemen. The Duke, of course, is one of the dwindling band of mourners who actually wears the campaign medals of World War Two and lays his wreath in memory of the dead who fought alongside him.

As well as these great rituals fixed immutably in the royal calendar there are other more moveable feasts. In 1990, for instance, there were two state banquets. These formal occasions actually involve two fixtures at a time, a home one at Buckingham Palace and an away match organised by the visiting Head of State's embassy. Then there's the presentation of Gold Duke of Edinburgh's Awards at St James's Palace. Because it is his own invention it is a relatively informal affair though – also, paradoxically – because it is his own invention, it has a very real sense of occasion. Ladies wear hats. People are nervous.

Nineteen-ninety also had some original one-offs, notably the Queen Mother's ninetieth birthday celebrations, the launch of HMS *Lancaster* on the Clyde, a Guards Museum Gala at Hampton Court, an RAF fly-past to mark the fiftieth anniversary of the Battle of Britain. There is always a lot of dressing-up in the ducal year and the necessity to be able to change clothes at speed. Even in 1954 the Duke was clocked by an impartial observer in Cardiff changing from the uniform of Colonel of the Welsh Guards into a blue suit. 'Guards officers may be interested to know that the Duke's time for the change from uniform to mufti – that is to say from the moment of disappearance into the City Hall to the time when he was back again in his car – was a mere five minutes.' This quick-change artistry is often the despair of his less accomplished members of staff.

Uniforms are an essential part of the Duke's wardrobe and you only have to look at a selection of these to see it. As with other aspects of his life one might suppose that this would pose problems of loyalty and allegiance. Inter-service rivalry is a fact of life; so is inter-regimental. 'Sailors,' concedes one senior Guards officer, 'don't naturally feel an affection for the Guards, but he's come in and he's developed a real understanding. I think he has developed a high regard for the pongos.'*

The Duke is now the senior Guards colonel, a role which has a real and not just a symbolic meaning. The other Guards colonels who include his son, the Prince of Wales (Welsh Guards), his wife's cousin, the Duke of Kent (Scots) and the Grand Duke of Luxembourg (Irish – he actually served with the regiment) convene for an annual meeting in his library at the Palace on the night before the Queen's Birthday Parade. There they will discuss an agenda prepared by the Major-General commanding London District before repairing to eat in the Chinese Dining Room. Items could include anything from buttons to defence cuts. He does not have quite his wife's awe-inspiring attention to detail. The other year she observed that at one point in the parade the troops were marching too fast. No one else noticed except for a retired general, who – in the manner of some retired generals – was watching the parade on television with a stopwatch. He confirmed the Queen's assessment.

The Duke – it is said – might miss that sort of finer point but he does take a keen interest. Indeed senior Guards officers have been surprised and impressed by the degree of his understanding and support.

---

* Originally naval slang for soldier, now more widely used across the services.

The other year, for instance, he observed that at one point when the Guards perform a particularly inelegant re-alignment there was no music. This meant that the audience's attention was drawn to the inherent clumsiness of the movement and the crunch of boots on the parade ground. 'Why no music?' he wanted to know. Music is now played at that moment. Not that he always gets his own way. From time to time the Army changes its basic weapon and adopts a new rifle. The time-honoured tradition is that the Guards always drill with the real thing, but the new weapon has considerable drawbacks from a drill point of view. It weighs nine pounds and is too short to be grounded. This means that it has to be regularly transferred from one shoulder to another. The Duke argued that the old weapon should be retained for the Birthday Parade. He was over-ruled.

So even such an apparently unchanging piece of ritual as the Trooping changes with the years. In fact this particular parade in this particular form is a comparatively new invention. The first formal record of Trooping the Colour appears in the Coldstream and Grenadier Guards' order books for 1749, but in earlier times the Monarch rarely attended. Prince Albert went once or twice but although Queen Victoria was an enthusiast she did not always take the salute and in 1845 even viewed the parade in secret from a small green 'chariot' where according to her diary she was 'quite incog'. She added that she had enjoyed 'an admirable view of the parade without being *found out*'.

Throughout her reign the Queen actually reviewed her Guards on horseback, only ceasing in 1987 when her horse, Burmese, was pensioned off. The Duke has also always ridden in the parade and continues to do so. He does so, for once, not because he is the husband of the Queen but because he is the Colonel of the Grenadier Guards.

Every year's parade is televised live; so is the Remembrance Day service at the Cenotaph; and so is the State Opening of Parliament. Although the Duke's wedding in 1947 in Westminster Abbey could be received on TV only in the London area, when his son was married in St Paul's Cathedral in 1981 the ceremony was shown live and in full colour around the world. In California it was half past four in the morning, yet still they turned on their sets in their millions; 38.8 millions watched in the United States alone.

Television has transformed much of the royal ceremonial in which the Duke takes part and the Duke has always encouraged the televising of these events. His father-in-law, King George VI, was unhappy about the idea of television cameras intruding on what he believed to be the essentially solemn and semi-private nature of such rituals. The

Duke has always welcomed public interest in royalty, seeing rightly that without such interest its future would be threatened.

'No society that values its liberty,' he has said, 'can do without the freedom to report on, comment on, discuss and indeed to gossip about people, institutions and events.' To have the bonding, almost tribal, effect that the great royal occasions have on public life they not only have to go on taking place in a grand, dignified, if at times extraordinary fashion; they also have to be *seen* to be doing so.

Most of the great ceremonial events in the Duke's calendar are undertaken with the Queen. When he is on his own the Duke tends, understandably, to be more relaxed and less formal. Because of his large, separate portfolio many of his engagements are undertaken individually with the smallest possible team in support.

Tim O'Donovan, a London insurance broker who makes this into an improbable hobby, has done a detailed breakdown of the Royal Family's activities for 1990. O'Donovan's findings are published in *The Times* each year, and although he concedes the statistics oversimplify a complicated picture, they are revealing. One overseas engagement is seldom *quite* like another and even one lunch can be more gruelling than the next. He calculates that the Duke was abroad on official tours for seventy-seventy days of the year – five less than his daughter and forty-nine more than his wife. On those days he undertook 260 separate engagements – almost certainly an understatement.

I turned the pages of Commander Sillars's file for 1990. February was interesting. That was the month in which the idea of my book was first formally floated before the Duke: Thursday 1 . . . 1100 Arrive Auckland . . . visit Commonwealth Games Village . . . 1320 Depart Auckland . . . 1420 Arrive Huka Lodge . . . Overnight Government House . . . Sunday 4 . . . Visit RNZAF Whenuapei. Present Standard to 425 Sqdn . . . 1145 Depart in HMNZS *Tarapunga* . . . attend Waitangi Celebrations. And so it goes on. A day at Stewart and Codfish Islands, a night at Wanaka, a flight to Taypu, a visit to Montana Vineyard, dinners, garden parties, welcomes, farewells.

That was what it looked like from the bald statements in the file. In fact the Duke never got to the Montana Vineyard. Suddenly news came through of an appalling hurricane that had devastated Western Samoa and Niue two days before. The Duke immediately decided that he should offer the islanders his and the Queen's 'support and sympathy'. This involved a wholly unplanned detour of thousands of miles, leaving the Queen to visit the vineyard and complete the engagements on her own. They were reunited in Auckland a few days later.

One missing spot in this tour of the southern hemisphere was Vanuatu, 1,500 miles east of Queensland and the only place in the world, as far as I am aware, where the Duke of Edinburgh is worshipped quite independently of Her Majesty the Queen. This worship is uncluttered by commerce, television, soap opera, or the tabloid press. Alexander Frater, a fine writer who was born in these islands where his father was the local doctor, has written of how, 'as the shadows of the great banyan trees lengthen and flying foxes flicker through the dusk, there is one particular chunk of worn basalt to which the Iounhanan give their undivided attention. And that is the Duke of Edinburgh stone.'

It is years since Frater visited the tribe that worships the Duke but when he did he had great difficulty in persuading them to discuss their religion let alone remove the framed photograph of the Duke from the cave where it is an object of veneration. Money – quite a lot of it – had to change hands. The photograph shows the Duke in a jacket and tie and appears to be personally signed.

These people, the Iounhanan, are described by Frater as being 'permanently spaced out on kava', the local root-based hooch which is very considerably stronger than Scotch. The effect of this is that the men sit in their huts smoking pipes and staring into space while the women do all the work. The women wear grass skirts and the men nothing but nambas or penis gourds, straw codpieces which hold the sexual organ in a permanently erect position. Or so Frater alleges. He even says that the chief, who in those days was an elderly man named Kalpapung, has sent a namba to Buckingham Palace so that the Duke may wear it on his visit. If the Queen accompanies him she must be careful not to see him drinking kava because, if she does, the local rules insist that she be executed summarily and on the spot with a single blow on the head with a giant root. If she does not accompany him the Duke will be allocated three wives bearing a dowry of pigs and pillows. If he wants more he may have to wait but the head man authorised Frater to inform him that there would be no problem over this.

None of the tribesmen could remember how the Duke came to be their god but the local tradition is that it was a coup by a British Resident Commissioner in the running war with the French. The Commissioner heard that the Iounhanan were on the look-out for a god who would have to be a Big Man. The Duke was the biggest

British man he could think of and the tribe accepted his suggestion with alacrity.

Understandably, perhaps, the Duke has never paid them a visit.

The Duke returned to England from New Zealand in mid-February 1990. At the end of March he travelled to New York to give the Raphael Salas lecture at the United Nations, support various WWF events and attend a performance of the Broadway production of Andrew Lloyd Webber's *Aspects of Love* in aid of the Award Scheme World Fellowship. In April he was home for a state visit on the third, a seven-a-side rugby tournament on the eighth and straight on to Geneva for a committee meeting before a day in Rome and then Heathrow Airport, Royal Train and the Maundy Thursday service in Newcastle-upon-Tyne. In May there was a brief trip to Washington (again for WWF), in between Wales, Brussels and Balmoral. In July he was in Sweden for the first World Equestrian Games (started at his suggestion), before hurrying home for the fiftieth birthday of his cousin ex-King Constantine. I can't see much foreign activity until November: Rome . . . Luxor . . . Karachi . . . Hong Kong . . . Ishigaki . . . Guam . . . Port Moresby . . . Cairns . . . Brisbane, Melbourne, Sydney, Perth . . . Visit zoo . . . meet premier . . . presentation barbecue . . . refuel Jakarta . . . refuel Colombo and Karachi . . . visit Oman . . . refuel Bahrain and Alexandria . . . depart Nice . . . Lunch for Reagans.

For more than forty years the schedule has been punishing, though not as punishing as it would be for the rest of us. This is not meant as a criticism. Indeed it was his old friend and travelling companion, Lord Buxton, former head of Anglia Television, who drew my attention to the relative ease of tours with the Duke.

He had accompanied the Duke to the Vatican to see the Pope recently. This was a World Wide Fund for Nature initiative. The Duke had masterminded an inter-faith conference in Assisi, where there was much lobbying of all religions to get them to take account of 'green' issues. As a result of this the Pope actually included an ecological passage in his Christmas broadcast and the Duke decided that a WWF response was in order. More than that, it should be personally delivered, which is how and why he and Aubrey Buxton arrived in Rome one day, dispensed with all formalities at the airport, were escorted to the Vatican in a convoy with heavily armed carabinieri hanging out of every aperture, and arrived about twenty minutes after touch-down.

You and I would still have been in a queue by the luggage carousel while the Duke and the Pope were kissing hands.

This is in no way to diminish the ducal work-load, simply to put it in perspective. Chris Patten, the chairman of the Conservative Party after Mrs Thatcher's departure, put it another way when he talked about the side-effects of being a public figure. Patten revealed that he did not know a single Minister who owned a raincoat. High profile prevents you getting wet. Actually the Duke does have a raincoat, but someone else carries it until it starts to rain.

To sustain a schedule as punishing as the Duke's, you need superlative staff work and a raft of umbrella-holders, uniform packers, memo-drafters and general factotums.

As I write this I am surrounded by evidence of this necessary staff work in the shape of no less than six capacious brown expanding files left by my father as evidence of the American tour he organised for the Duke in 1966. Its main purpose was to raise money for charity and to boost British exports. The actual trip only lasted from 9 March to 23 March, but its planning appeared to take up an entire year of my father's life. Dipping into these files I begin to see why.

The president of the Mokuleia Polo Club wanted the Duke to play in a polo series sponsored by the English Speaking Union of Hawaii. Someone called Robert Pentland Jr wanted Sir Stafford Sands to bring some people to dinner in Nassau for $1,000 a head. The president of the Economic Club of Detroit proposed a 'fun episode' – which seemed to involve the Duke making a speech to the local business community. Jimmy Carreras, head of Hammer Films, wanted the Duke to clear the introductory speech he proposed making at the beginning of each function. Someone in Beverly Hills complained that no one had been in touch with Cary Grant. My father, taking a leaf out of the Duke's book, has put in the margin of this letter two exclamation marks and a question mark and written 'Rubbish'.

Several companies in Chicago claimed to have received exclusive instructions to service the Andover aircraft of the Queen's Flight. Too many people were invited for a cocktail party hosted in Chicago by the London store Aquascutum so it had to be moved from a private apartment to a hotel. And so on. It is not surprising that my father seemed to be away a great deal at this time of his life, nor that when he did surface he seemed, despite his usual energy and ebullience, to be in a daze.

In the event the tour, at the invitation of Variety Clubs International and the Committee for Exports to America, was a successful

Sir Hugh Casson thinks that the studies for the final portraits of the Duke are nearly always better than the finished works. This sketch by Annigoni bears him out. It is a particular favourite of Queen Elizabeth the Queen Mother and hangs at her London home, Clarence House.

Princess Alice and Prince Andrew of Greece. These two de Laszlo portraits of the Duke's parents hang in his private study at Buckingham Palace.

Edward Seago was the official artist on the Duke's world tour in 1956 and 1957. Here he shows the Duke, an avid pupil, at his easel on the deck of the Royal Yacht, *Britannia*.

These three examples of the Duke's own work show Alltanaguibhsach House on the Balmoral Estate in Scotland, Her Majesty the Queen at breakfast in Windsor Castle and a still life of gladioli.

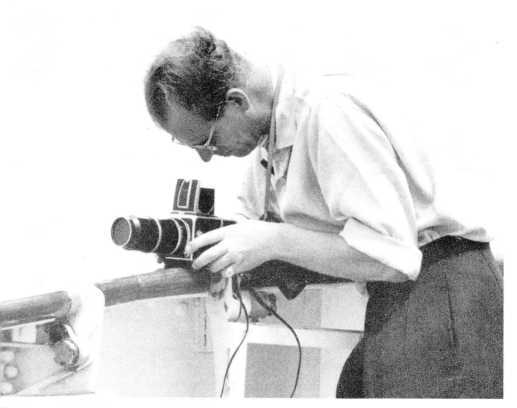

The albatross in flight *(left)* was captured by the Duke using his trusty and well-beloved Hasselblad camera with which he is shown on the Royal Yacht, *Britannia* during his 1956-7 tour. 'Jak', in the London *Evening Standard*, turned the picture to his advantage.

"BLOODY PHOTOGRAPHERS!"

The wedding of Princess Elizabeth and the Duke of Edinburgh, 20 November 1947.

1 Prince George of Denmark. 2 Nada, Marchioness of Milford Haven. 3 Princess George of Greece. 4 Princess Andrew of Greece. 5 King Peter of Yugoslavia. 6 Queen Alexandra of Yugoslavia. 7 Countess Mountbatten of Burma. 8 Princess Margaret. 9 Earl Mountbatten of Burma. 10 Count of Barcelona. 11 Duchess of Kent. 12 Prince Bernhard of the Netherlands. 13 Princess Juliana of the Netherlands. 14 Marquess of Milford Haven. 15 Prince William of Gloucester. 16 King Haakon of Norway. 17 The Queen of the Hellenes. 18 Prince Charles of Belgium. 19 Prince George of Greece. 20 Princess Elizabeth. 21 Queen Mary. 22 Lieutenant Philip Mountbatten. 23 Prince René of Bourbon Parma. 24 Queen Victoria Eugenie of Spain. 25 Prince Michael of Kent. 26 Princess Alexandra of Kent. 27 The King of Denmark. 28 The Queen of Denmark. 29 King George VI. 30 King Michael of Romania. 31 Crown Princess of Sweden. 32 Prince Michael of Bourbon Parma. 33 The Queen. 34 Duchess of Aosta. 35 Prince Jean of Luxemburg. 36 Princess Eugenie of Greece. 37 The Duke of Gloucester. 38 Prince Richard of Gloucester. 39 The Duchess of Gloucester. 40 Princess René of Bourbon Parma. 41 Princess Helena Victoria. 42 Princess Marie Louise.

fund-raiser, mainly for the Award Scheme, and it all passed off with-out disaster though there were some ugly moments. A letter from Admiral Bonham-Carter, the Duke's treasurer, gives an indication of the sort of storm which often lurked on the horizon. Someone from another charity came in 'with a terrible bleat' about having been carved up by the Variety Club. 'He got pretty short shrift from both His Royal Highness and me,' wrote Bonham Carter. They told him it was 'sour grapes' and he left chastened. My father, however, was asked, in a final line, 'Be kind'. This sounds as if he was being asked to pick up the pieces of a bruised ego.

My father's two worst moments were when he got the Duke to the airport an hour too early. 'Now what are you going to do with me?' asked the Duke with one of his looks. And at Twentieth-Century Fox, when the reception line unaccountably froze, 'Call this Twentieth Century Fox? I call this Twentieth-Century ******* disaster,' said the Duke.

The 1966 tour was only possible because of the Queen's Flight, one of whose Andover aircraft was the main transport, frequently flown by the Duke himself. Since 1952, when the Duke first learned to fly, aeroplanes have been a unique combination of business and pleasure for him. It is a rare opportunity for being in complete control even though all his flights are technically designated as training flights and he is always under the command of a professional RAF or Royal Navy pilot. For almost twenty years his personal pilot has been Squadron Leader Geoff Williams alias 'Kitty Three'. All the Queen's Flight pilots have the call sign Kitty, ranging from the CO, who is 'Kitty One' down to 'Kitty Eight' who is a spare.

Williams now flies the specially adapted British Aerospace 146 which has superseded the long-serving Andover. At the Queen's Flight headquarters at RAF Benson near Oxford, Williams keeps the Duke's logbook and the St Christopher medallion, a present from the Goldsmiths and Silversmiths Company, which hangs from a special silver screw in the aircraft whenever the Duke takes to the air.

I wondered how the Duke had adapted to flying a new aircraft type in his mid-sixties. Presumably even an experienced pilot finds such a transition quite difficult. 'Oh,' said Williams, 'you give him all the books and notes. He reads them through and then he knows them better than you do. Then he went up to Hatfield where BAC make the 146 and did five or six sorties in the simulator. Right from the word go he was absolutely at home with it.'

The Duke learned to fly in the Mike Parker days and in this, as in

so many things, they were the keenest possible rivals. The upper ech-
elons of the RAF, egged on no doubt by Winston Churchill with his
vociferously expressed fear of royal flying, were obviously apprehensive. From the first the Duke displayed a predictable aptitude. As an
accomplished horseman and sailor with a fascination for design and
technology, flying was always likely to come naturally. The problem
was that he, again predictably, approached it with a degree of élan
which was not for the faint-hearted. As Basil Boothroyd observed,
'One of his difficulties was to strike a working medium between keeping the rules and bending them.' One fine summer day his instructor,
Flight Lieutenant Caryl Gordon, told him that the Commander-in-
Chief had specifically insisted that the Duke should do no more aero-
batics. The Flight Lieutenant however turned a blind eye.

Both Williams and Air Vice Marshal Sir John Severne, who served
as an equerry in the fifties and then returned in 1982 as Captain of
the Queen's Flight, are agreed that he is an extremely able pilot. He
first went up in a Chipmunk trainer at White Waltham where a
special Home Command instruction unit had been established on 12
November 1952. On 20 December, after only ten hours' flying, he
went solo for the first time and managed a perfect take-off, circuit
and even an exemplary three-point landing. In 1956 he converted to
helicopters. John Severne explained to me that there is a school of
thought that says you should never fly fixed-wing aircraft and helicopters in the same day. The techniques – which he demonstrated
without my fully understanding them – are diametrically opposed.
The Duke however was accustomed to flying, say, from London to
Aberdeen in a fixed-wing Andover, landing, alighting, walking across
the tarmac and into the left-hand seat of a Wessex helicopter and
taking it straight up, up and away. The Duke says it was no more
difficult than switching from driving a car to riding a motor-bike.
Now however, in deference to anno domini, he has given up helicopter
piloting and is even threatening to abandon fixed-wing flying once he
has passed seventy. Williams thinks this would be sad and not necessary. So does his 'Senior Partner', Prince Bernhard of the Netherlands,
who still regularly flies his own aircraft even though he is almost ten
years older than the Duke.

Despite his years of incident-free flying it took just one highly publicised moment to provoke a furore of press criticism. This followed
a reported 'near-miss' when the Duke was at the controls. There is
some difficulty over this. The rules are that such incidents should not
be discussed publicly on the very reasonable grounds that if they do

get wide, and adverse, publicity people will be reluctant to report them. The Palace and the Queen's Flight maintained the prescribed silence at the time, but found it galling to be accused of carelessness or dangerous flying when in fact what had happened was that all the fail-safe systems worked perfectly. The Duke was making a descent near Heathrow Airport and had been advised to go to a certain height but, due to a misunderstanding, began to go lower than he should. As they went through the cleared height the navigator immediately warned the captain, who adjusted the aircraft to the assigned altitude. However, there was a British Airways 747 close enough for it to be advised to take evasive action. There was no danger to anyone, as the subsequent official report proved. The correct procedures were followed and the 'Jumbo' was indeed well out of harm's way.

Another incident which was not reported was the one in which, after take-off from Geneva, the plane, with the Duke at the controls as usual, ran into an electric storm of such violence that a thunderbolt actually passed through a wing. Williams still has the panel with the hole to prove it. At no time did the Squadron Leader feel it necessary to take over from the pilot who was well able, in his estimation, to fly through the trouble as competently as he himself.

Certainly the Duke's experience seems prodigious. He has put in some 5,150 flying hours and has piloted an extraordinary variety of different planes including Concorde and a Vulcan bomber. In 1959 he became the only member of the Royal Family ever to fly his own single-seater aircraft. This was a tiny Turbulent G-APNZ usually piloted by John Severne, then his equerry. In it Severne won the King's Cup in 1960, becoming National Air Racing Champion at an average speed of 109 mph – 50 mph slower than an earlier Captain of the Queen's Flight, Sir Edward Fielden, when he won the same competition in 1932. Unfortunately Severne is shorter than the Duke so, when the Duke flew the plane, the top of his head was exposed above the end of the windshield. He found it exceedingly cold.

The 146 aircraft seems to be the Duke's preferred mode of travel, mirroring the universal move from sea to air. The Royal Yacht, *Britannia*, is still used, but the sort of prolonged sea voyage which the Duke made in 1956–7 today seems inconceivable. Those who took part in those trips still recall the experience with an almost misty eyed nostalgia. Anne Griffiths, then one of the girls in the office, remembers entering a hut in the Antarctic where she and a colleague met two scientists who had not seen a woman in the best part of a year. The men insisted on retaining locks of their visitors' hair as a souvenir.

Parker says, 'It was a brilliant idea of Prince Philip's and deserved much greater recognition . . . the object was to put *Britannia* to her greatest use in visiting beleaguered British people deep in the oceans around the world – Ascension, St Helena, Gough Island, Tristan da Cunha, the Falklands, South Georgia, Chatham Islands, Deception Island and some bases in Antarctica only open twenty days a year. It was quite a sacrifice for all – our first Christmas away from home since the war to boot.'

The Duke's account of the voyage in *Birds from Britannia* is well worth reading. It was a seminal experience in a number of ways. He painted oils under the supervision of the expedition's resident artist, Edward Seago, who also painted the Duke at work on deck with easel and brush. He developed his photographic technique with his Hasselblad camera and showed a well-concealed sympathy for the professional lensman – 'After two hundred yards on my pony I felt very sorry for anyone who has to carry large and awkward camera cases about.' Above all he learned about wild birds. 'Up to that moment,' he wrote, 'I don't think I had ever deliberately taken a photograph of a bird in my life. My ignorance of birds was sublime; if pressed, I would have admitted that apart from the more obvious game-birds the others came in three categories: sparrows, seagulls and ducks.' Within weeks, however, he was becoming a positive poet of ornithology, able to recognise 'Sooty, Wandering, Black-browed, Buller and Shy Albatrosses; Grey-faced, White-headed, Antarctic and White-bellied Storm Petrels; a Grey-headed Mollymawk, a flock of Prions, a silver-grey Fulmar and a Sooty Shearwater'.

As always, of course, it is just when you catch him being poetic that he becomes prosaic. On one of these *Britannia* voyages they picked up the United States Ambassador to a Central American republic because he was supposed to be keen on birds.

Standing on the bridge one day the Duke and his guest scoured the horizons, searching in vain for some sign of life.

Eventually the Ambassador turned to the Duke and said, 'I venture to suggest, Your Royal Highness, that there seems to be a remarkable dearth of ornithological activity in these parts.'

The Duke looked at him for a moment.

'You mean there are no bloody birds,' he said eventually.

Every so often the expedition used to send a bulletin for the benefit of the folks back home. The Duke is particularly proud of the one describing the visit to Tristan da Cunha. At the time there were about 250 people living on this 45-square-mile volcanic dot in the middle of the Indian Ocean. The Royal Yacht anchored somewhere off Edinburgh, named after that earlier Duke, Queen Victoria's son Alfred, late of the Royal Navy. This was a rather unimaginative place name beside some of the others such as 'The Place where the Minister Landed His Things' and 'The Point Where the Goat Jumped Off'.

At 9.30 a.m. the island administrator Mr Forsyth-Thompson, with Mrs Forsyth-Thompson and the chief, Mr Willie Repetto, were rowed out by longboat and greeted the Duke who was dressed in the uniform of an Admiral of the Fleet. The Duke took the helm and sailed ashore where he was greeted by cheers from the fishermen on the beach and their ladies on the cliffs above.

The instruments of the Royal Marines band were carried from the beach by ox-cart, all donkeys having been removed to the far side of the island for fear they should eat the 'arch of welcome'. The Duke inspected the crayfish canning plant, met the doctor, schoolteacher and agricultural adviser together with their wives and was shown some knitting, some model boats and marbles made from the eyes of dried bluefish. These were two short because the chief's cat had eaten some the previous night.

After a reception at the library, and lunch at the administrator's, the royal party went to the new hall for the laying of a commemorative stone. After laying it the Duke presented the island with a portable gramophone and watched a football match played on a 'rugged pitch which gave a distinct advantage to the side playing downhill so long as they were able to pull up before the cliff edge'. The game ended Tristan da Cunha 2, *Britannia* 2, and was followed by dancing to the Royal Marines band and the local accordion ensemble. Finally the Duke was rowed back to the yacht by longboat.

An irresistible day which must have given enormous pleasure to all concerned. Tragically the island had to be evacuated a few years later when quite unexpectedly its volcano erupted after having been dormant for several hundred years.

Few days in the Duke's life can be quite so magical, especially now that there is so much less pink on the globe. Nevertheless there are still plenty of places where the flag can be waved to mutual benefit and enjoyment and even now the Duke remains, with the possible exception of the Princess Royal, the most indefatigable member of a widely travelled family.

# 'Blood's a Rover'

'Clay lies still, but blood's a rover;
Breath's a ware that will not keep.
Up, lad: when the journey's over
There'll be time enough to sleep'

*Reveille*
A. E. HOUSMAN

No matter how much one reads about the Duke, or how many people you talk to about him, there is no substitute for actually watching him in action.

In the autumn of 1990 a perfect opportunity presented itself: a brief visit to Glasgow, Edinburgh and Coventry, using train and helicopter and paying a wide variety of visits in the shortest possible time. To my surprise I was lucky enough to be invited along with the Brigadier, the policeman and the valet.

The Brigadier and I were supposed to travel to Euston Station from the Palace with Barry Lovell, the valet, and the bags, in one of the royal vans, but Barry couldn't be raised and we had no car of our own. After endless phone calls and pleas to policemen we were rescued by a chauffeur from the Royal Mews in a vintage unmarked Rolls-Royce, a Paxton greenhouse on wheels, which creamed through London to Euston at breakneck speed with traffic parting before us like the Red Sea before the Israelites, getting us to Euston shortly before 11 p.m.

The Duke had been at a private Trafalgar Day dinner at Admiralty House. The Royal Train was parked at the platform nearest the east end of the station, and we were just able to get our bags on board in time to stand nonchalantly by the door as he arrived. There seemed to be a large number of men in bowler hats. The Duke, to my surprise, arrived in his personal green electric van and full Admiral of the Fleet evening dress. The ceremony was scant and he walked on board with maximum expedition as we bundled in after him. Inside he held the door open for me and asked, genially, 'Like a drink?' There was a bottle of Famous Grouse and another of Malvern water on a side table. I said yes please and he poured me a stiff one, with water, another for himself and a beer for the Brig. Then we sat down. The Brigadier was in the armchair facing the engine, the Duke by the window, me on his left. On the low table in front of us a plate of miniature sausage rolls and sandwiches and nuts. 'Have something to eat,' said the Duke. 'Keep the wolf from the door,' and seconds later we pulled out of Euston with me sipping nervously at my Scotch.

It does not seem to matter how grown up you feel most of the time, royalty is alarming. It inhibits. For some minutes I kept pretty quiet while the Duke and the Brigadier spoke among themselves. Then suddenly the Duke made a dive at my ankles, fished out his briefcase and said he had to work on his papers. So for the next few minutes the Brig. and I chatted. It was a curious conversation. The Duke *was* going through his papers, but all the while with one ear cocked. When, for instance, I was showing off about helicopters and the *Daily Mail* Air Race all those years ago, he suddenly chipped in with 'Depends whether or not you've got two engines'. Oh, right. If one engine you have to hug the river, if two you can over-fly London.

And so to bed. The steward came in and asked about breakfast orders. The Duke went for haddock. 'Kippers,' I said. 'Kippers would be great.'

'Kippers!' said the Duke, with his look, quizzical, amused, insisting that you explain yourself properly.

'Oh, all right, kipper. *A* kipper would be wonderful.'

We laughed.

Next morning my kipper, beautifully filleted, was served with a style I don't normally associate with British Rail.

'Have some cream with them,' said the Duke.

'Cream?'

'They can be terribly dry otherwise,' he said, and so I poured a trickle of cream over them. They were extremely good. Next night I said I'd like the Dover sole. My father, who had travelled on the Royal Train some twenty-five years before, had been surprised to see the

Duke having sole for breakfast. I ordered the sole for him. An absurd act of remembrance. 'Have some scrambled egg with them,' said the Duke.

'Scrambled egg with sole! You're joking.'

'Not at all. It's very good.'

'Are you sure?'

'Yes.'

'Well if you say so.'

And so I breakfasted off Dover sole and scrambled egg. Unorthodox, but very good. Worth a try.

There were teething problems on the train. The bathroom door kept locking itself and the hot water supply had given out. Later I mentioned this to Sir Peter Parker, who was chairman of British Rail when the train was delivered. He was aghast! Incidentally someone has made the point that there is no such thing as the 'Royal Train', just royal railway coaches. Fair enough. The only thing I could see in this train which marked it out as the Duke's was an enlarged copy of his senior citizen's rail pass in a frame by the door. The configuration of the saloon was two-seat sofa with back to engine and one armchair opposite. This had been raised on the Duke's instruction so that the occupant can see out of the window better. On the first evening the Brigadier sat in it. The Duke was anxious to know if it was comfortable. Attention to detail – very typical.

He riffled through his papers very fast that first night. He's obviously good at assimilating a brief. It was also almost the only time I really got a glimpse of what some observers consider the famous short fuse. 'I can't stand the way these people are always adding things to the schedule,' he complained. And next morning after breakfast, he muttered away at his various briefs. 'Not a word about what the thing *does*.' Or, 'How on *earth* is one expected to read these sticky pages?' This muttering never carried over into conversation. It was a private, personal mutter.

At breakfast he wore a sort of Lovat green cardigan and open-neck shirt, pink and white striped. All the newspapers were on board and in a masochistic way he seems to turn first to the tabloids. 'That's because you can't read the big ones at the table,' he interjects. On day one he was fulminating about the awfulness of the gossip columnists, one of whom 'has discovered that the roubles that came out of Russia for Arthur Scargill couldn't have come out without the Kremlin giving it the OK. Well I should have thought that was self-evident.' On day two it was another tabloid columnist who had written a paragraph about the expense of 'the Royal Train'. There had just been a sub-mission to Parliament about the royal expenses and everyone had picked up on the train. Keith Waterhouse had written the same piece the day before, rather better. Today's was a mocking, facetious paragraph, entirely predictable, along the lines of 'Wouldn't you like to have a special train all of your own at the taxpayer's expense?' The Duke was plainly irritated by it and I did find it a bit startling that he should be reading these predictable pieces in the tabloids. Not good for the blood pressure. He read the more serious papers too and when the Brigadier and I came in to breakfast he was listening to the BBC *Today* programme on his Roberts' portable radio.* England had just beaten Poland 2–0 at Wembley in a World Cup qualifier. We discussed Gary Lineker, of whom the Duke seemed to approve. A few weeks later he presented him, as England's football captain, with the trophy England won for Fair Play during the World Cup finals.

0930 The Duke of Edinburgh, accompanied by Brigadier Robertson, Mr Heald and Inspector Brownridge arrives at Glasgow Central Station in the Royal Train.

The words are from the internal Palace memorandum. Platform 12 as a matter of fact. We had 'stabled' briefly in a siding a few miles out of town and now we slid in between the grubby commuter trains with their passengers' heads suddenly jerking up in surprise as our shiny coaches eased into 1990's European City of Culture.

One minute the four of us – Duke, Brigadier, detective and me – were standing around chatting idly, the next we came to a halt, our door immediately opposite the red carpet. People in uniforms and chains of office standing apprehensive outside. Two, three, door opens. Two, three, Duke exits. Two, three, Deputy Lord Provost curtseys. Two, three, rest of party alight and fade into background, Inspector Brownridge scanning all horizons in one well-trained stare. In seconds the Duke has worked his way past the Vice-Convenor of Strathclyde Regional Council, the Assistant Chief Constable of Strathclyde Police and the Area Operations Manager of British Rail, and then we're out of the station almost at the run and into the waiting cars. The Brigadier and I are in the second car, behind the big black limo which has a sticker in the rear window saying 'Glasgow's Miles Better'. Motor-cycle police buzz like wasps to and fro beside us. It is

* Roberts are the only indigenous British radio manufacturers and have supplied the royal radios since the Queen Mother bought one for Princess Elizabeth at the Army & Navy Stores in 1939.

only a few weeks since Ian Gow, the Conservative MP for Eastbourne, was murdered by the IRA. It occurs to me that the Duke is a prime target. Not a comfortable thought.

We are heading towards 89 Tollcross Road where the Parkhead Housing Association has a new development. It is a grey morning and despite all the good works and renovation Glasgow on a grey day still has a capacity for greyness equalled by few British cities. Those monolithic Victorian buildings look grey, the tenements look grey, even the ground of Glasgow Celtic, one of the world's great football teams, looks grey under its gaunt gantried floodlights.

At the housing development there is another reception line. There are a lot of reception lines in royal life. Routine for the Royals, the split second of a lifetime for those who stand and say hello. The star here is John Ferguson, chairman of the association and a local bus driver. He is a jovial, perky soul not in the least fazed by royalty. There are also a bevy of councillors and Sir James and Lady Mellon. He is chairman of Scottish Homes. The Duke has a special interest in housing because he is president of the National Federation of Housing Associations and has chaired a high-powered enquiry into housing which has produced some controversial recommendations including the replacement of mortgage tax relief by a means-related scheme. The received wisdom on the findings is, to put it simply, that what the Duke and his colleagues said is absolutely right, but that so far it has been politically impossible.

This is clearly a subject in which the Duke is interested and which he knows well. This particular scheme will provide sixty-five homes. At various times it has housed a church, a bakery, a petrol station and even a famous cinema, the Parkhead Picture Palace, but for fifteen years the site has lain derelict. The owners were untraceable so the land was eventually acquired by a Compulsory Purchase Order. The housing association which has developed it was started by locals in 1977 and already has 670 properties in management. The Duke has been well briefed and he obviously knows the right questions to ask, whether he is looking at the architecture of the flats or at the plans or simply chatting to officials or occupants. There is a lot of pointing, jabbing a finger at door jambs, eyes crinkled, head on one side. 'Did you have to knock everything down? . . . How very far-sighted! . . . What exactly will you do with this open space? . . . So there are two flats here and then . . . no, but . . . you'd have done better to put the living room here and the bedroom there.' Well, no, actually he's wrong there, as Mr Ferguson politely but firmly points out. The existing configuration is the appropriate one because of the main road which runs immediately outside. If you did it the Duke's way the occupants would get no sleep. The Duke smiles and nods. Point taken. His conversation is like ping-pong, every ball batted back at once. I am struck by the number of 'buts'. 'No, but', 'Yes, but', 'But what I'm getting at', 'But don't you see', 'But surely'.

On the other hand he likes to be argued with. A little later we all take a tea break in the spanking new and spotlessly decorated flat of a family described in our programme notes as 'Mr and Mrs Stephen McShane and their eight-month-old baby'. There is some good-natured banter to begin with. The Duke asks if they have had to make use of the new pawnbroker's shop yet and we learn that Mr McShane is a dab hand with a wok. It sounds a ridiculous scene: the Duke and Sir James and Lady Mellon and all sorts of other grand enchained figures crammed into this little Glaswegian flat being served tea and biscuits by beaming Scottish matrons. But when you are actually there in the middle of it all it seems entirely normal. The Duke is pleased to be there, the McShanes are pleased too. We are all pleased, all polite, all interested.

Then the Duke starts to talk about housing associations. His theme is that housing is too important to be left to bureaucrats. I can see one of the councillors becoming agitated about this. He is a small man, quite anonymous, but he does not like being told that housing is too important to be left to people like him. Eventually he speaks up. 'With respect, sir,' he says, and then launches into a defence of his council's housing record. He is polite, but adamant, he fights his corner with dignity and vehemence. The Duke listens and fights back. 'You shouldn't subsidise the house, you should subsidise the person,' says the Duke. And again, 'You can't build an "affordable" house . . . affordable to whom?' . . . 'No, no' . . . 'How else?' . . . 'Yes, but . . .' The intricacies of the argument are not, I think, what matters. The point is that it *is* an argument. Views are being exchanged even though they are not being changed. No rank is pulled and each man expresses himself in a robust fashion without fear or favour. Both stick to their guns, but both give the impression of learning from the other. The discussion ends in a draw, amicably. It has been mutually instructive.

Outside in the drizzle the Duke unveils a plaque. I feel I have seen this before. Duke up against a wall, beaming. Onlookers a small knot of dignitaries and flat-dwellers. 'All I want to do is to congratulate the housing association on this great success. This represents what the housing association is all about.' He waves at old ladies who wave back with something approaching frenzy. He is asked to sign a visitors' book. The last entry says 'Automotive and Highways Workers, USSR'. 'I can't add my name to that, can I?' he asks, grinning broadly. He does. Somehow we have run ahead of schedule. This is an opportunity to meet some extra people and penetrate some unexpected places.

There is the pawnbrokers'. In we go, chatting to all and sundry, opening safes, examining contents. We call in at Haddows, the wine merchants, where we chat up two smiling girls. We inspect Smellie and Weir who purvey glass and china and various other items of bric-à-brac.

The end comes with an unnerving suddenness. One minute we are all affable breeziness, waving up at the girl on the fifth floor who is gawping out of her window or exchanging jokes with the old ducks gathered outside the Parkhead Public Library, the next we're making a dive into the cars and the whole procession, with its motor-cycle outriders, is swinging across the city to Moffat Street where at 11.10 precisely the Duke is to visit the Strathclyde Distillery, part of Allied-Lyons plc, whose chairman, Sir Derrick Holden-Brown, has flown up from London especially for the visit.

The distillery is not, as its bosses keep saying rather apologetically, a thing of beauty. It is an industrial plant producing 34 million litres of alcohol a year. For forty-seven weeks of the year it is operating flat out, twenty-four hours a day, seven days a week. It consumes a hundred thousand tons of wheat a year. David Beattie, chairman of Hiram Walker Ltd (the structure of companies as large and diverse as Allied-Lyons is positively Byzantine) told me that Strathclyde is probably the third biggest such distillery in the United Kingdom.

We start off with a display cabinet full of token bottles of various different company brands, some extremely famous, such as Teacher's whisky and Beefeater gin; others such as Glendronach and Balblair less so. Then we are taken to the mash house and outside to the fermentation tanks where the brew is bubbling away like something in a witch's cauldron. How many times must he have seen this before, I keep asking myself, and yet he manages to seem alert and interested, though not as much of an obvious expert as he was back at the housing association. I am amused by his first question which is, 'Is there any effluent?' It occurs to me that if you are not really interested in the principal matter in hand, namely the distillation of spirits for the making of hard liquor, it is a good strategy to turn the conversation into an area about which you do know and about which you are concerned. Thus his first question is, in effect, what are you people doing about pollution? Luckily this particular distillery seems to recycle everything and there is no waste. Just as well.

The next most enjoyable moment comes in the managing director's office where we are gathered to hear the distillery's senior Scotch boffin and senior gin boffin give a short lecture on formulae and recipes. The Duke sniffs at various samples, wrinkles his nose and pulls his face in the – obviously – required manner and then asks questions about the many different and unexpected ingredients which can go into gin. Cardamom, for instance. And juniper. The Duke wants to know where Strathclyde gets its juniper berries. It turns out they're imported.

'Imported!?' The Duke is scandalised. 'But good heavens, there are juniper bushes all over Scotland. Why on earth do you need to import them?'

I miss the answer to this very reasonable question because I think I know what's coming next. He's going to start juniper farming at Balmoral. I even whisper my prediction to the policeman next to me.

The Duke is laughing. 'Well,' he says, 'I can see I'm going to have to go into juniper berry production at Balmoral.'

Am I hopelessly optimistic or am I beginning to know my man?

In conclusion he signed another visitors' book with that firm, slightly backward-sloping 'Philip' and is presented with a cheque for charity, a bottle of gin and a bottle of Scotch.

After I had left my papers in my cabin – enormous by usual railway standards with the bed set along the line of the train not across it so that you lie feet first – we returned to the saloon where the Duke was already in the armchair with a gin and tonic. He is now reading *The Scotsman* and occasionally gives us the benefit of a few lines out loud. In today's paper there is a story based on some manifestly maddening book called *Secrets of the Royals*. *The Scotsman* has latched on to some story about Queen Mary's last wishes and he spends a few minutes explaining how ludicrous it is. I notice the copper bracelet he is wearing on one wrist – for the arthritis presumably. He has large hands, and the arthritis in them is a nuisance. Michael Mann, the former Dean of Windsor, told me to watch the way he fidgets, rubbing a knee or playing with his ear, because he is in pain. To be honest I don't see much evidence of pain. He would, I am sure, go to considerable lengths to conceal pain even if it were acute, but you can usually tell. Either he is a consummate actor or it is not as bad as all that. And he eats carefully and modestly, with no wine because it is too acid. For lunch today he has ordered, from a wide range of richer more extravagant alternatives, egg mayonnaise and roast chicken. Mind you, when the roast chicken arrives and turns out to be all breast he is not pleased. 'I like legs,' he says to me and the Brigadier, but he does not complain to the staff.

'Golly,' I wrote in my diary a little later, 'lunchtime conversation with the Duke!' We seemed to cover an enormous number of topics, and he calls your bluff whenever you chance it. We mentioned Sinaia, the little Romanian town in the Carpathians where the Royal Family had palaces and where he stayed as a child in the Carpathians. I said that Ceauşescu had maintained them beautifully even though he hadn't gone there much on account of some morbid fear of being infected with damp rot or death-watch beetle. This naturally led on to Communism, the revolution, state of the nation and 'intellectuals', teachers, state of their morale, 'progressive ideas', corporal punishment, morality, integrity, a sense of duty, capital punishment, journalists' standards, moral and ethical, the poll tax, humour, Billy Connolly and adapting books for TV.

Suddenly he broke off in mid-sentence to watch a kestrel by the side of the track hovering and about to swoop. He looked on intently for a few moments and then reminisced about one day at Sandringham when he drove halfway up the sea wall to watch birds and a kestrel came past so close and fast that it almost took the end of his nose off.

And then it was back to the dangers of centralised government; the virtues of strong provincial government — as in Germany; the concentration camps — the difference between 'people not knowing, and people not wanting to know'. And then suddenly we were coming into Waverley Station, Edinburgh, and we had to put on a public face again.

The Duke has been Chancellor of Edinburgh University since 1952, the year of the Queen's accession. Sir David Smith, the Vice-Chancellor, a slight, dapper biologist, co-author of *The Biology of Symbiosis*, has held his post since 1987 and was a twenty-two-year-old post-graduate scholar at Oxford when the Duke was originally installed at Edinburgh. He is our host this afternoon, although he delegates responsibility to academics in the three very different faculties we are to visit: Divinity, Sport and Music.

I am in the police car following the royal limousine. Security here seems less obtrusive than in Glasgow though it is there in the background. Every part of our progress is talked through to HQ on the inter-com by one of the two policemen in my car. There is a sinister-sounding sign on it which says, 'This car must be hand-washed.' This is a warning which has nothing to do with preserving chrome finish.

First stop is the 'divvers' library. Edinburgh is famous for its school of divinity and the room is packed with students pretending to work. The problem of this sort of visit is obvious. The Duke wants to be seen as a working Chancellor and he wants to see the university at work. He does not want a special show laid on. He wants to see the university behaving as it does, day in, day out, and these students at their desks are indeed ordinary students going about their studies just as they do every day of the academic year. And yet it is not every day that their royal Chancellor drops in to have the intricacies of Christian scholarship explained to him. There is a sense of giggle, of peeping from behind hands . . . of performance. It cannot be helped.

The dons lead him to a screen at one end of the room. The computer is called Ibycus. The whole of Greek literature up to the year 600 is stored on a single hard disk. Search and ye shall find. They search and they find. The teaching technique is the same as it was in the whisky distillery and as it will be tomorrow in the Land-Rover factory. An expert is explaining his expertise in what he hopes is layman's language and yet one senses that the Duke is determined to prove that he is not just any old layman. He is, as the dons concede, used to reading lessons in church. He knows the Gospel According to Saint John, because he has read it at the lectern so many times these forty years and more. More than that, of course, he has been indulging in dialogue with deans since 1960.

'Isn't there a theory that the gospels were collected together?' (He knows very well that there is such a theory – he is probing, throwing up an inviting full toss.) 'Is Josephus there?' . . . 'and the Gnostics?' And then there is a learned discussion about the cutting off of ears in the garden of Gethsemane and a parallel incident a hundred years before. The dons seem impressed. 'You'd better come back for a full tutorial some other time.' Laughter.

He progresses back through the student body. 'You're all deep into divinity, are you?' It seems they are.

We move on to the Centre for the Study of Christianity in a Non-Christian World. This is 'an international and inter-confessional community devoted to the study of Christian history, thought and life in a full world context.' This means a multi-national receiving line. The Duke glides down it. The name Kasselman is dropped and fielded. Someone says something about Hindus. 'What's that got to do with Christianity?' It sounds a brusque question. Perhaps it is, and yet in context it is not nearly as gladiatorial as it seems. It is the sort of question a robust teacher would ask in a tutorial. I am reminded of Christopher Hill, once my tutor and the ultimate Marxist historian of the seventeenth-century radical and working-class movements, saying with a twinkle, 'Now Mr Heald is going to tell us *all* about the diggers and levellers.' The Duke's technique is not dissimilar.

Somehow the combination of physical exertion and high technology, characteristic of the contemporary approach to athletics, is *very* typical of him. So he seemed very much at home in the sports hall. At the same time he always manages a little bit of obscure one-upmanship. The president of university sports, a student from south of the border, had discovered an obscure Scottish game, a Gaelic form of hockey. The Duke wrinkled his nose. 'There used to be shinty played in Inverness,' he said. Unanswerable. Hockey, of course, was very much his game. It was Hahn's favourite at Gordonstoun and on ships all over the world the Duke has always been a vigorous exponent of 'deck hockey'. As one long-standing adversary remarked, 'I always felt he'd take you off at the knees if they were between him and the ball.'

Sir David seemed only marginally interested in this part of his university, though he was in fact doing an excellent job of delegating the exposition to the people in day-to-day charge, and what, after all, could the Vice-Chancellor usefully contribute to a conversation between the Duke and a sweaty girl in a leotard doing the splits on a Nautilus machine? We left them to it. 'It gives a lot of people a wee boost,' said the Vice-Chancellor, adopting a trace of Scots vernacular. 'He's very good on impromptu occasions like this, very good at the incisive question. And he seems to do it as if he is really interested.'

In his previous job, as Vice-Chancellor at St Andrews, about an hour away in the Kingdom of Fife, Sir David's Chancellor had been the eminent classical scholar, Sir Kenneth Dover. 'Who's he?' I hear a strangled cry. The answer is that Sir Kenneth probably knows more about the Greeks and their culture than any man alive, that he was for more than a decade the head of an Oxford college, and that he lived at 49 Hepburn Gardens in St Andrews and was therefore always available for a cup of tea and a knowledgeable chat. His sort of Chancellor is the antithesis of the Duke and they both have their advantages as well as their drawbacks. Accessibility is not the Duke's strong suit, fenced off by the Buckingham Palace switchboard, Brian McGrath, the Brigadier and all that they imply. On the other hand a visit from the Duke generates buzz, excitement and a heightening of morale. Even republicans seem quite to enjoy him.

The Rector of the University is that spiky, droll, very Scottish media personality, Muriel Grey. It is a position to which you are elected by the student body. On every count you would expect them to be at daggers drawn, but they are – by all accounts – if not the best of friends at least the best of working partners. Despite his position in the pyramid of power and the social status with which he was born and into which he has married, the Duke appears to get on well with republicans and anti-monarchists. Indeed you could argue that he gets on better with them than with the more dyed-in-the-wool traditionalist. He likes argument.

The Kenneth Dover sort of Chancellor is low risk, low profile, on-tap. The Duke is the opposite. It is not a question of better or worse, though there is no doubt which is the more comfortable. 'Comfortable' is not a word one associates with the Duke. 'And then there's security,' says Sir David, with, I thought, some feeling. Despite the Duke's well-known and manifest dislike of all but the most essential security, he is a person who generates a flap wherever he goes. He does not enjoy this as much as some might suppose. His daughter, who knows him better than most, feels that he is not naturally a person who enjoys centre stage. He can do it, but under 'normal' circumstances – whatever they may be – he is someone who is perfectly content to merge.

From sport we turned to music. Not, I assumed, the Duke's most passionate pursuit, even though he once asked Benjamin Britten to write a *Jubilate* for St George's Chapel, Windsor. The focal point here was a harpsichord collection, one of the world's finest.

'It was begun in the sixties when we had some money,' said the Dean of the Faculty, Professor Kimbell.

'So this is how you wasted it,' said the Duke, quick as a flash.

A typical response. Written down baldly in this way, it sounds offensive. Yet it was not intended to be taken like that. It was banter. Robust, certainly; and not perhaps the usual cut or thrust of the senior common room; but, in context, perfectly acceptable. A tabloid newspaper could, however, have had a field day with it: 'A waste of money, says Chancellor. Prince Philip yesterday blasted Edinburgh University for squandering public funds on a harpsichord collection.'

Luckily there was no one to record the remark, to take it out of its context, lay it on a front page and add to the tabloid canon of ducal boobs. It was what it was meant to be, a piece of innocent private banter.

'This is a harpsichord,' said the professor, 'that's a virginal.'

'Yes, but . . .' said the Duke.

In and out of the instruments we weaved. Every so often an academic sat and played a reedy piece on an antique keyboard while we listened quite enraptured; exposition was followed by interlocution: 'You mean to say this isn't Japanese . . . Oh, it's what the Navy call "an organ, portable, small" . . . Not as good as a harp . . .' Bagpipe chanters are called in evidence; there is a discussion about leather hammers; another about the relative merits of raven's and rook's feathers; harps are invoked. I am impressed. So is the Duke. Immediately after a learned discourse on double keyboards he shrugs, grins, bends his knees, and says, disarmingly, 'I may sound frightfully well-informed about this. But it's all based on a children's lecture I heard last year at the Royal Institution.' The self send-up came at just the right moment. It broke the ice and made him human again, stopped him seeming a pompous know-all.

And so to tea. The students have taken over the catering at Edinburgh and it was a marvellous Scottish tea with smoked salmon sandwiches, scones and cream, cakes. The Duke and I were separated. I found myself talking to aspiring journalists, he to grandee fundraisers, including the former Palace press officer, Michael Shea, himself a graduate of the university and now a highly paid PR man in 'the private sector'. At the end of this interlude he and I touched base, briefly. 'I haven't seen him for a while,' said Shea, 'but he is extraordinary. She . . .' – and here he indicated a learned historian – '. . . has done a thesis on Highland regiments from 1828 to the early twentieth century and he was capping her stories every time.'

After tea we had a welcome break. I was flagging. I like to think I am a reasonably well-educated generalist, but on housing associations, distilling, divinity, Nautilus machines and harpsichords I had been hopelessly outgunned. He had, of course, been better briefed. But even so . . .

The interlude was at Holyroodhouse, the palace at the end of Edinburgh's Royal Mile. The Duke's visit was unusual as the Royal Family seldom go there except in July. We were to dine at the Castle which sits on a rock at the other end of 'The mile', dominating this craggy, beautiful capital city, and now we had a couple of hours to bathe and change into evening dress and take stock. Barry Lovell, the Duke's valet, had gone on ahead of us, so that when I was shown into my bedroom I found everything – the moth-eaten dinner jacket I had owned since school almost thirty years before, my father's patent leather boots, a pair of worn black socks – laid out with the sort of precision they obviously teach in the Royal Marines. Barry had worked for an ex-treasurer and equerry of the Duke's, General David Alexander, and he came with a personal recommendation. The Duke was initially disconcerted by Barry's appearance – 'Why didn't you tell me he looked like an ice-cream merchant?' – but they have been together for more than ten years. Barry probably now knows him as well as anyone and he is adept at helping to make the Duke one of the quickest changers in the world. Lounge suit to Admiral of the Fleet in five minutes flat. It *is* impressive, but you have to remember that the Duke has never had to go through the torment of lesser mortals. 'Darling, where have you put my cuff-links?' is not a phrase he ever has cause to utter to *his* wife.

The Duke had his own quarters while the rest of us were housed on a first-floor corridor overlooking the gardens. Every one of our changing rooms had its own printed name plate on the door and the bath towels were the biggest I had ever encountered. The shower in my bathroom was a brilliant Heath Robinson contraption. In the ground floor drawing room, shared between the Brigadier and myself, the housekeeper served a Scottish tea as impressive as the one we had just eaten at the university. More smoked salmon sandwiches and oatcakes and honey. I cannot understand how so many courtiers manage to be quite so skinny.

'Prince Philip,' said the Brigadier, 'wants to know if you're all right. I mean, is there anything you want to know?'

How curious, I thought, that he should ask the Brigadier to ask me instead of asking me straight out. He, who is famous for being so direct and confrontational. Perhaps it is years of life in the Palace?

Naturally there were endless questions I wanted the Duke to answer, but as with most people direct face-to-face inquisition is not always the best approach. The most revealing replies often come when the person you're interrogating does not even know they have been asked a question. In any case Brian McGrath had warned me that the one certain way of not getting anything out of my subject was to take out a notebook and start firing staccato 'yes or no's' at him.

There were small questions – detailed logistical matters like a letter from his father which Princess Sophie said she had given him; there were big questions – philosophical thoughts about nationality and influence; and there was one niggling technical question – the publishers and I had been worrying away at the book jacket. This last struck me as an obvious opener. The Duke is riveted by design and very good at it. Hugh Casson had ruefully told me how he always went unerringly for the weak spot. Quite recently Casson had persuaded the Duke to open a new office building for him; this contained a chairman's suite with bathroom. The design of this was faulty, because the handle of the shower cabinet was in the wrong place. It would not be possible to get in and out without scalding yourself. Casson hoped – against hope – that the Duke would not notice, but naturally and inevitably he was drawn to the shower cabinet as if by a magnet and – how could it be otherwise? – he spotted the design fault immediately. 'What a ridiculous place to put the handle!' he said.

The Brigadier and I were bidden for a drink at ten to seven. The Duke, watching TV from an armchair, remote control at hand, had, without meaning to, become engrossed in a programme about women in sport and now he was into the news. He had meant to get on with some work, but the sporting women had caught his imagination. The programme was evidently full of unexpected historical footage. We all three watched silently until the final item, in which we were shown striding about the pavement outside the Parkhead Housing Association development. It was hardly headline treatment, but it was fair and perfectly accurate as far as it went. After the news we watched the weather and then there was a natural break into which I slotted my first question which was the one about the book jacket.

Much incredulity. 'I'm not a book designer . . . what an extraordinary idea . . . red, white and blue? . . . really?!'

For a moment I thought that I had miscalculated. I floundered, tried to explain that every single book about a member of the Royal Family had a red, white and blue cover with a suspicion of gilt and a very boring stock photograph, small, in the right-hand corner and that we were keen to avoid this particular form of cliché. He seemed disinclined to believe this. I said that I thought green might be an interesting colour but that 'marketing' wisdom was that green-coloured books never sold unless they were about cricket. The Duke looked even less inclined to believe what I was saying, but then, as I had hoped, the cogs started to grind. I remembered Lord Zuckerman's advice: 'Study his mind.'

'Edinburgh green,' he said. 'Edinburgh' green is his official colour, very dark, almost olive, rather grand. 'What about green and gold and red? And you could use the cipher.' The cipher is an elegant, curlicued design, much featured, for instance, in the literature of the

Award Scheme. It has a coronet on the top and a pattern underneath which manages to suggest both crossed 'P's and crossed sabres without being, quite, either. Now he was up and running. A book jacket began to appear before my eyes – a panel of red here, a panel of white there, the cipher superimposed just so. In the event, of course, the professional designers had their own ideas, but his were interesting and could have worked though I do think you need a picture of him on the jacket and not just art-work, even if it is as personal as the cipher. Interesting that he should not have proposed a portrait.

'How are you getting on?' he wanted to know. He meant with the book.

'It's fun,' I said.

'Fun!?' He could not believe it. 'Fun! It's not supposed to be fun.'

'Well, yes, actually, it *is* fun.' I told him about my conversations with Princess Sophie and with Prince Bernhard; about travelling around trying to get to grips with his childhood, about his old school contemporaries, Jim Orr and Robert Varvill . . .

'Robert Varvill!' he interjected. 'What's he up to?'

I told him he was alive and well and living on Chichester harbour.

The Duke seemed pleased, just like any old boy being reminded of a schoolboy chum and finding that he was still around and in good form. Then we started to talk about Gordonstoun and Kurt Hahn. This was safer ground and the Duke was speaking with interest and enthusiasm. Then he suddenly looked at his watch. We were in danger of being late for dinner at the Castle so we shot off along the dark-flagged corridors of the Palace, bade farewell to our host and hostess, and headed for the waiting cars.

There were soldiers and pipers, mainly from the King's Own Scottish Borderers, at the approaches to the Castle; a flurry of indecision as we alighted; and then we were in a crowded room full of what, irreverently, I have described in my diary as 'red-faced buffers in kilts, wives to match.' Royal biographers should not perhaps write such descriptions and my fellow guests were charming, polite, welcoming to a fault. If their faces were red, the room was crowded and we were drinking Heidsieck '81. Nevertheless at Table M where I was positioned in the Great Hall, one of the diners was Brigadier Sir Gregor MacGregor of MacGregor, 23rd Chief of the Clan Gregor, Grand Master Mason of Scotland and a former Commanding Officer of the Scots Guards. Not that one should be unduly impressed by external evidence. It was just that the MacGregor looked so very like a Brigadier Clan Chief and many of the rest of the guests looked so very like him. In that halberd-hung hall, as the pipes played 'The Pibroch of Donald Dubh' and 'A Lament for Alasdair Dearg MacDonell of Glengarry', and we waded through five courses before the Drambuie truffles and the 1975 Dow's port, I felt very foreign and very fat and full. The Duke, at the high table alongside Sir John Macmillan, Commander of the Army in Scotland and Governor of Edinburgh Castle, looked lean, hungry and entirely at home.

The pretext for this feast was to raise funds for the Queen Victoria School in Dunblane. The School was founded in 1906 as a memorial to Queen Victoria and to all those Scots who were killed in the Boer War. All the present 270 boys in the school have at least one parent who served in the forces. Our programme said that after dinner: 'His Royal Highness Speaks' and then, 'Lieutenant-General Sir John Macmillan replies.' The Duke spoke, and spoke well; nothing sensational but just the relaxed, breezy, good-natured, mildly fund-raising words the occasion demanded. The general however did not reply. Some mistake. An inexplicably crossed wire. For several minutes we hung around drinking port and then I realised to my consternation that the Duke and the Brigadier had made their excuses a good ten minutes ahead of schedule and were heading off towards Waverley Station. I hastily said goodbye to my neighbour, Sir James Cayzer (the fifth baronet), and to the MacGregor (the sixth baronet) and hurried after the royal party, just making it to the car in time.

The train seemed almost familiar by now and I was becoming dangerously used to the red carpet on the platform, the late-night Famous Grouse, the early-morning tea, the efficiency of the whole operation with a British Rail timetable that had some of our timings down to the last half minute. Next morning our breakfast conversation was dominated by news of the Eastbourne by-election result. The contest was caused by the IRA's murder of the Conservative MP, Ian Gow, and the Conservatives failed to hold it. This led to talk of the poll tax, almost certainly the biggest reason for the anti-government swing. The Duke cannot, of course, talk party politics, but as a considerable landlord in Scotland, where the tax was first introduced, he is something of an expert on its ramifications and repercussions. It seems a pity he is not allowed a public opinion on it. He might have given the government pause for thought.

At Coventry we slid into the station at ten to ten. The Lord-Lieutenant, the Earl of Aylesford, in his blue uniform with sword and spurs, introduced the High Sheriff and the Lord Mayor and the Clerk to the Lieutenancy and the Assistant Chief Constable and the Area Manager, British Rail.

This morning's first stop was Progress House, headquarters of the Examinations Board of the RSA. The RSA was founded in 1754 as the Society for the Encouragement of Arts, Manufactures and Commerce. It received its Royal Charter in 1847 when Prince Albert was its president and the Duke has occupied his great-great-grandfather's position since 1952 – just under ninety years after Prince Albert's death. A quick word with a posse of schoolchildren – 'You ought to migrate to Scotland, you get more time off up there' – and then into the modern building which he was to open officially, even though it was already in full operation. There are a hundred and fifty staff in occupation already. In the last full year of operation they dealt with 890,000 entries in 184 different schemes. In the warehouse where he made his speech there were stacks of scrolls ready to be awarded. I noticed the Diploma in Secretarial Procedures and the Diploma in Retail Distribution. After the formal speeches there was a forty-five-minute tour of the building and then the party all got back into the official cars and headed off for the last visit of the tour, to Land-Rover, a few minutes away in Solihull.

The Duke had been here twice before, and knew the product. Land-Rover hold all four Royal Warrants for supplying vehicles for the Queen, the Queen Mother, the Prince of Wales and the Duke himself. Together with the Barbour raincoat and the green wellington boot (supplied by the Gates Rubber Company of Dumfries, Scotland), the rugged four-wheel-drive Land-Rover is virtually synonymous with the Royal Family in shooting and fishing mode. This time the Duke was to present the company with the Queen's Award for Export Achievement so it was no wonder that Sir Graham Day, the group's chief executive, seemed particularly pleased to see him. He was meeting a satisfied royal customer and picking up an accolade as well. Sir Graham, of course, is a senior captain of industry who was chairman and chief executive of British Shipbuilders before joining Rover in 1986. He is also a Canadian, hailing from Halifax, Nova Scotia, and I wondered if it was this which made him seem less fazed than some Englishmen when confronting the Duke. There was a moment when the operations director, in his formal talk, said that the factory was 'the most integrated plant in the West Midlands'.

The Duke was in bantering mood. 'Also the biggest traffic jam,' he said.

Sir Graham smiled. 'Traffic jams mean prosperity, sir!' he replied with an expression which was just as bantering, but firm with it. In my notes I wrote an immediate aside to myself: 'But it's good natured.' Reproduced without that caveat the exchange could look prickly and chippy. It was neither of these, but I did feel that a lot of Englishmen, even very senior ones, might have more trouble in dealing with this sort of conversational gambit. Canadians and Australians have informality and egalitarianism bred in the bone; even English republicans have problems with class and above all with royalty.

The Duke obviously did know the product well though he also asked pertinent questions about management structures and relations with the unions. At lunch (Parma ham, salmon and prawns, *crème brûlée* – how on earth *do* they cope?) he and Sir Graham sat next to each other and talked with animation, the Duke nodding, frowning, questioning, learning. The Lord-Lieutenant caught me trying to eavesdrop – I was below the salt – grinned impishly and made an ear-flapping motion to let me know that I had been spotted.

One tiny incident stuck in my mind from lunch. These days the Duke does not drink wine, but someone had boobed and his usual half pint of pale ale had not been provided. There was a flurry of embarrassment and presently a waitress appeared with a beer on a salver. That was all he drank during the meal. Afterwards, touring the shop floor, he would stop regularly and chat to various workers and I, following behind but standing well away, would later ask some of them for their impressions. One of the first conversations was with a small rather bothery man in overalls and late middle age. 'I could smell the beer on him!' he said, with a sneer. 'What we want is a decent pay rise!' I could picture this man that evening at home or in the pub with his mates. 'Spoke to the Duke of Edinburgh this afternoon. I could smell the beer on him.' And how long would it be before the Chinese whispers had transformed it into, 'The Duke of Edinburgh was at Rover the other day. Blind drunk!'? Maybe not, but it set me wondering.

He was the only worker I spoke to who adopted that line. Much more typical was another man who said, 'We like having well-informed visitors whoever they are. The Royal Family were some of the first people to buy a Range-Rover so we're always pleased to see them. I've not met him before but he was much as I expected. Well-informed and curious.' No sycophant he, but open-minded.

It is an impressive plant; mile upon mile of slowly moving vehicles in various stages of assembly; each emerging product swarmed over by workers prodding, screwing, peering, frowning, testing. Up and down the official party marched, pausing in time with the eager, curious Duke. Some of us looked more incongruous than others. The Lord-Lieutenant was the most obviously out of place in his peaked cap with his sword and his spurs. He played up to his image. At one point he picked up some strands of highly coloured wires and wrinkled his nose. 'I've been looking for something to tie my fishing flies with,' he said, 'this would be just the thing.'

At 1455 a spanking, state of the art Range-Rover conveyed us to an open space where, despite the foul weather, there was a waiting scarlet Wessex helicopter of the Queen's Flight. The Brigadier told me I should sit in the back with the Duke. I protested that the Duke must have had enough of me by now, but the Brigadier was adamant. 'If he has, he'll go to sleep,' he said. And he was right.

'I used to fly these things,' said the Duke, looking rather wistfully in the direction of the flight deck. I said I knew that and asked if he missed it. He said he was trying to give things up slowly, one at a time, because it was less painful that way. The Wessex was 'a bit lumbering . . . not very fast.'

Outside in the rain the Lord-Lieutenant and the High Sheriff of the West Midlands and the Mayor of Solihull were standing at attention in their chains of office. The Duke waved; the Earl saluted; the engine surged and we swayed up, up and away. I watched the three stiff men turn to matchsticks and then fade from sight altogether. For some reason it was an extraordinarily poignant moment and I felt terribly, terribly sad.

And then in my notes I see that I have scrawled, 'He's eating a mint chocolate (How Crawfie can I get?).' For the first few minutes of the flight the Duke scrutinised a report on participation in his Award Scheme; then he passed it to me and went to sleep. Not the sort of fitful shallow daydream that is the best most of us can manage but a proper sleep. I mentioned it to his sister-in-law, Princess Margaret, a week or so later. 'My father could do that too,' she said, 'I think it's an old naval trick.' But she had taught herself too, so maybe it's something that comes easily to royalty.

A few minutes before touch-down the Duke shook himself awake. The visibility had not been good over the home counties, but London was clearer. We flew low over the Albert Hall, banked above Victoria railway station; a man in an office window waved; and then there was the back garden of Buckingham Palace. The Duke gazed out as we touched down. The lawn still looked as dry and khaki as an Indian polo field. 'The lawn still hasn't recovered from summer,' he said.

The official programme, which I shall always treasure, says, in the orotund tones of Palace bureaucracy,

1600. Arrive at Buckingham Palace where Mr Heald takes his leave.

I am sure there is a correct courtier's way of doing this but no one told me, so I simply said thank you very much for having me and goodbye. And so we parted. Commander Sillars gave me a cup of tea, carried my case to the Privy Purse door, and I took a taxi home feeling like Alice coming out from behind the looking-glass.

A breathless hush is not acceptable as the only verdict on a trip like this, though a certain not very audible breathlessness is surely allowable. Housing association, distillery, university, fund-raising school dinner, opening of RSA building, motor factory, and all this with the briefest of pauses in between. No discernible gaffes; pleasure given and taken; give-and-take all round. I do not believe any fair-minded person could fail to have been impressed. The Duke, after all, was pushing seventy at the time of this expedition and he has no need to do it. He is past retirement age and in any case no job specification has ever been written for a Prince Consort in all but name. No reasonable person could honestly ask for greater effort or a higher standard of performance.

I had talked to a variety of people all along the route, gathering impressions. In the aftermath, once the dust had settled, I asked one or two others for their thoughts on royal visits in general and the Duke's in particular. Given the circumstances, it is hardly surprising that the responses were favourable. The West Midlands' High Sheriff, for instance, could hardly be expected to be hostile but the way in which he was enthusiastic was revealing. In conversation he said that the Duke's opening line was a question: 'How long have you been High Sheriff?' Other members of the Royal Family will say, 'Oh, we all do that,' but the Sheriff had already met half a dozen of the Duke's relations and this was the first time he had been greeted with a question. Provided the other person knows the answer – and royalty can numb the brain in the most unexpected way – it is obviously a good way of easing tension. This particular High Sheriff, David Burbidge who runs his own kitchen furniture company, *was* able to tell the Duke how long he had served and found the approach stimulating and refreshing.

'When the Duke of Edinburgh first arrives for a visit one is immediately struck by the combination of his commanding presence and his warmth and dry humour,' he wrote, adding that, 'His involvement in a royal visit immediately implies a high level of achievement and a very high standard should be expected.'

Burbidge argues that the success of a royal visit depends on 'two essential criteria'. The first is the individual's feeling about the Royal Family and the second is people's desire to be patted on the back. This is a universal urge but if it is to be worthwhile the pat on the back should be administered by someone who can evince some enthusiasm and some knowledge. It is dispiriting to be presented with a prize by a visibly bored guest of honour or even to receive a rave review from a critic who has manifestly failed to read the book. The Duke is good at seeming interested – a corollary being that he is not always accomplished at disguising boredom. Both attributes suggest that he is not as much of an actor as some public figures. When he appears interested it is because he *is* interested; when he seems bored he *is* bored.

'It is this close interest in the things that he is seeing that helps to add even greater significance to the visits,' says Burbidge. 'Everybody likes to show off about the things they have done well and it is so much more satisfactory to be praised by somebody who understands fully what he is seeing and who only gives praise when it is fully deserved.'

Graham Day of Rover writes, 'Prince Philip aside for a moment, there are both external and internal benefits gained by Rover in consequence of an industrial visit by a member of the Royal Family. Internally as I am sure you observed, such a visit gives our employees much pleasure. The very long connection with the Royal Family is valued by the employees in emotional terms and, also, I know that they understand the commercial significance vis à vis customers at large. Externally, in the surrounding community, a visit by a member of the Royal Family is, properly, an occasion. Such a visit, therefore, tends to further cement the ties between the community in which the industrial undertaking is located and the industrial undertaking itself. Also externally, the media interest in such a visit emphasises to the larger marketplace the link between the Royal Family and the product which is produced.

'The visit of Prince Philip in many ways adds emphasis to the points I have made above. Again as I am sure you will have observed, Prince Philip is open, friendly and very much at ease as he meets and speaks with a number of our employees. Consequently, they are at ease in speaking with him and this underlines the pleasure which they derive from his visits. As a professional observer, it will not have escaped you that our female employees are particularly attracted to Prince Philip. Understandably a similar manifestation was apparent when Prince Charles visited Cowley about a year ago.'

He adds that the Duke understands the company's cars and is familiar with them and that the firm's Royal Warrants and the personal association with the Royal Family are particularly useful in the export market, and he concludes: 'I know it would be difficult, if not impossible, to quantify the benefits which I perceive Rover receives. However, I and my colleagues are confident that the company receives very real benefits through the reinforcement of product image, which is critical to our marketing success and, as I have said, the very real pleasure and satisfaction it gives our employees.'

At the very last the objective rather hard-nosed captain of industry allows a personal note to enter his calculations. 'I make no apology for saying to you, in addition, that I am an unabashed royalist and these visits also give me much pleasure.'

In a way, that last line is more telling than the more measured earlier judgements. This short journey with the Duke was unique but not, judging from his diary, untypical. It was revealing and instructive in a number of ways but in the end what was remarkable was the evident pleasure everywhere. Some people looked apprehensive or nervous (not as many as I would have expected); a great deal of hard work and spit and polish had obviously gone into preparing for him; working days had been disrupted. But everywhere there was a sense of occasion and a sense of fun, all the more so because he too seemed to be enjoying himself, to be interested in people and their work, to be making an effort. This seldom communicates itself in print or on the screen perhaps because, as anyone who has ever watched a live sporting event and then read about it or watched it on TV will know, it is incredibly difficult to capture the electricity of real life in print or on celluloid. The sense of occasion gets lost.

It is easy to understand how these royal visits excite people for whom they are a once-in-a-lifetime experience; very much more difficult to understand how you can retain your zest and enthusiasm when you are the royal visitor. In a sense every day in the Duke's life is a royal occasion, but on this programme he never seemed simply to be going through a routine or undertaking a chore. He seemed to be having a good time. Which inevitably made it easier for everyone else to do the same.

# 14

# 'And Must Unbend His Mind'

'A man, though wise, should never be ashamed
Of learning more, and must unbend his mind'
*Antigone*
SOPHOCLES

One of the peculiarities in running such a diverse portfolio of patronages and presidencies is that those who run each organisation with which the Duke is associated like to think that their links with him are in some way special, if not unique. Time and again a retired general or bishop or academic or all-purpose personality such as Gyles Brandreth will rather coyly show you one of the Duke's home-typed letters, topped and tailed in the large loopy script: 'Dear Gyles', at the beginning; 'Yours sincerely, Philip' at the end. This sounds flatteringly personal.

The fact that he is able to juggle the great and the good like so many Indian clubs is a considerable feat. He cannot really attach equal importance to each one of his causes and commitments and yet each one's boss genuinely seems to believe that in the final analysis he is the one with the special relationship. In fact the Duke never consciously displays any favouritism and goes to great pains to make every organisation with which he is associated feel that they enjoy a unique and special relationship. Even so some people do become jealous if they sense that the Duke is giving more attention to someone else. I asked him, for example, if he had worked out a programme based on a set of priorities for the foreseeable future. It seemed reasonable. As you near your three-score years and ten you must have *some* sense of time suddenly becoming in short supply and if you are as busy as he is you must parcel it up according to a sense of what matters most. Mustn't you? 'No,' he said. And that was it.

By the same token, how do you evaluate his achievements when, on the one hand, he is so manifestly reluctant to distinguish between them himself and, on the other, so many different people believe that the greatest achievement of his life is the one most clearly associated with themselves?

Sir Peter Parker, for example, believes that the Commonwealth Study Conferences are 'the most original thing he has done in my experience of him'. Sir Peter would say that, wouldn't he? He was the first-ever conference secretary and the man most responsible for making sure that it actually worked.

Sir Peter and the Duke first crossed paths in 1953, the year of the Coronation. He was an unlikely royal acolyte; sometime Chairman of the Oxford University Labour Club and parliamentary candidate for Bedford in the 1951 election campaign; he played Lear opposite the Cordelia of Shirley Williams. She was later a Labour Cabinet minister and a founding member of the ill-fated Social Democratic Party. Parker also played Hamlet under the direction of the great, if wayward, theatre critic Kenneth Tynan. At Cornell and Harvard Universities he held a Harkness Commonwealth Fund Fellowship to study 'Social Responsibility in Industry'. A 'pinko', an aesthete, an intellectual and an egalitarian, Parker seemed disbarred on every count from being any sort of adviser to a royalty then regarded by many as conservative, philistine, and class-bound.

At a loose end after his academic studies he trawled through the phone book, found something called 'the Industrial Welfare Society'* and was taken up by its director, 'an original' called John Marsh, who had survived the Japanese 'Railway of Death' and consequently lived every moment as if it was a totally unexpected bonus. In the autumn of 1953 Marsh called Parker to say that he would like him to help out with 'a new problem'. The 'problem' was the Duke.

Parker concedes that the name Industrial Welfare Society was 'old fashioned' and 'cracked'. Despite this, it was a pioneer in personnel and organisational practice and was supported by all the important

* Now known as the Industrial Society.

figures in trade and industry. For years its patron was the Duke of York, later King George VI, who lent his name to a series of annual camps for industrial apprentices and other young people in the nineteen thirties. After the King's death in 1952, the Duke was asked to take over.

His response was to the point. Yes, he would take it on, but only if he could be of some use. What exactly did the IWS want of him? Kindly clarify. 'A typical slam-bang, naval officer's letter' is Parker's estimation.

Marsh responded in kind. The Duke recalls: 'He came to me with the idea of a Commonwealth Industrial Relations Conference. Even in those days I was not completely naïve and I could see that I could not possibly have anything to do with that subject. As it happens, I had just come back from a visit to Canada, where I had seen a number of new industrial and mining developments which involved building new towns for the employees. I therefore suggested to him that a better idea would be to arrange for potential managers and trades union leaders to visit good and bad sites in this country to study the relationship between industry and the community and to learn together from direct experience of the urban industrial situation. He accepted the idea.'

The Minister of Employment, Sir Walter Monckton, nodded an absent-minded approval and before anyone considered the implications the scheme was up and running. On the very day of Marsh's call to Parker the London *Evening News* ran a leader about the conference even though, as Parker recalls, 'the precise aim, programme, membership, funding and organisation were still dangerously undefined.' Parker winces at the memory. 'It was a chaotic situation,' he says.

Prematurely publicised in its half-baked state, the conference ran into flak from left to right. The employers thought the whole concept implied criticism of their role in the conduct of industry; the employees were 'aghast' at the idea of a royal personage sticking his oar into industrial relations. The Duke says, 'I specifically insisted that it shouldn't have anything to do with industrial relations.' But at first his message did not get through. Arthur Deakin of the Transport and General Workers' Union was of the opinion that if it went ahead the conference would be 'the greatest tragedy in the history of industrial relations in this country'.

Underpinning this rare display of unanimity were two criticisms which have dogged the Duke throughout his royal life: 'Who does he think he is anyway?' and 'I thought royalty wasn't supposed to get involved in politics?' Taken to their logical conclusion these twin ideas meant that the Duke was not allowed to express himself on any matter more controversial than the weather. And even that can turn political. 'A sudden chill went through the establishment,' says Peter Parker, 'and everyone asked "What exactly is going on here?"'

In this instance the Duke enjoyed powerful support. Sir Harold Hartley was already in place as a loyal and zealous adviser. That archetypal Balliol man – he even married the Master's daughter – is one of the unquestioned influences on the Duke's life. He was not only a brilliant scientist, the tentacles of his influence extended throughout the British academic and business establishments. Peter Parker himself, although still a young man at the outset of his career, went on to be boss of Britain's railways and chairman of more public companies than is, especially for a socialist, quite decent. And despite that initial hostility Prince Philip showed that he was already adroit at winning new friends and influencing new people.

The crucial meeting was at Buckingham Palace in July 1956. The agenda was a paper prepared by Peter Parker, entitled, 'The Social Responsibility of Industry'. Parker thought it bland stuff but the use of the word 'social' was a mistake. It sounded, in those far-off days, provocatively radical and the bosses rose to the bait with a prepared statement from their president, rubbishing everything in it. The two Parkers, Peter and the Duke's secretary Michael, were seated immediately behind their boss and they saw him stiffen in the face of this verbal onslaught. Instead, however, of losing his temper, he beamed down the long thin table (a 'ridiculous' table, says Peter Parker who believes, as an article of faith, that all conference tables should be round), and said, 'I am sorry, I must have missed something. I couldn't altogether follow that.' A shrewd move, this pretence of ignorance, naïvety or simple innocence. When he asked if the speaker would mind repeating it, he was on to a winner. Second time round it sounded flat and unconvincing. The bosses were floundering.

The Duke doesn't recollect the first council meeting as being quite so dramatic. Peter Parker on the other hand was observing him closely, and thought the whole occasion charged with drama.

The Duke won the conference round and, in retrospect at least, there were a number of crucial turning points. One of the bosses was Sir Simon Marks of Marks & Spencer. For most of the meeting Marks was silent. Parker, Peter, had prepared two conclusions, one indicating failure, the other success. Just when it seemed that the meeting would find for failure Marks could contain himself no longer. The

Walking out to bat in one of the cricket matches that raised money for the National Playing Fields Association, with which he has been associated since 1949.

The Duke leading from the front as stroke of a whaler representing his ship HMS *Magpie* in the Mediterranean Fleet regatta, 1951. They won the Destroyer Command Officers' race by half a length from a field of fifteen.

The Duke and the Prince of Wales have both been passionate about polo. The Duke had a considerable reputation for being noisy on the field of play.

HIT-UP SESSION FOR PRINCE PHILIP AND PRINCE CHARLES AT CENTENNIAL PARK TO SELECT POLO PONIES — NEWS ITEM

"Dodge the older one fellers — he's very outspoken."

Although widely regarded as a natural forward the Duke played most of his polo at back – mainly because he never had enough opportunity for practice.

In August 1967 the Duke tried his hand at bicycle polo and is seen here during a six-a-side match on Smith's Lawn, Windsor.

At the helm of *Coweslip*, the 'Flying Fifteen' presented to him by the people of Cowes, Isle of Wight. His companion is the legendary sailor and small boat builder, Uffa Fox.

Although he came to shooting late in life the Duke is a keen and accomplished shot and has strong views about the place of game conservancy in the preservation of wildlife. As the hat suggests this is a German shoot.

The Duke seldom has the opportunity to fish, but he is passionate about 'dry-fly' fishing which he was first taught before the war by his brother-in-law the Margrave of Baden.

The Duke has been a keen pilot ever since first learning to fly at White Waltham in 1952. His earliest aeroplanes were the de Havilland Chipmunk, North American Harvard, Airspeed Oxford and de Havilland Devon. The team photo (*upper right*) shows him with his pilot Squadron Leader Geoff Williams and the rest of the crew during a tour in 1988. The two lower pictures show him with the single seat Turbulent in which Air Vice Marshal Sir John Severne, then his equerry, won the Queen's Cup in 1960. On the left Severne is cranking the engine and on the right the Duke is making his first solo landing.

Since retiring from active polo in 1971 the Duke has become an enthusiastic carriage driver. As President of the International Equestrian Federation he was instrumental in framing the first international rules for carriage driving and has himself competed at international level.

'fail' statement did not even mention the Duke by name but simply said that there had been a meeting at the Palace. 'We can't leave your name out from whatever we say,' ventured Marks. 'It would be like playing *Hamlet* without the prince.'

The Duke's riposte was speedy and apposite. 'Well,' he said, 'a lot of people prefer *Hamlet* without the prince. Very unstable fellow, the prince.' Laughter. Collapse of opposition. Duke wins day.

Peter Parker told me that story in his office at Portland Glass where he is now chairman. At sixty-six he seems almost busier than the Duke not only with his chairmanships but with an endless stream of supplicants asking his help in raising the odd million for their pet projects. He is one of the great fund-raisers and still a prime mover in raising money for the next of the Duke's conferences. As an ex-actor he tells a story well and the Duke's *Hamlet* remark sounded brilliant on his lips even thirty-four years after it was first coined. Later when I read it in Parker's biography, and again when I myself put it on paper, it seemed a little limp and forced. This is often a problem with the spoken word: print diminishes it. There is something about the Duke's off-the-cuff repartee which exaggerates the effect. Face to face he is a lively performer and his remarks seem incisive and amusing; they make people laugh, they energise, they are life-enhancing.

It is clear that the genesis of this first conference was immensely exciting to people who were not essentially cerebral or intellectual. Quite ordinary men and women became imbued with a sense of occasion, of treading new ground. This was an event. Parker wrote:

We were being driven towards the central question of industrial societies which had not been asked before: how to reconcile the imperatives of industrial and technological developments with the needs of the individual and the community? Industry and social life interact at every point: it follows they can only be studied intelligently as a whole.

These sentences, however, simply do not convey the atmosphere of the moment.

The Duke and his colleagues now had to translate Parker's words into action. At Balmoral he stared long and hard at a blank sheet of paper while his guru, Sir Harold Hartley, rang round the great and the good and asked for ideas. Eventually the Duke got his inaugural speech written, the conference took shape.

'I think,' says Peter Parker, 'that I recognise the mystery of personality at three hundred yards on a misty day and he had it. That was his first real exposure to this sort of thing. It was hard grind to achieve that conference.' When it took place in Oxford the Duke opened it, he sat through all the sessions, and he gave the closing address. On the penultimate night he stayed up with Parker and his colleagues helping to prepare the reports so that they could be on everyone's breakfast tables. 'He knew just how to be "that little touch of Harry in the night",' says Parker, 'and he handled the day of reporting in an absolutely starry way. It's a quality I recognise because it's a theatre quality. He had it. Mountbatten had it too, but in a more obvious way.'

After three weeks the Duke, in the Sheldonian Theatre, sent the delegates away with a ringing admonition to apply what they had learned in Oxford to their working lives. Parker is convinced that he detected a note of wistfulness in the Duke. Many of these young men were the same age and Parker felt that what the Duke was *really* saying was, 'You chaps are lucky – you're going back to real jobs.' The implication being that he was the only one who did not have a 'proper' job to return to. The Duke denies this with the exasperation of someone who is always having to deny similar allegations. Parker, for his part, felt that the Duke was the sort of man who could have made a fair fist of running British Airways, as indeed Sir Harold Hartley had already done: 'I was chairman of BOAC and creator of BEA,' he once said, with an eye for accuracy rather than self-glorification. Prince Philip would have liked to have done that and could have pulled it off. Instead he was simply acting as a sort of glorified cheer-leader for others.

'I have certainly never felt "frustrated" in any way,' insists the Duke. 'The point has always seemed to be to find ways to use my position to be constructive. I am not surprised that others cannot see this, they have never been in my position!!' The double exclamation marks are his! His observers, and well disposed observers, not enemies, remain sceptical. 'The point,' said one, 'is that every time he is really able to concentrate on something he knows he has to let go.'

The Duke says this is quite wrong: 'I can pick and choose.' He adds that for twenty-two years he ran the International Equestrian Federation; he has headed his own Award Scheme for thirty-five years; he has retained his links with the National Playing Fields Association since 1949, and his WWF connections go back to 1961.

In the case of these Study Conferences he has never let go, they have continued to take place in different countries of the Commonwealth every six years. The Duke has continued to nurse them along, preside over their deliberations and make sure that they adhere to the principles established all those years ago in Oxford. It is a formidable achievement and scarcely known, let alone acknowledged outside the circles of those who have taken part. It is not the stuff of newspaper headlines.

He himself knows why. Introducing one of his anthologies he cautioned, 'Most of the material was either written or delivered for a particular audience on a particular occasion and in rather special circumstances. When an essay or a speech is read several years later by someone not directly involved with the original occasion . . . the impression is bound to be different.'

How true, how very true! After that first successful conference was over Oxford University Press produced two fat volumes summarising its deliberations. Try as one may, it is difficult to catch the excitement of the event from those musty pages. The names of the speakers were once great in the land but now, alas, they are the stuff of history past: Sir John Maud, Permanent Secretary at the Ministry of Power; Lord Citrine, chairman of the Central Electricity Authority; Alfred Roberts, General Secretary of the Amalgamated Association of Card, Blowing and Ring Room Operatives; J. Crawford Gale, president of the National Union of Boot and Shoe Operatives; Dame Florence Hancock, Chief Woman Officer at the Transport and General Workers' Union. I do not list these names to denigrate them. They were much in the public eye in those days, but they are not now much remembered outside the particular worlds in which they used to be such giants.

In Oxford these star speakers addressed themselves to a whole variety of subjects connected with the central theme. Thus – 'The Varying Pattern of Industry'; 'The Human Problems of Industry'; 'Why Does Man Work?'; 'The Two Partnerships – Man with Man and Man with Nature' (this from Sir Harold Hartley himself); 'Thoughts of an Ecologist on Industrialisation' (this was Sir Frank Fraser Darling). The Commonwealth itself was fairly represented with men like Harry Oppenheimer from South Africa and W. J. Bennet of Atomic Energy of Canada; one talk was on 'The New Dimensions of Woman's Life in India' and another on – this is my own favourite – 'Health, Welfare and Safety in New Zealand'.

Occasionally a phrase or an idea still leaps off the page as when Hugh Casson, pithy and forthright as always, addresses himself to the aesthetics of the industrial landscape and says, 'The look of industry can be shortly summarised. It is a dirty look.'

Peter Parker says that 'the records of the conference, far too little known, show his summings-up during the final days of reporting back at every conference, his comments always impromptu, public, vivid, uninhibited, revealing and sharply to the point.' After the formal sessions, the young leaders of the Commonwealth undertook a series of study tours. These included such locations and experiences as: coal mines, day nurseries, a cargo ship, the Oxford Circus Underground station at rush hour, a meal with twenty Yorkshire mill girls, being entertained by the City Livery companies, the London sewers, the fish market in Hull, a Border tweed mill, a huge engineering works, the goods depot of a main line railway station, a youth club, a university common room and a Cardiff pub. Then, replete with such a wealth of first-hand experience of 'real life', the delegates returned to Oxford for the final sessions in which they discussed their findings.

The seventh of these conferences, in 1992, returns to the city of the original dream. Oxford and the Sheldonian will once again play host, and thirty-six years after he first presided the Duke will take the chair again. The Duke of Kent is now Chairman of the Trustees and the Duke of Edinburgh is at last showing the first signs of relinquishing this baby of his. Already the Canadians, who will host 1998, are wondering who will chair *their* conference. The Duke will be seventy-seven by then, but . . .

If, as Peter Parker suggests, the public's perception of these conferences is minimal, they still touch the Establishment. At a fund-raising dinner at the Royal Mint Court on Guy Fawkes' Night 1990, an astonishing collection of men with their fingers on the nation's purse strings included the former Chancellor of the Exchequer, Nigel Lawson, his erstwhile colleague, Lord Young of Graffham, Maurice Saatchi of Saatchis, Sir Evelyn de Rothschild of Rothschilds, the chief executives of Tate & Lyle, Vickers, British Airways and British American Tobacco, the senior partner of Price Waterhouse and enough similarly placed business and City mandarins to underwrite the Duke's conferences for eternity.

Little of this spills over into public knowledge, another illustration that much of what the Duke does, seminal and influential though it may be, remains a surprisingly well kept secret. And yet there are leaders all over the Commonwealth – Bob Hawke, the Australian premier, to name but one – for whom these conferences are among the most formative experiences of their lives.

John Hunt – leader of the 1953 Everest expedition, and later Lord Hunt – remembers meeting the Secretary of State for Education, Sir Edward Boyle, at a reception in the mid-fifties just after Hunt had left the Army in order to be the first director of the Duke of Edinburgh's Award Scheme.

'He didn't like it one little bit,' says Hunt. '"Oh," he said. "So you're running the Award Scheme." And turned his back. And walked away.'

A disconcerting experience. Hunt, after all, was an authentic hero, and Boyle was someone he admired. Perhaps this is the inevitable reaction to any innovation. There is always an 'Establishment' defending its own position, resistant to any newcomer, particularly when this particular world is so crowded with organisations such as the Scouts, the Boys' Brigade, boys' clubs of every description, and schools which felt they provided as much extracurricular activity as anyone could possibly need. 'What's the point in doubling up?' asked the Scouts. Hunt says, 'I put the opposition down to the simple sin of jealousy.' In the case of the Award the 'Establishment' was sceptical, even more so because many of them believed that the true *éminence grise* behind the Scheme was that awkward, ambivalent, essentially alien figure, Kurt Hahn.

Hahn's Moray Badge, started while he was headmaster of Gordonstoun, was indeed the prototype. Conventional English wisdom at the time believed that character was formed by caning and cricket. Hahn didn't seem to believe in either. Claude Elliott, Provost of Eton and president of the Alpine Club, gave Hunt a long lecture telling him he was 'on the wrong tack'. Most of these critics were won round, but it took time. It helped that the Duke at that time was a popular figure and a natural role model. When Hunt agreed to leave the Army and help start the Scheme he did so partly because he admired the Duke but he was nervous of Hahn and made one stipulation – that he should not have Hahn breathing down his neck all the time. It was nothing personal. He admired Hahn but the man was a mesmeriser and Hunt did not wish to be mesmerised.

Perhaps I should declare an interest here and say that my father left the Army in 1956 in order to become Hunt's assistant and was later a trustee of the Award. As an adequately rebellious teenager I regarded the Award with an eye as jaundiced as Sir Edward Boyle's. Ever since the beginning there has been debate about whether or not the Award reaches those who most obviously need it. Critics have argued that it appealed mainly to those who would be doing something worthwhile anyway. This has always irritated the Duke because he was conscious of the danger from the first and has fought against it. Nevertheless the accusation is still being voiced, and repudiated. In 1990 a report by Her Majesty's Inspectorate complained that 'success has until now been predominantly with motivated and more able young people', and

'There has, in general, been little impact on disadvantaged adolescents in urban and inner city areas, particularly with young people from ethnic minorities.' The rejoinder, in essence, is that the Award sets high standards and would be failing in its aim if it dropped them. High standards, on the other hand, can be a deterrent.

What I also remember, vicariously, of those early years was the shoestring nature of the operation, the strong sense of pioneering new ground, and a definite feeling that it was an experiment which might not work. Indeed it was originally a 'pilot' to be tried out over a three-year span and then reassessed.

Thirty-five years on, this widely suspect embryo has become a fact of life, as much of an institution in its way as those organisations that were so resentful of it when it was first conceived. School prospectuses include references to it alongside boasts about university scholarships and rugby victories; job applicants use it to impress employers; local government eulogises it; and – symbol of the age as much as of the scheme – Mars Bars sponsor it.

In 1990 I attended the Award's Council in Northampton. The Council is always in a different place and happens every other year. This time we were in a modern conference centre cum theatre called the Derngate where the previous attraction had been George Melly and where we were to be followed by the English Brass Ensemble, and, shortly afterwards, pantomime. Traditionally the Duke chairs this meeting, although hitherto he had been present on only one of the two days. Finally he asked the director, Major-General Michael Hobbs, 'Why don't you let me chair *both* days?'

Hobbs was taken aback. He had assumed that the Duke was far too busy and that even one day of chairmanship was an imposition. He simply hadn't dared ask for a second day. Generally speaking there *are* too many invitations in his life so it is hardly surprising that General Hobbs made the assumption. However not only does the Duke have a stunning appetite for such tasks, he also has a higher level of dedication to the Award than practically any other organisation with which he is involved. It is after all, unequivocally and obviously, his own creation and has grown from nothing to an international organisation which functions in more than fifty different countries – not always under the same name – and in which two million young people have participated.

The original idea was to do something about what was known, in the early fifties, as 'the gap', for those leaving school at fifteen and entering compulsory military service three years later. With employers reluctant to take on people who would be whisked off to the armed services after only three years, the plan was to have entry at fifteen and departure at eighteen. When, however, Hunt convened a conference of experts he was told that this would never work. You would have to hook boys while they were still at school and therefore you *must* lower the age to fourteen. Unless young people were 'caught' while still at school they would elude the net altogether. This decision was made in the Duke's absence and Hunt had to tell him over the telephone. He was not amused. 'I had a job to persuade him,' says Hunt, 'and he made some fairly caustic remarks down the phone.' Hunt smiles. 'Not being as used to the great man as I have since become I found it a very daunting experience. But to his eternal credit, he let it go.'

At first there was no Scheme for girls but that decision was swiftly changed and today there is no sex discrimination. Indeed, at the Gold Award ceremonies at St James's Palace there seem to be as many young women as men. There are six ceremonies every year with one session in the morning and one in the afternoon. The Duke attends them all, though there are now so many Gold winners that it is logistically impossible for him to hand out each one in person. Instead he moves from room to room, mingling, congratulating, bantering. He was notably good at relaxing everyone on the occasion I attended, but even so it is interesting to see how daunting a royal presence can be even to the best and brightest. At one point he stopped to ask a girl what she had done for the 'service' part of her Award. You could see her mind go completely blank. Eventually, with a big effort at composure she was able to remember that 'I worked in a mental hospital' but for a moment she was frozen. Yet she was formidably intelligent and mature, a university graduate working in a high-profile City merchant bank.

Apart from these six days a year handing out Awards, and one other in Edinburgh, the Duke takes two trustee meetings a year at Buckingham Palace. He also undertakes as many fund-raising events as he can fit in, though Prince Edward is now playing a major role in this. He is the only one of the Duke's children to hold a Gold Award and it is always alleged, in jest, that when he was presented with it he was the only winner not to bring his parents. Prince Edward now devotes between twelve and fourteen weekends a year to Award work. But the most important aspect of the Duke of Edinburgh's work for the Scheme is the constant stream of advice, help and encouragement he gives. He is a huge support.

At Northampton in the Derngate the Duke sits up on the platform throughout the day's proceedings. The hall is crowded with 'experts' of one sort or another but the Duke is comfortable, at ease, apparently as expert as anyone present and very obviously in charge, right from his downbeat entry and cheery, casual, 'Good morning, do please sit down' to his equally cheery thankyou at the end of the afternoon. 'Oh, and a special thanks to all the staff here at the . . . what's the place called? . . . ah, yes, Derngate.'

A look through the list of those attending makes you realise how far the Award has come from the day that Sir Edward Boyle turned his back on John Hunt. There are people here from the Prison Department of the Home Office, St John Ambulance Brigade, the Jewish Lads' and Girls' Brigade, the Red Cross, the Scouts and the Guides, the British Forces Youth Service and the Nationwide Anglia Building Society. There are Members of Parliament, Directors of Education, County Councillors, heads of youth and community services, headmasters, and chief executives of Library Boards.

In his opening remarks the Duke asks, 'Is the Scheme still relevant after thirty-five years?' The cast list suggests it is and the day's debate reinforces the view, particularly the testimony of four Gold Award holders. The most moving of these is from a girl who is paralysed from the neck down and has lost the power of speech. After each one the Duke says a brief thank you and picks up a particular point on which to comment. Then there is a question and answer session with the Duke very much in command, not just of the technicalities but also of his audience. He is good at giving what could be a tedious occasion some light relief.

Man: 'You've got the name wrong.'

Duke: 'Oh, I think you're right.'

Man: 'It's probably my handwriting.'

Duke (grinning): 'Yes.'

Someone else makes an interesting point about the demands of the 'Expedition' section of the Award, observing that the stipulation is that a distance of fifty miles should be covered but that fifty miles of Dartmoor is not the same as fifty miles of Bavaria where his Sea Scouts appear to have been.

Duke: 'Ah, this is the great flexibility factor we've been talking about.' And then, a deadpan aside, 'Though I just wonder what Sea Cadets are *doing* at 7,000 feet?'

After lunch, which is a standing buffet with the Duke queueing for his meal like everyone else, then mingling and talking, the highlight is a discussion of the hostile HMI report by the man who wrote it. Brave of him, I think, to come into the lion's den, though he slightly cops out by maintaining that his report was not that hostile and was misrepresented by the press. Actually I think it *was* hostile in part, and the press reporting was quite fair. After all, the opening summary reported that 'Most participants are white, motivated and more able young people', and that 'Approximately seventy per cent of those who begin the Award fail to complete its Bronze stage.' The Duke and the General say this figure is plain wrong and that between fifty and sixty per cent complete the Bronze stage. The final sentence reads, 'For urban adolescents, particularly from ethnic minorities, the Award's image and methods require attention in order to promote flexibility to meet individual needs.'

The Duke looks long-suffering but exhibits what for him is Job-like patience. He explains that over the last thirty-four years this has always been a problem but that if you are to be fair about the Awards they must be on offer to everyone. The argument is complex but conducted with restraint on both sides. However, when one person in the audience says that the Award Scheme was 'far ahead of its time', there is a loud chorus of 'Hear, hear!'

Afterwards there is a section on 'Business Support' with a statement by the man from Mars. This, inevitably, is a bit of an anticlimax. No controversy.

We run late in the end and the Duke says, 'I see you are very anxious to go to tea which means I must be very quick in winding up.' He sums up succinctly and with expedition. The dominant sense behind his remarks and, indeed, of his whole performance is that he has lived with this scheme from its infancy. I guess there are remarkably few – if any – in the hall who can say the same. This gives him a massive advantage because he can say, as he does, 'That's not how it seemed at the time,' or 'That is not how we envisaged it.'

In this, as in so many spheres, the Duke has spent a long time at the top, and this experience, properly tapped, can obviously be invaluable.

As head of any organisation the Duke is seldom, if ever, just a titular head, though some organisations are more president-proof than others. MCC, the great cricket club, for instance, changes president every year and this naturally restricts the chances of any individual one managing to interfere with the even tenor of the regime administered by the full-time professional staff and one or two long-term committee members. The Duke has twice been president and opened the new Mound Stand. A few months later, sitting in the pavilion, a senior MCC official turned to the Duke and asked, 'How do you like our new Mound Stand?' The MCC man appeared to have forgotten that the Duke had performed the opening ceremony. However, MCC is not one of the associations by which these days he seems to set enormous store. Indeed, when asked to write a short essay about cricket's headquarters for an MCC-sponsored book he, for once, declined. When he was asked to be president of the Lord's Taverners, a charity organisation named after the original pub building at one side of the ground, he found a compromise: he became permanent 'twelfth man'. This means, in theory, that he is responsible for the team bag and for bringing out drinks in intervals between play.

Generally speaking, however, if you take him on you get real commitment, support as well as constant appraisal and analysis, criticism and encouragement. A letter to the chairman of the National Playing Fields Association provides a typical example.

The first sentence is a thankyou for a letter and two enclosures – one called 'Mean Streets' and the other 'Inner City Village Halls'. On a positive note, he next commends the new hall on Merseyside which he has just opened. Then comes the 'but'. He thinks the design could be refined to save money. There is a lot of wasted space above the changing rooms and the office. Why not think about shifting all this outside into a 'lean-to' attached to the main hall? That would give greater flexibility.

Gyles Brandreth was only one year old when the Duke first took on the NPFA so a quick restatement of the early aims obviously seems appropriate. Keeping children off the streets was the most important idea and, in the Duke's estimation, still is. 'But', or for once 'however', comes next, as inexorably as light after dark. He wants the schools to provide 'playing facilities and leadership' in term time and he wants local government to license local bodies to use the facilities in the holidays. This represents a departure from the original aims but implicit in what he writes is a sense that nothing can ever stand still. Change and innovation, a response to new situations, these are all an important part of his character.

The final paragraph starts with an upbeat 'naturally delighted' before descending into a final critical conclusion. He had noticed, 'as I flew in by helicopter', that this new hall was surrounded by open space and playing fields. The real problem was getting such halls into areas where there was no such open space. End of message. 'Yours sincerely, Philip.'

The letter is full of the experience of more than forty years, of observation, of cogent suggestion and, above all, shows a real interest. Yet, note the construction. 'Great success, but . . .', 'very important. However . . .', 'naturally delighted, but . . .' There is praise here, certainly, but never unqualified. Is the boss, I wonder, ever unstinting? Is success, in his eyes, ever unqualified? Might he not be, perhaps, a little more generous? Is he ever all carrot and no stick?

He *was* nearly all carrot at a fund-raising luncheon at the Royal Automobile Club where Brandreth was trying to raise money. The gathering was a mixture of sporting and other personalities – the athlete and prospective parliamentary candidate Sebastian Coe, the broadcasters David Frost and Brian Johnston, the actress Joanna Lumley (placed next to him at lunch) – friends of the NPFA, and the targets: directors of companies who might give money. Within weeks Brandreth had twenty-one donations of five thousand pounds and one of fifty thousand. You cannot entirely attribute this to the charisma of the Duke, but it certainly helps, and it was a remarkably productive lunch coming, as it did, just as the country began to dive into recession.

One could go on about the Duke in chairmanic mode virtually for ever. One could write whole books about the Award Scheme or the Study Conferences or National Playing Fields. He himself *has* compiled whole books about carriage driving and on conservation. He chairs, or has chaired, countless committees and organisations on everything from the Coronation to housing; he heads the Royal Commission which still administers the proceeds of the Great Exhibition of 1851 and he has his own personal charitable Trust Fund. In each case, of course, the substance differs but the style is recognisably the same. The Duke who established the Study Conferences or who presides over the Award Council or who raises money over a National Playing Fields luncheon is recognisably the same model, no matter which particular cause he is attached to at any given moment.

The ability to master so many different briefs, to keep an eye on so many different activities, to be able to bore in on minute details such as the position of changing rooms in the Wirral, to energise so many other people is impressive, but there is a double caveat which he has expressed himself.

'I happen,' he says, 'to find myself in rather an individual position. I am involved in the activities of a great many groups but the sheer number of these groups makes it impossible to belong completely to any one of them. Furthermore in many cases my involvement is as an active or titular head and that in itself tends both to isolation and objectivity.'

It cannot be easy to be associated with *quite* so many groups, nor always to be at the top of them. It is, I suppose, in the nature of the job and there is no point in the hypothetical at this stage in the Duke's career. Yet does viewing such a wide canvas from such an exalted position lead to an unusual and not always accurate perspective? Always the chairman, and never the office boy, must make it difficult to comprehend exactly what goes on at the pit-face; and to wear so many hats at one and the same time must mean that just occasionally the fit is less than perfect. Mustn't it?

# 'Between the Scylla and the Charybdis'

'This is what the Church is said to want, not party
men, but sensible, temperate, sober, well-judging
persons, to guide it through the channel of no-meaning,
between the Scylla and the Charybdis of Aye and No'
*History of My Religious Opinions from 1839 to 1841*
CARDINAL NEWMAN

The Duke's mother became a nun and his great-aunt a Christian martyr and saint, so religion runs in the family. In his latter years, the Duke has become intrigued by theology and debate about the meaning of life, the origin of the species and the future of mankind, while his son, the Prince of Wales, has a strong Christian belief which sometimes seems tinged by mysticism.

The Duke himself answered my question about his late flowering interest in religion in a matter-of-fact manner, with no reference to his antecedents. 'I was dragged into religious things,' he said, 'by being invited to become involved in the re-organisation of St George's, Windsor. Theological dialogue was really forced on me. I have never had any great difficulty about being an "ordinary" Christian. Trying to get the major religions to take an interest in the conservation of nature is dictated more by a wish to promote conservation than to any great theological theory.' Whether Christian belief comes before the conservation of nature in the Duke's life is a matter for conjecture. Certainly they are closely interwoven and the World Wide

Fund for Nature is now – thanks largely to him – in partnership with the world's religions and their leaders.

His great-aunt Ella or, more formally, Elizabeth was a Hessian princess, the sister of the Grand Duke Ernest Louis who commissioned Peter Ustinov's grandfather to build a Russian Orthodox church in Darmstadt, and the sister of Princess Alix who married Tsar Nicholas of Russia. She was married to the Grand Duke Serge. Like her sister and the Tsar she too was killed by the Bolsheviks in 1918. Her death was peculiarly horrible. She was thrown down a mine shaft and then, according to most accounts, pelted with stones. The Duke says, however, that it was, if anything, worse still. The Bolsheviks tossed down a hand-grenade which mortally wounded her. It took her three days to die and throughout her agony she consoled herself and her companions by singing hymns. Somehow her body was later transported to Jerusalem where she lies buried in the gardens of the Orthodox church in Gethsemane.

The precise nature of Princess Alice's beliefs was elusive. It certainly eluded the Dean of Windsor who occasionally visited her for prayer at Buckingham Palace in the sixties. However she was profoundly religious, always, at least after the war, appearing in her austere grey habit with the single exception of her son's wedding in 1947 when she got out her jewellery and wore a dress. She revered the memory of Aunt Ella and her son says that her desire was to establish a nursing order based on Ella's ideas. Princess Alice so loved Ella that she expressed a wish to be buried alongside her at Gethsemane, in Jerusalem. Her daughter Sophie was dismayed by this and her son, the Duke, pointed out that there would be a number of logistical difficulties in conveying her coffin to Jerusalem. Besides, the family would be unable to visit her grave.

The Princess could see no problem.

'There's a perfectly good bus service,' she said with asperity.

After the Princess's death in 1969 her coffin lay in the vault at St George's Chapel, Windsor, while arrangements were made for her burial in Jerusalem. The negotiations were interminable and dogged with misunderstandings. Once, for example, the Duke and the Queen were on a state visit to Jordan, when a strange bearded priest presented himself at the royal palace and asked to speak to the Duke. The authorities were unimpressed and turned the man away. It was only later realised that he was the priest in charge of the Orthodox church in Jerusalem and that he had wanted to discuss Princess Alice's funeral. This unintentional rebuff did not help matters and the negotiations faltered. It was not until 1988 that the innumerable difficulties appeared to have been overcome. The Right Revd Michael Mann, the Dean of Windsor, and domestic chaplain to the Queen, agreed to accompany Princess Alice's coffin to Jerusalem, although he was not entirely optimistic. He was stoically down to earth about the project. If he did not succeed he would just have to bring the coffin back again. For security reasons the Duke was unable to go himself, but the Dean and Princess Sophie set off and accomplished their mission although not without difficulty. Both of them talk very movingly of the nuns singing the burial service in the garden under the olive trees, of the place's peace and tranquillity and of the sense of fulfilment in at last laying Princess Alice to rest alongside Aunt Ella as she had always wished.

The Duke had always tried to be a dutiful son to his mother, bringing her to live at the Palace when her health began to fail. She sounds splendidly spirited, though, like her son, not always easy. 'Doctor!' she exclaimed, when a lady-in-waiting, on the Queen's behalf, suggested that she really ought to see one, 'I'm far too ill to see a doctor.' And then, having recovered through willpower rather than medication, she announced, 'I am well enough to see a doctor now.' There are echoes of the Duke in that story which is regarded by everyone to whom I have spoken as entirely characteristic of the Princess. However even though from 1960 onwards the Duke began to take an increasing interest in religion it does not seem, overtly, to have had anything to do with her.

The man who seems to have sparked his interest in religious matters was the Right Revd Robin Woods who was appointed to the Deanery of Windsor in 1962. Woods's father had been Bishop of Lichfield and, as Lord High Almoner, had become associated with the Royal Family through the annual Maundy Thursday almsgivings. At the beginning of the 1960s Robin Woods was an Archdeacon in Sheffield working with the industrial community – a far cry from a 'Royal Peculiar' such as St George's.

The previous Dean of Windsor had grown old in the job and died in 1961, leaving behind an institution which had become introspective and parochial to the point of decrepitude. 'Full,' as one critic unkindly said, 'of a whole lot of canons all eating their heads off.' One day, Woods was asked by an old friend, the Revd Ted Ward, who was chaplain of the church in Windsor Great Park, if he would come and preach before the Queen on the Sunday after Ascension Day. This would be followed by lunch at the Queen Mother's home, Royal Lodge, with members of the family. Sermon and lunch obviously went well and afterwards Ward recommended, rather overzealously in

Woods's recollection, that before starting off for Sheffield he and his wife Henrietta should go for a walk round the Savill Gardens. A few minutes later Ward suddenly appeared from behind a rhododendron with the surprising news that the Queen would like him to become Dean of Windsor.

Though flattered, Woods was reluctant. The deanery had the reputation of being a dead-end job; the canons, regarding themselves as being immutably bound by royal statute to go on doing nothing very much, were likely to be troublesome; the daily services were attended by 'precisely nobody'; and the Archbishop of Canterbury, Michael Ramsey, advised against him taking it. It was, however, intimated to Woods that the Queen and the Duke were most unhappy with the present state of affairs. 'If I took the job,' he recalls, 'it was made clear that I would be expected to turn everything upside down.' This was a challenge and, ultimately, he accepted, receiving a formal letter from the Prime Minister, Harold Macmillan, in July.

At first the Duke, according to Woods, 'had absolutely no time for the Church of England'. He was not even keen for Prince Charles to be confirmed and during the confirmation service rather ostentatiously read the Bible. Archbishop Ramsey drew Woods's attention to the matter after the service and said, in decidedly unarchiepiscopal language, that he thought it 'bloody rude'. The Duke baulks a little at Woods's description of his religious state and points out that he always went to church on Sunday. He has also always been quick with biblical quotation and reference. Nevertheless he was neither religious in any very contemplative sense nor was he enamoured of the woolly-minded side of the Church of England. And relations between the Royal Family and Archbishop Ramsey were often a little strained.

Fundamental to Woods's plans for turning everything upside down at Windsor was the idea of establishing a St George's College which would act as a sort of training school for high-flying clergy in mid-career as well as a place where leading members of the laity could come and confer within a religious context. The Duke envisaged a clerical counterpart to the staff colleges run by the armed services.

Woods made it work. Paying tribute to his achievement the Duke says, 'He succeeded in giving the whole of St George's an entirely new and eminently practical direction for the future,' adding that 'Robin was kind enough to discuss his plans with me and I found the whole process of developing the structure and programme for St George's House entirely fascinating.'

At first the Duke's interest did not seem particularly religious or theological. Practical as ever, he was anxious to help the Dean raise the necessary £350,000 to convert the existing buildings into a residential conference centre. The Duke's contacts were invaluable though it also helped that some of the Dean's trustees were Knights of the Garter whose headquarters are at Windsor. Since the fourteenth century the Garter has been one of the grandest and most exclusive orders of chivalry in Britain. It is difficult to think of more influential fund-raisers.

On 23 October 1966, in the week of the Aberfan tragedy in Wales, St George's held its first weekend 'consultation'. The overall subject was 'The Role of the Church in Society Today'. Lord Caccia, Provost of Eton College and former Ambassador in Washington, led off; Lord Salisbury, the great Tory *éminence grise*, followed, and after dinner the Duke spoke for forty minutes – 'quite brilliantly' according to Robin Woods – on 'What does the Nation expect of the Churches?' Lively debate ensued among the assembled thirty-five dignitaries, before the Duke, the Dean, Field-Marshal Sir Gerald Templer, and Sir John Maud adjourned for a drink together, finally turning in at 12.30 a.m.

The Dean's relationship with the Royal Family became increasingly intimate as time passed. His own five children were similar in age to Prince Charles and Princess Anne, and he himself became close to Prince Charles while preparing him for confirmation. The Queen and Duke usually spend weekends at Windsor Castle and it became customary for Woods to drop by for a drink on Saturday evening. He recalls one occasion when the Queen's page rang to say that Her Majesty wanted to see him at once. He had been gardening and, being still in mufti, said it would take him a moment to change into the formal clerical outfit in which he normally presented himself. The message came back that urgency was more important than costume – the Queen was in riding gear and would not be changing. From that moment on Woods never dressed up for informal audiences such as these. In January 1966, the Duke, who had hitherto always addressed him as 'Dear Mr Dean', could stand it no longer. 'Dear Robin,' he began, 'I don't think I can force myself to go on calling you "Dean", it's so impersonal.'

At first the exchanges between the two men had the strong practical element I would have expected from the Duke. He found '"Ethics and Management Training" a particularly interesting subject for discussion'; he thought that 'what needs to be discussed is the extent to which a job is for the purpose of enjoying some other things in life or to what extent a job is life itself'; he suggested getting some engineers to come to St George's to 'discuss the social and human consequences of technology'; and what about 'preparing for retirement' as a theme for a clergy consultation?

But there is a growing reflective and philosophical dimension too. A letter from the Royal Yacht off Australia in 1969 runs to ten pages and deals extensively with a book called *Religion and Change*. He does not think the author makes enough of the distinction between the 'organic or myth-based religions' and the 'revealed' faiths. He offers views on God in the abstract, he distinguishes between the way the Disciples interpreted the teaching of Christ and the essential timelessness of the real message. The importance of the individual is often paramount. In the end, he argues, it is 'the acceptance of the Christian idea by people as individuals which will influence universal problems.'

At times it is he who begins to sound like the Dean, an accusation whose truth he sometimes acknowledges. 'Oh dear, *I* seem to be preaching now!'

In 1970 Woods was offered the diocese of Worcester. Before receiving any formal official advice a long handwritten letter arrived from Balmoral. He was moved 'to hear from the man I had come to respect very deeply, not only for the integrity of his religion but for his ability to judge men and situations'. Woods thought it 'full of wisdom and insight'. The Duke however, on re-reading it, said he was half-inclined to tear it up, as it wasn't helpful. It does actually present the essentials of the choice very clearly but most significant is the Duke's statement about his and the Queen's own feelings.

'In the first place,' he wrote, 'you can take it that neither the Queen nor I would want you to feel that you should stay at Windsor for our sakes. I know this sounds rather unkind, but what I mean is that we would not want to stand in the way of your opportunity to serve the Church in a more responsible way. It has been simply marvellous having you at Windsor and your help and guidance for us and for our children has been invaluable, but frankly I think the Church needs your services more urgently than we do.'

The Duke was even-handed in his advice, more than usually clear about both sides of an argument. In the end Woods went to Worcester and he was succeeded by Launcelot Fleming, the sixty-five-year-old Bishop of Norwich, a noted Antarctic explorer in his youth. Fleming who died in 1990, served five years as Dean before being succeeded by the Right Revd Michael Mann. As Bishop of Dudley Mann was a suffragan to Robin Woods at Worcester and had an unusual background – Harrow, Harvard Business School, King's Dragoon Guards, and Colonial service in Nigeria. He was also a military historian of note. He had much in common with Robin Woods, incidentally, having been a Forces' chaplain and mentioned in despatches, and was to prove as much a theological and religious confidant of the Duke. The Duke likes the sort of directness that an association with the Forces seems to confer.

As a result of his association with Bishop Mann, the Duke published a number of volumes of what one might reasonably describe as a philosophical nature. The first appeared in 1982. Entitled *A Question of Balance*, it is a collection of essays based on addresses the Duke had given to general rather than specialist audiences and is edited by the Dean. He begins with a close textual analysis of Marx's communist Manifesto out of which Marx comes badly – 'His arrogant conviction that his theory comprehended all human problems, his aggressive style, his predilection for totalitarian solutions and dictatorship and his advocacy of State control have had results which not even he could have foreseen.' They encompass 'Truth', 'Clashes of Interest', 'The Individual and the Community', 'Community Health', 'Philosophy, Politics and Administration' and they conclude with an essay called 'Satisfaction and Contentment' based on his opening address to the 1980 Commonwealth Study Conference.

This last begins with a quotation from Shakespeare's *Julius Caesar*. The Duke throws it off with some nonchalance, explaining that his 'piece' was really an expansion of it. The short piece goes on to rehearse a number of the Duke's preoccupations with technology, the individual, morality, intelligence and so on but the most interesting point about it – in my opinion – is the Shakespeare quotations. Many years earlier Peter Parker, helping set up the first, 1956, Study Conference, suggested that T. S. Eliot might speak. The Duke thought for a moment: 'Deep, but narrow,' he said. Parker says, 'I think this was the most surprising remark I have ever heard him make.' In November I was sitting in the audience at Northampton when the Duke was chairing the annual Council of his Award Scheme and a Gold Award holder told us how part of her studies had taken her to South Wales in search of the world of Dylan Thomas. The Duke seemed delighted by this and paused to muse a little on the unexpectedness of the Award Scheme leading along such a path. After all – though this he did not say – Dylan Thomas would have made the least likely candidate for the Duke of Edinburgh's Award one could conceivably imagine. Thomas, after all, was a drunken layabout. The Duke takes mild exception to this observation, remarking that Dylan Thomas was 'a brilliant poet.' Whether or not he would have wanted or qualified for the Duke's Gold Award is an irrelevance to him.

That meant three instances of the Duke's interest in poetry. Not what I had expected. At lunch at Clarence House I turned first to the Queen Mother and asked about her son-in-law and poetry. She gave me one of her famous beatific smiles, but made it plain, in the nicest possible way, that she thought I was mad. I explained and although she obviously believed me she was very surprised indeed. Everyone, she supposed, had secrets, even those one thought one knew. Then she spoke across me to Princess Margaret. 'Did *you* know that Philip read poetry?' The Princess gave much the same disbelieving look that her mother had employed seconds earlier. She had never heard of such a thing, and when I explained, she too seemed most surprised.

After that Northampton meeting I sent the Duke a copy of my favourite Dylan Thomas poem, 'Do not go gentle into that good night', with a request along the lines, more or less, of 'poetry – discuss'. It did not get me very far. 'I have read Eliot and Thomas,' he wrote, 'and I have also read Jung.' When pressed he replied, via his private secretary, that his views on poetry were far too conventional and conservative to be of interest to anyone else.

My point was that I was surprised to find him expressing any view on poetry – conventional and conservative or not.

When I went to Wolfsgarten to see his old friend Princess Margaret of Hesse und bei Rhein, she said that whenever the Duke came on a visit she always made certain that he had some time on his own to walk round the garden. She particularly emphasised the idea of time on his own without interruption or chatter and it confirmed my impression of the Duke being a man much more prone to contemplation or even introspection than he is keen for the rest of us to know. I mentioned the Wolfsgarten walks to Princess Anne. 'Well,' she said as if I had got quite the wrong end of the stick, 'it's an extremely attractive garden.' This is precisely what I would expect her father to say.

The next slim volume of a philosophical nature appeared in 1984 under the joint authorship of the Duke and the Dean. This was entitled *A Windsor Correspondence* and stemmed from a lecture by Professor Sir Fred Hoyle entitled 'Evolution from Space'. The Duke read the lecture, thought the Dean might be interested and sent him a copy. The Dean was very excited by it, largely because he thought it suggested 'Science and Christianity seem to be moving towards each other.' The Duke's response to the Dean's response is a classic example of his 'Yes, but . . .' style of debate though it is expressed slightly differently. 'I agree,' he begins, accepting the Dean's verdict that Hoyle's theory of evolution was not a new one but simply pushed 'divine intervention a bit further back'. Then he begins the bulk of the letter with the phrase, 'Having said that, I must take issue with you on some of your other points.' Which he does at some length.

Now they are well into discussion. The Dean strikes back, 'It is not only evolution that . . . where I might place a different emphasis . . . and so on.' The disagreement is often quite profound. The Duke says, 'Whether God became man in Jesus Christ is a philosophical question.' The Dean is not having this. 'The belief that "God became man in Jesus Christ" is not, in the Christian view, a philosophical question; it is a matter of faith.'

The Duke's riposte includes the last paragraph of Darwin's *Origin of Species* and the Dean comes back with a form of 'pax', suggesting that they are arguing along parallel lines. He quotes Darwin too. The Duke's next letter backs off with 'I did not mean to imply,' but still his next paragraph begins with the inevitable 'However'. In the next letter the Dean appears to throw in the towel: 'Sir, I think I am in complete agreement.' He qualifies it for another forty-four lines before the correspondence is concluded – quite rightly, for the protagonists have exhausted the argument.

There are three more separate correspondences: one on fundamentalism, one on science and religious conservatism and a third on evolution and morality. As published correspondences go they are not in the same league as, say, the Lyttelton/Hart-Davis letters. As the Duke himself would be the first to concede, he is no philosopher or theologian.

But this is to miss the point. The point is – the Duke's letters are full of this finger-jabbing phrase – that the Duke of Edinburgh carried on a correspondence with the Dean of Windsor about the meaning of life. The Queen's husband wrote long letters to his domestic chaplain in order to discuss 'ideas'. Publishing them was the Duke's idea and the Dean was originally opposed to this. He argued that 'it would be irresponsible of me to publish the sort of language you write in' and also that publishing them would create an inhibiting precedent. If all royal chaplains published their letters no one would feel able to write freely and you would destroy trust. The Duke thought about this, consulted the Queen and stuck to his guns. He wanted the public to see that he was an ordinary enquiring person, not simply a public cardboard cut-out.

The Dean says that the public and private reaction to this was gratifying in the sense that this was how they perceived the correspondence. People respected the curiosity.

The third of the Duke's philosophical works is called *Survival or Extinction* and is subtitled 'A Christian Attitude to the Environment'. This is a work of co-authorship, the Duke's and the Dean's names appearing with equal prominence on the title page, and is also in part at least a distillation of seven 'consultations' at St George's. The various participants are listed at the back of the book, beginning with Her Grace the Duchess of Abercorn, 'Counsellor in Transpersonal Psychology', and ending, after almost a hundred names, with Mr Giles Wyburd, 'Director ICC, United Kingdom'.

This is less of a work of philosophy and dialectic than the other two and fits more easily into the lobbying pigeon hole. This is the Duke trying to persuade the Church(es) to take an interest in the conservation of nature, not the Duke pondering the meaning of life. In that sense it is a much less surprising, more recognisable Duke than the other more reflective character.

In his introduction to *A Question of Balance* the Duke discerns a common thread in his writings. 'I keep coming back to the importance and the central position of the individual and the crucial part that human nature plays in every aspect of communal life.' There are good reasons for this, not the least being that he is, as we have already observed, 'in rather an individual position'. He is involved 'in the activities of a great many groups but the sheer number of these groups makes it impossible to belong completely to any one of them'. Also he is either 'an active or titular head' of every group to which he belongs. There is nothing more isolating than being at the top of any organisation, or that more sharpens one's sense of individual importance.

He has written that 'religious conviction is the strongest and probably the only factor in sustaining the dignity and integrity of the individual.' A good contentious line, but not one, I suspect, which he would have penned before he first got to know Robin Woods and St George's in the 1960s. That religion, and an interest in the questions implicit in a study of religion, have come to be important to him is self-evident. You could just put this down to his restless spirit and enquiring mind. Certainly he has an interest in 'ideas' which is most un-English and none the worse for that. Perhaps that is part of the equation but I do not believe that we can discount the influence, genetic or overt, of his great-aunt Ella or his mother Alice.

Nor can we abandon the notion – it is, after all, the Duke's own –

that it was his interest in conservation that really led to his fascination with religion. I first encountered the environmental Duke at Strasbourg in 1970 with Stanley Johnson, author of such expert tomes as *The Politics of the Environment* and former adviser on environmental protection to the European Commission in Brussels. Johnson is a professional in the world of environmental politics; he knows what he is talking about but he does not work for any of the organisations with which the Duke is connected. He is an impartial authority and he rates the Duke highly. 'Pretty good on wildlife. His interests are not as wide-ranging as his son's, but he knows his stuff. Broadly speaking I'd say he's a refreshingly good thing.'

This single topic of conservation has probably consumed more of the Duke's time than any other and he has become an important player on the world stage.

At his first encounter with the Duke, Johnson, at a conference to mark European Conservation Year, cheekily smuggled an American folk singer and activist called Suzanne Harris into the conference hall where she sang a ballad called 'We're using up the world, can't you see?' The lyrics were not wildly inspired and the microphone failed, but she got her photograph taken with the Duke and delivered her message. The nature of the subject is such that, sadly, you very often need something gimmicky and apparently trivial to get it across. The Duke himself is well aware of this and knows that a single quotable page is worth hours of well-documented verbiage. In Strasbourg he was at his most pungent, telling the delegates that, 'All the impassioned speeches will be so much effluent under the bridge unless they are followed by drastic political action.' When a questioner asked about a European population policy the Duke said that the French might like to start sneaking contraceptives into their baguettes. These lines were widely quoted while deeper, more profound, less colourful ones were ignored.

'At a time,' says Johnson, 'when everyone else was being thoroughly wimpish about the problem, the Duke spoke out. He's always been sound and consistent on population.' The Duke's own four children seem to run counter to his argument, but he did have a royal succession to secure.

The Duke was first seduced by the great outdoors as a child when his German cousins introduced him to country pursuits. The dawn strut of the capercailzie captivated him and he remains fascinated by birds and animals in the wild. To this essentially emotional response to nature he has, in his mature years, grafted on a formidable mass of knowledge and a passionate concern about the whole future of the planet.

Lord Buxton, one of the original founders of the World Wildlife Fund, explains that over a long period he has 'gradually developed from ornithology to conservation of habitat and then from that to global issues'. In Britain, says Buxton, he is sometimes regarded as 'a cantankerous old so-and-so', but abroad he is thought of as 'a very exceptional world leader'. Wherever he goes he is regarded, says Buxton, as 'Mr Environment'. If, as it should, the world decided that there should be some international organisation, perhaps created through the United Nations, to deal with the global problems of the environment, Buxton is convinced that the Duke would be the unanimous choice as its head.

In a sense he enjoys that position already as the International President of the World Wide Fund for Nature, and WWF is the largest private international nature conservation organisation in the world. He took over at WWF in 1964 from his friend and senior partner, Prince Bernhard of the Netherlands, who said, 'I was able to convince him that he was the only person in the world who could take it on because we needed a person who had an entrée to heads of state and government ministers. Letters from him *have* to be answered. People *have* to respond to him. Nobody else would do and there wasn't anyone else. It was lucky that he had an enormous interest in nature conservation. So we found the right man for the right work and he has done it fantastically well in my opinion.' The Duke himself confirms that he took on the job, in part because of his interest in 'natural history', but adds, that 'it would be foolish to deny that a title always looks good at the head of a charity.'

Today, Prince Bernhard enjoys the title Founder President and remains active in everything to do with conservation. He and the Duke meet regularly to co-ordinate their travels, carving up the world between them, lobbying heads of state, attending fund-raising banquets, inspecting WWF sponsored projects and generally trying to alert the world to the danger it is in. 'The whole business of the conservation of nature has had a significant influence on my life and thought,' says the Duke.

The evolution of his interest in this subject is instructive and relates closely — I think — to his increasing interest in religion and mythology. Aubrey Buxton recalls the Duke coming to stay in Norfolk — Sandringham is not all that far away. They went duck shooting 'on a most unsuitable morning' and he hardly had a shot at anything, but they had a marvellous time watching a pair of goldfinches. He always seems to have found birds, even small ones, more interesting than any other sort of wildlife. Buxton remembers another occasion, in Tanzania, when he and the Duke set off in a column of Land-Rovers to search for lions.

'Look sir, lions, sir,' went up the cry. The rest of the party were engrossed by the lions but the Duke and Buxton were evidently unimpressed. Someone turned round to find us 'looking in the opposite direction at a small brown bird'.

If you read the Duke of the nineteen-fifties on 'nature' and then contrast it with the Duke of the nineteen-eighties you find a fascinating difference. The younger Duke is excited by the sheer adventure of discovery. One minute he is wading out to join shouting and shrieking Gilbert Islanders on a fishing spree, the next he is being exasperated by the white terns that came and hovered over his Hasselblad camera, but then shot off as soon as he got them into focus. He records the same Gilbert Islanders singing a dialect version of 'It's a long way to Tipperary' and 'Some fur seals and two southern right whales having a high old time in the bay'. Words like 'delightful', 'charming', 'enjoyable' and 'amusing' flood the pages. It is exuberant, curious, funny but seldom contemplative or reflective.

Now listen to him, lecturing in the mid-eighties. 'Man's relationship to the natural world is not a matter of science,' he told the European Council of International Schools at Montreux in Switzerland. 'It is a matter of concept and conscience. The "big bang" theory may explain to the satisfaction of physicists the origin of the universe and of our planet Earth, but it does nothing to answer such questions as "What are we doing here?" "What is the point of existence?" "Is there anything beyond this life?" "Was the world created by a Supreme Being?" "Is everything that happened since the creation part of His plan, or is it all a matter of chance?" Questions which men have been asking ever since they discovered speech.'

Well, up to a point. Today's Duke spends much of his time contemplating those kinds of questions, gnawing away at them like a dog with a bone, but the Duke of thirty and forty years ago was a different animal, full of zest and curiosity but far too restless and hurried to bother himself with the fundamental questions, 'which men have been asking ever since they discovered speech'. As he matures he has become demonstrably more contemplative and reflective than he was in the past.

He is the first to admit that this message does not always get through. 'Conservation,' he has conceded, 'has a lot of dedicated and knowledgeable supporters, but it has failed to make much impression on public opinion in general.' In recent years he has targeted the Churches as natural allies in the cause on the grounds that, 'If God is in nature, nature itself becomes divine, and from that point it becomes reasonable to argue that reverence for God and nature implies a responsibility not to harm it, not just for our own selfish interests, but also as a duty to the Creator.'

In 1986, the twenty-fifth anniversary of the WWF was celebrated at Assisi, home of St Francis, patron saint of birds and animals. The idea of Assisi was the Duke's own. The conference and celebration were designed to forge 'a permanent alliance between conservation and religion'. The Buddhists, says Lord Buxton, were much the best, and the Christians much the worst, but the Hindus, Christians, Buddhists, Muslims and Jews all issued 'Declarations on Nature'. So successful was the onslaught on the Roman Catholic conscience that the Pope himself has gone green, up to a point at least. He does not seem yet to have taken on board the Duke's concern about population explosion and the need for a proper programme of birth control. However he has included ecologically sound passages in his recent messages and he and the Duke met in April 1990 to celebrate the appointment of WWF as 'consultant to the Roman Catholic Church in programmes related to nature conservation'. The notion of the Queen's husband acting as the Pope's adviser on nature conservation is a strange one which does not seem to have permeated the national consciousness. But the Duke argues, persuasively, that the idea of conservation is not just 'a newly invented, self-centred European, middle-class capitalist campaign', but has 'been taught by the deities for centuries'.

The coming together of religion and conservation may well have a sort of global logic, but it also marries two of the Duke's own preoccupations as he hurries through his autumnal years. He has become, to the surprise of many who knew him as a younger man, something of a green mystic, almost a guru in his own right.

# 'The Image of War'

'. . . it's the sport of kings, the image of war without its
guilt, and only five-and-twenty per cent. of its danger'
*Handley Cross*
R. S. SURTEES

He is, says one former employee, 'one of those maddening people one knew at school who are able to be good at games AND work.' Oddly enough, of course, he was not like that at school. Always athletic and competitive but never that keen on written work. Now he has acquired intellectual disciplines to match the athletic and sporting attributes but he has never stopped playing games. His leisure-time has always been fully occupied and he remains the epitome of the sporting prince. Since he heads so many charities, like the Central Council for Physical Recreation, the London Federation of Boys' Clubs and the National Playing Fields Association, that makes a sort of public as well as personal sense. His own equestrian activities and interests certainly enhanced his twenty-two years as president of the International Equestrian Federation and a lifetime of committees has been made incomparably more useful because he is, and has been, so much more of a player than a spectator.

I had vaguely thought that his sporting interests tended to be outside the English mainstream. I was thinking that he had never been a soccer player and that polo was not exactly the people's sport. He disagreed with me, of course. He *had* played a little tennis, and some golf, but it took up too much time. He was a regular squash player – convenient because Buckingham Palace has its own court. He was a keen rugger player – nearly always in the three-quarters – and, of course, there was cricket.

It is difficult to work out how good the Duke *really* is at anything. One school of thought will always profess to be amazed that he can do anything at all. His daughter feels this strongly. So gilded is the royal cage that the average man in the street assumes that its occupants are totally unable to fend for themselves without benefit of equerry, lady-in-waiting or other specialised help. Even shopping. At the other end of the spectrum there are sycophants for whom the Royal Family have only to buy an ice-cream to excite eulogies. By the same token, if they do find themselves in a competitive situation, the Royals soon discover that their opponents either pull their punches or become overzealous.

The late Bernard, Duke of Norfolk, was an avid cricketer who had his own ground at Arundel Castle, the most beautiful in England. When he batted, the form was that the first ball he received was an innocuous half-volley which even he, poor cricketer that he was, could push through for a single run. The score book at Arundel is full of entries which read, 'His Grace. Bowled Major Cartwright. One.' Once, playing the local town team, His Grace was confronted with a ferocious fast bowler who had not been told the rules. He beat him with his first ball and His Grace was not amused. The point is that it is seldom a fair contest. Indeed this is one reason, I suspect, why the Duke has tended to compete in relatively confined, comparatively exclusive areas such as polo and carriage-driving where his competitors are more likely to treat him simply as another player.

Cricket, the most English of all team games, is a great leveller and a good test for a player, however grand or humble. In 1949 the Duke was president of MCC, otherwise known as Marylebone Cricket Club, and despite that parochial-sounding name, the most famous cricket club in the world, maker of the game's rules, touring club extra-ordinary, synonymous sometimes with England itself. He was also president of the National Playing Fields Association. That year, Errol Holmes, an England all-rounder and former captain of Surrey, was asked to organise a fund-raising cricket match and, meeting the Duke in the committee room at Lord's, headquarters of MCC and of world cricket, invited him to take part.

The response was predictable and typical. 'I don't think so. Village cricket is more my standard and I suppose you'll be asking all the experts to play in this match. I shall be out of my class.'

Holmes was not too dismayed by this because he had a feeling that

the negative answer left room for manoeuvre. He arranged an interview with Mike Parker, the equerry, and selected a National Playing
Fields side to play against a Hampshire county side. The NPFA team
consisted of first-class players, including some famous international
test players, but had one vacancy for A.N.Other in case Prince Philip
changed his mind. The team was to be called the Duke of Edinburgh's
XI.

Holmes was nervous about the Duke's playing ability and arranged
to go and watch him play in a village match in Kent. On this occasion
the umpire unhelpfully gave the Duke out first ball leg before wicket.
That meant there was no way for Holmes to tell whether his potential
captain was any good or not.

The match was scheduled for September, when the Royal Family
were at Balmoral for their annual Scottish holiday. Mike Parker, a
useful wicket-keeper and keen cricketer himself, said that his boss
would do it if he possibly could. No promises.

Just before the game was due to begin, the news came through that
although the Duke had an injured hand he would fly down and have
a go. He arrived at Dean Park, Southampton, just before the start of
play at 11.00 a.m.

Hampshire batted first and after an hour and a half the Duke
said to Holmes, 'If I'm going to bowl at all I'd better get on with
it.'

I had assumed that his competitive approach and strong upper body
would have made him into a snappy fast medium bowler in the mould
of an all-rounder like Ted Dexter, but instead the Duke's preferred
mode of delivery was flighted off-spin. In his second over Dawson, a
Yorkshireman who played for Hampshire, hit the ball in the air to
Freddy Brown, a sometime captain of England. Brown caught it. The
Duke's first first-class wicket! The capacity crowd adored it.

Hampshire were all out for about 250 runs in three hours. Then
the Duke of Edinburgh's XI went in and the most exciting England
cricketer of his generation, Denis Compton, flailed around, ably supported by other England cricketers such as Walter Robins. Holmes
and the Duke were sitting next to each other and the cricketer ventured some avuncular advice. 'This is a wonderful wicket,' Holmes
told the Duke. 'You'll find it even easier than village cricket. Just
play at the pitch of the ball and if you get out having a swish it won't
matter – we've still got to go for these runs.'

Almost at once a wicket fell and Holmes suggested the Duke went
in straight away, ahead of himself. 'I don't mind,' he said, put on

Holmes's gold, scarlet and black hooped I Zingari club cap, and strode to the wicket.

'Short and sweet,' said Holmes. His second or third ball was an easy full toss outside the off-stump and he hit it for four through the covers. Another ball went for four over mid-on and then he was out for twelve 'having a go'. Thunderous applause. The Duke's XI won by a single wicket with one ball left and the National Playing Fields Association benefited to the tune of £1,100.

It was such a success that the Duke could have set up a regular fund-raising team if he had had a mind to. Instead it was decided that this particular NPFA fixture would be an annual event. He might play some jolly, purely recreational cricket but this would be his only public performance before paying customers.

Unfortunately even an annual appearance proved difficult. The following year the ground at Edinburgh was waterlogged, and the game called off, and in 1951 and 1952 the Duke was otherwise engaged. The next year was Coronation Year and Holmes thought it would be fun to stage a match at Arundel between the Duke of Edinburgh and Bernard, Duke of Norfolk, who, in his hereditary capacity as Earl Marshal of England, had stage-managed the Coronation. Holmes asked Norfolk to use his influence to persuade Edinburgh to take part.

'Why is there so much difficulty over Prince Philip playing?' asked a friend. 'After all, Bernard, you're a Duke and you're playing.'

Norfolk put on his most inscrutable expression – and he had a particularly inscrutable, inscrutable expression. 'Yes, my dear,' he said, 'but you must remember that there are Dukes – and Dukes.'

This time everything went according to plan. The Duke and Mike Parker arrived on Saturday evening from Cowdray Park where the Duke had been playing polo. Indeed he was still in his polo kit. After dinner they all played games on the billiard table, at which, Holmes observed, the Duke of Edinburgh excelled. After church the following morning the cricket began in front of a large crowd. Admission was free though cars were charged ten shillings each for parking. Before lunch the Duke took a good catch at slip, but the highlight came when the Duke of Norfolk went in to bat and was soon clean bowled by the Duke of Edinburgh. 'I am sure I am speaking for everybody here when I say how glad we all are to see you, sir, here today,' said Norfolk in an impromptu speech a few minutes later. He looked rueful. 'That is, everybody except myself . . .' Much laughter. In mid-afternoon the roles were reversed, with Norfolk bowling to

Edinburgh. Edinburgh carted the bowling all over the field and poor Norfolk had the misfortune of hitting the stumps without dislodging the bails. Edinburgh was eventually out for eighteen. His equerry later made an identical score, causing one spectator to shout, 'Who's afraid of making more than his boss!'

Nineteen fifty-four was a non-ducal year but in 1955 another duke entered the arena. This time it was Beaufort and the game was staged on his cricket ground at Badminton. Mike Parker and the Duke arrived by helicopter and joined a sporting house party which once again played boisterous after-dinner games on the billiard table. At least, Holmes claimed they played billiards. The Duke recalls no such thing. Holmes, however, set down his recollections only a year or so after the event while the Duke was remembering after more than forty years.

The Duke of Beaufort was a non-playing captain and his team was led by Sir William Becher, Bt., who once played for Warwickshire and has been the mainstay of I Zingari, the most famous amateur cricket club in the world, since the end of the Second World War. Sir William won the toss and batted. After a while Tom Graveney, one of the greatest of all England batsmen and then at the height of his powers, came in to bat, and the Duke of Edinburgh, greatly daring, put himself on to bowl. Almost at once his off-spin induced Graveney to mis-hit and spoon a catch to Holmes at mid-wicket. Here, once more, the Duke chips in to disagree. He says Holmes was fielding at long-leg. Holmes himself claims that it was 'mid-wicket'. In this instance I think the reader should decide for himself. In any case, Holmes maintained the chance was 'awkward' and he failed to get a finger to it. 'I picked up the ball,' he said, 'returned it to the bowler, who smiled broadly at my apology, and the game proceeded.'

When his turn came to bat, the Duke hit a brisk twenty-two and moved Errol Holmes and the 15,000 spectators to transports of delight. Holmes reported:

He drove to the off, and Charles Cobham said, 'I've seen many worse shots than that in a Test Match.' He smacked the ball to the on side, like one who had been playing cricket all the summer, whereas, in truth, the only practice he had since the match at Arundel in 1953 had been two or three nets. The multitude, almost delirious with happiness at the sight of their Prince showing such ability in such company, thundered applause as the royal runs flowed from his bat. 'How on earth does he do it?' said I to Charles Cobham, and the President of MCC could only shake his head in wonder and admiration.

When the Duke was out and walked back to the pavilion, 'smiling modestly', Holmes tells us that

the applause echoed and re-echoed throughout that ancient village. It was all very moving, with the evening sun streaming down on that unforgettable scene, and one could sense the feeling of happiness, almost of thankfulness, which one old countryman aptly translated into words when he said to me, 'He's the Prince of Cricketers, too.'

This is heady stuff and when I asked his opposing captain, Billy Becher, to tell me his verdict he was not quite so euphoric though he was still generous. 'If he hadn't been to Gordonstoun he could have been a very useful club cricketer,' he said. 'He was a natural.' And then, musing a moment, he added, 'I do hope they don't send Prince Charles's sons to Gordonstoun.'

Coming from Sir William this is high praise for he must have played against, or watched, every good club cricketer in the last fifty years – not to mention most of the best international players, too. And he is not particularly lavish with his praise.

The Duke *was* captain of cricket at Gordonstoun for what it was worth, which, on his own admission, is not a lot; but the point is that he is a naturally talented athlete and games player. He has, or had, a good eye; a sense of timing and balance; he is a perfectionist; and perhaps, above all, he is highly competitive.

He might have played more cricket were it not for the Queen and his uncle, Lord Mountbatten. 'I made the serious mistake of underestimating my wife's interest in horses,' he says. This was in Malta in 1949 when he was stationed there with the Navy and his uncle was commanding the 1st Cruiser Squadron. When Princess Elizabeth came out to Malta she was offered the choice of watching her husband play cricket or Mountbatten play polo. She always opted for the polo. The Duke realised that if he was to see anything of her he would have to accept his uncle's offer to teach him the game and provide him with ponies. So began a twenty-year love affair with the game.

He first rode a horse in Romania, staying with his friend and cousin (once removed), King Michael, when he was five years old. He didn't ride again for about ten years and then only when rich friends and relations 'were prepared to trust me with one of their horses'. He just had time, before the war, to hit a polo ball from astride one of his uncle's ponies, but did not become consumed with the Mountbatten passion for the game until post-war Malta. As he points out laconically, there was little opportunity for polo when you were ferrying convoys or hunting E-boats.

Under the pseudonym 'Marco', Mountbatten wrote a famous book on polo so he was an ideal teacher, and the Marsa Club was an ideal place to learn. The only worse thing than a bad pony, in the Duke's estimation, is bad weather which produces horrible playing conditions. The ideal is a smooth, hard surface under blazing sun. Major Ronald Ferguson, father of the Duchess of York, played alongside him at back during an equally long polo career. He once told me that the Duke was 'unquestionably a very vocal player'. He shouted a lot. Often colourfully.

The Duke himself has written revealingly about this. His view is that the decibel count is a good indicator of the standard of the polo. The noisier the players, the worse the game. Bad ponies also produce noise because the riders evidently like to tell their steed what they would like it to do and what they think of its ancestry.

'Shouting,' he continues, 'which is neither warning nor instructional, nor directed at the pony, is more or less without exception abuse. There is really not much venom in it and very frequently it is produced more by fright than by animosity.' He also believes that noisy players are usually the mildest and most cheerful of men off the field of play and that Anglo-Saxons are more vocal than Latins.

Although comparatively few people play polo, there are clubs all over the globe – and the Duke managed to perform in the Americas, Africa, Australia, India, Pakistan, and Singapore as well as the United Kingdom, though hardly ever, he says, in Continental Europe. He has played indoors in Canada. In those early Maltese days he went on a polo trip to Rome accompanied by Princess Elizabeth. Not only did they meet the Pope, he also played on a Sunday, thus running foul of the *Daily Express* and its Presbyterian proprietor, Lord Beaverbrook. 'Too much Pope and Polo', said the *Express*.

After Malta he joined Cowdray Park where he and two other naval officers decided to form a Royal Navy team under the captaincy of a Marine general called Sir Robert Neville who had played for Mountbatten's 'Bluejackets' before the war. Unfortunately Sir Robert had a bad accident before the season started and they recruited an ex-Indian Army player instead. However, they still called themselves 'The Mariners' and played in the square-necked white shirts that sailors wear under their blue jumpers.

Cowdray Park provided enjoyable polo but it was a tiresome cross-country drive from Windsor and the Duke fancied a club nearer home.

He therefore persuaded Sir Eric Savill, Deputy Ranger of Windsor Great Park, that polo would be just the thing for Smith's Lawn. He then induced a polo enclave from Henley-on-Thames to up-sticks and join him at Windsor where, in due course, this enterprise became the Household Division or Guards' Polo Club. Right on the Royal Family's weekend doorstep, it has proved highly convenient for both himself and his polo-playing son, the Prince of Wales, and the annual International Day in August has become one of the high points in the polo calendar. For most of his playing career Smith's Lawn has been the Duke's home ground and he played in the red and green livery of Windsor Park. Their colours were his own design.

Polo is a dangerous game, however. The Duke, who took his share of falls, remembers once being catapulted over the head of a pony which crossed its legs while galloping flat out. He recalls that he just had time to say to himself, 'This is going to hurt.' Which it did. To this day he can hardly bear to watch a dancer doing the splits because it reminds him of the time he caught his knee against the knee of another player going in the opposite direction. He thinks he lost at least one weekend a year through injury: bruises and contusions, a broken ankle, a torn riding muscle . . . and 'the older I became, the longer it took to recover from an injury'.

Finally, an injury to his right wrist began to turn arthritic. His solicitous head groom suggested that as many of his ponies were on a drug called Butazolidin he might like to try it, too. For a time he did, and it worked as well for him as it did for his horses, but after a while he began to notice side effects. In any case he was nearing fifty, which he had marked down as a suitable age for retirement. So, with great sadness, 'I gave up both the drug and the game in 1971.' Considering how relatively little time he had given to the game, his top handicap of five was extremely creditable – not up to the standard of the 'hired assassins' who play for money but a great deal better than that of many of the rich 'patrons' who hire the 'assassins'.

The Duke is not by nature a sedentary person and he needed a substitute for the polo which had been his main sport for more than twenty years. There are relatively few sports which you can sensibly take up at fifty but in carriage-driving he found one which has occupied him even more fully than polo and which has many of the elements he so enjoyed in that game. It involves horses; it has speed and spills; it is competitive; it is social.

Even as late as 1968, and despite the fact that being a member of the Royal Family involves a great deal of ceremonial carriage-driving, he was not even aware that competitive carriage-driving existed. Prince Bernhard had already persuaded him to stand as his successor as president of the International Equestrian Federation, or FEI. This is the international governing body of show-jumping, dressage and three-day eventing and the Duke was its president for twenty-four years; making way in 1986 for his daughter, the Princess Royal.

According to the Duke, anyone wanting to organise a carriage-driving event must obtain and read the following publications, all 'written as a result of bitter experience':

The latest edition of the FEI *Rules for Driving Events*.
The latest edition of the FEI *General Regulations*.
The latest edition of the FEI *Veterinary Regulations*.
The FEI *Checklist for Organisers of Driving Championships and International Events*.
The FEI *Memorandum for Ground Juries, Technical Delegates, Course Designers and Organisers of International Driving Events*.

When he penned this advice in 1982 he also revealed that the FEI Driving Committee was split by disagreement over two issues. In the first, the 'reactionaries' were opposed to new designs of carriage (too expensive) while the 'progressives' – of whom he was one – favoured experiment in the interests of safety. There was also hot debate about whether to work towards a standard distance between cones in obstacle driving and a 'minimum track-width for carriages'.

From all this it can be deduced that the International Equestrian Federation is all-powerful within its own world; also that it is highly specialised and technical and prone to controversy over what, to the outsider, may seem impossibly arcane.

Prince Bernhard wanted the Duke to take his place at the FEI for some of the same reasons that he had wanted him to succeed him as president of the WWF. He had enthusiasm, contacts, and an international position which meant he would always be listened to with respect.

'It's funny,' said Prince Bernhard, 'Philip played polo. I have never played polo. I was in our national team for show-jumping and dressage, both of which he didn't do, and I have never been able to drive a four-in-hand or whatever he does. But our love for the horses is identical – each in a different kind of sport.'

Prince Bernhard talked of the difficulties of the Mexico Olympics, not least when a sudden midday thunderstorm flooded the three-day event course. The Duke was then FEI president and Prince Bernhard president of the Appeal Jury. Everyone who competed after the deluge appealed on the grounds that it was unfair but the two presidents dismissed all the appeals. There was another problem over an inaccurate measuring of the show-jumping course. 'A lot of laughs, but a lot of hard decisions,' says Prince Bernhard. At the Stockholm Olympics there was a row over whether non-commissioned officers could win medals. And there was a recurring and acrimonious debate about amateurism and professionalism.

It all sounds very wearing and the president is vulnerable in all sorts of ways. 'That's one thing about him which I admire very much,' says Prince Bernhard. 'He is extremely strict in ethical subjects. For instance, at the Tokyo Olympics we were both offered a free watch by Seiko. I would have accepted it and thought nothing of it, but he wouldn't accept it on principle so when I thought about it I wouldn't either.' Of course, Prince Bernhard was badly burned after accusations involving impropriety with the Lockheed Aircraft Corporation, so his remarks in this respect are poignant. 'Obviously if I smell something, I don't like it. But he is so strict that he will never accept anything even if there is no smell attached.'

The Duke gave an immense amount of time to the Swiss-based FEI, so much so that his daughter, also no slouch when it comes to effort, felt it necessary to explain from the outset of her reign that she would not be running it in the same way. 'I'm certainly not going to translate the international rule book every time it's changed — which is what he did,' she said. 'I don't have the capacity and I don't have the time.'

The person who introduced him to competitive driving was Eric Brabec, the Polish delegate to the FEI who suggested that it was high time there was a set of international rules to govern the sport. The Duke visited the Aachen International Horse Show and saw some driving, was intrigued, set up a committee under Sir Michael Ansell, the great show-jumping expert, and supervised the drafting of the first-ever rule book. Quite apart from the arcane intricacies of the sport itself there were considerable difficulties with translation. Many of these linguistic problems had to be solved by the Duke himself. He then suggested that Sir John Miller, the Crown Equerry, should enter a team of Windsor greys for the first competition under the new rules and, in 1970, was instrumental in establishing a driving competition at the Royal Windsor Horse Show where he acted as a referee.

By now, he was effectively hooked. The Royal Mews was full of horses and carriages; the Windsor stables where he kept his ponies were available; and he envisaged a handful of competitions during summer weekends. It looked like the perfect substitute for polo.

He began with a pair of horses in 1972. At first they were understandably sedate and could not be induced to get their feet wet, even in a small stream in the Home Park. This problem was solved by getting someone to stand on the other side of the water armed with sugar lumps. However, it was 'four-in-hand' driving that appealed to him and he still knew nothing about it. He therefore arranged for David Muir, who looked after the stalking ponies at Balmoral, to come to London and learn how to harness four horses together. Meanwhile the Duke bought a couple of text books and studied hard. That summer he set off down the drive at Balmoral behind a team of stalking ponies, instructions at the ready. 'Fortunately,' he says, 'all went well and I had started a new sporting career.'

At Sandringham he borrowed five Cleveland bays from the Royal Mews, enlisted the aid of Major Tommy Thompson, an accomplished 'whip' who had been Riding Master to the Household Cavalry, and set about learning the sport properly. After a month Major Thompson decided that his charge could be risked in open competition and the Duke and his bays entered the lists at Lowther in April 1973. The Duke got off to a bad start. It had snowed the night before and the going was sticky. In the dressage the Duke lost his way and accumulated enough penalty points to put him tenth out of ten. In the later phases of the competition he improved enough to end a creditable fourth. A year later there was a disaster when he hit a tree-stump in one of the obstacles, turned over and had to watch helplessly as his horses ran off.

To his surprise the sport's popularity increased in bounds. In 1973 Windsor hosted the second-ever European championships and he entered driving the famous Balmoral 'dogcart' which the Crown Equerry, Sir John Miller, had been driving in most of the earlier competitions. Alas, the Duke hit an obstacle and had to retire with a bent front axle. He believes that the dogcart must hold the record for the number of times it has been reconstructed. He also thinks it was the first carriage ever to be fitted with disc brakes.

At Balmoral he persevered with the ponies and has regularly entered events with them in Scotland and the north of England. Like polo, carriage-driving is international and surprisingly popular behind what some of us used to call the Iron Curtain. It is a curious paradox that during more than twenty years of the Cold War the husband of the Queen of England should not only have run the FEI but also be so well-liked by its East European Communist members. When the Duke finally decided to retire as president it was the Russians who were first in the long line of member countries to say that his going was a tragedy. The irony was, of course, compounded when he was succeeded, amid acclaim, by the Princess Royal. As a competitor, the Duke was a member of the British team in the European and World championships in Poland in 1975 and Hungary in 1978 and 1984. He has also competed in Holland, Switzerland and Sweden. A further bonus is that most of the events are held in the parks and estates of great country houses – including Sandringham. So he has seen a lot of Capability Brown landscape.

He has had his share of disasters – 'a spectacular turn-over' in the 1975 European championships when everyone else found it plain sailing – and of successes – he won a team Gold at Windsor in 1980 and a further three team Bronzes in other world championships. His best individual placing in an international competition was sixth in the world championships in Holland in 1982.

The sport is much safer than it used to be because of improvements in harness and carriage design. It is still easy to turn over if you corner too fast or hit an obstacle but the chances of a harness breaking are now much reduced. His worst harness failure was at Sandringham once when his team baulked at a small water-crossing and then tried to jump it. All four horses broke away from the carriage and the Duke did not have time to let go of the reins and was carried clear over the stream to the far bank, leaving Major Thompson alone in the carriage. The Princess Royal was riding nearby and suddenly found herself confronted with a single escaped carriage horse galloping towards her. 'She was,' says the Duke, 'a great help in coping with the crisis.'

One of the oddities of driving is that you carry your referee round with you. Once, at Mellerstain in Scotland, he hit a bump and was tossed from the driving-seat. His grooms immediately jumped down to catch the horses, leaving a shocked referee the only man on board. Another time, at the same place, the referee was so alarmed as the Duke tried to control a 'singularly silly horse' on a slippery slope where the brakes wouldn't grip, that he leapt off the carriage and then ran after it, jumping to the safety of the back step alongside the grooms. But the worst moment was at Windsor Home Park when his horses shied, a pole broke, he was thrown out and the 'off-wheeler' caught him in the hip and lower ribs with a huge hoof. No bones broken but he was sore for days. I sometimes get the impression that the Duke positively enjoys being thrown off horses or out of carriages.

Carriage-driving has also extended his interest in design and technology. The early carriages were antique vehicles built of soft iron and wood and emphatically not suited to the rigours of competition driving. The Duke reckoned that an all-metal carriage using a proper steel frame was the answer and he even persuaded Sir George Edwards, managing director of the British Aircraft Corporation, to make some special light-alloy wheels for it. Later he designed an 'equi-rotal' or 'bendy' carriage, like a two-wheeled cart with a pair of rear wheels hinged under the front. Several of these were built but though they worked well with pairs they were less successful with teams. He also produced a design for a revolutionary cross-country vehicle which attracted so much enthusiasm at the European championships in Zug, Switzerland, that today it has been adopted by practically everyone. So his influence on this rapidly growing sport has been profound.

In 1987, he gave up driving horses and switched his attention to ponies. At sixty-seven the physical strain of controlling four full-sized horses was proving too much and he decided it was time to try something different. So, on a dank, damp summer weekend at Sandringham, the Duke, number 76, was seen in the class devoted to teams of four ponies under 148 cm, competing against such diverse entries as Pro-Mill Engineering Ltd., Universal Salvage, Coastal Container Services and Mrs M. and Miss K. Bassett of Dorking, Surrey. His entry has a positively poetic ring to it:

HM The Queen, Buckingham Palace, London. Lownthwaite Lady III, Balmoral Bramble, Bannerdale Dawn, Sanja Ebony, Balmoral Cilla. Black gelding and mares driven to a Bennington Phaeton by HRH The Duke of Edinburgh.

He claims to be the only president of an international sports federation who has taken part in a world championship in a sport controlled by his own federation. This is not just an empty boast for the benefit of the *Guinness Book of Records*. If more such presidents got a competitor's-eye-view, perhaps fewer mistakes would be made.

Sport has always been important to the Duke and his keen participation has given him valuable insights in many of his public positions. Clearly his carriage-driving helped him in his twenty-two-year presidency of the FEI; his cricket gave him the necessary credentials to be

– twice – president of MCC. His long and active presidency of the National Playing Fields Association is obviously informed by his all-round sporting activity. So is his association with the Central Council for Physical Recreation – one of the first charities he took on. An element of outdoor pursuit and sporting interest has always been an essential part of his Award Scheme. His interest in the environment, and his presidency of the World Wide Fund for Nature, stems in part from his love of country activities. It also made him a much more useful, if sometimes beady, president of the Royal Yachting Association. When you look at the portfolio of his presidencies and patronages it is remarkable how many of them reflect his recreational pursuits, so that although they have all offered opportunities for letting off steam, making new friends, escaping from the office and all the other reasons for taking up active recreations, they have always been more than that. Part, if you like, of the job.

Although his main office is in the centre of one of the world's great cities and although many of his interests are urban and indoor he has been, essentially, a countryman, ever since his birth – not in smoggy Athens but in Corfu, in a house surrounded by olives and cypresses, oranges and lemons and eucalyptus. He insists, of course, that he left Corfu far too early to have any memories of it but it remains true that his earliest life was rural and that most of the rest of it has been spent either at sea or in a sort of countryside. Even Buckingham Palace has the biggest private garden in London.

His interest in country sports really began when his four sisters all married country landowners with large estates in Germany. An important part of the tradition and life of all four families was fishing, deer-stalking and 'occasional forays after capercailzie in the Black Forest'. He writes quite lyrically about this last:

There was nothing I enjoyed more than going out with my brothers-in-law in the early mornings, or just before dusk, to sit up with them for a roe-buck or to creep through the tall pines in the morning twilight in the hope of hearing and tracking down a capercailzie as it greeted the rising sun with its strange clucking display. A special treat was to go out to observe a black-cock 'lek', where a whole gathering of males strutted and displayed in front of a critical gallery of females on the lookout for a likely mate.

His first lessons in ecology and the study of nature came from the brothers-in-law and their keepers and foresters and he has always approached environmental issues from that point of view. Like most countrymen he is impatient with what he sees as the ill-informed, townee views of the anti-bloodsport lobby. Prince Bernhard, his predecessor as head of the World Wildlife Fund, as it was then called, is so impatient with the endless stream of people who write in to complain about the apparent contradiction in his concern for wildlife and his fondness for shooting it, that he has had a standard riposte specially printed. Prince Philip has not gone this far but he does become tetchy when confronted with what he sees as the knee-jerk reactions of those who think that killing animals, especially for sport, is wrong. Some very pretty animals – fox or seal – can be regarded as vermin; you need to cull deer to preserve healthy stock. And so on. The arguments are complex and probably irreconcilable. The crucial point is that the Duke believes absolutely in his point of view and has the dialectic ammunition to support it, partly through wide reading and partly through having been brought up in a landowning tradition in which wise husbandry was essential for survival.

He himself never shot anything as a child or even as an adolescent but his brother-in-law, Prince Berthold of Baden, did teach him the art of dry-fly fishing in which he himself had been instructed by the Salem school's English master. Berthold was totally addicted and very good, but apart from one or two occasions at his uncle's home at Broadlands on the River Test, one of the best fishing rivers in England, the Duke has never had much chance to pursue it. Salmon fishing, much loved by his son and mother-in-law, has never appealed to him in the same way and the nearest he has found to dry-fly fishing is wet-fly fishing for brown trout at Balmoral. Unfortunately the country there is too acid and infertile for the trout to grow big enough to be really interesting.

He first stalked Scottish deer just before the war and was surprised to find how it differed from German stalking. In Germany he had pursued his quarry in forests whereas in Scotland the deer were living on open, heather-covered hills. When he began stalking at Balmoral he did it like everyone else but the Duke is not a natural conformist nor a natural spectator. The usual drill is for a professional stalker to take an amateur rifle out on a beat and do the work for him. The stalker finds the deer, organises the approach, selects an appropriate target and then hands the rifle to the amateur so that he can administer the *coup de grâce*. When he has done this, the pro then guts or 'garalochs' the stag, summons the pony and, assisted by a ghillie, loads the carcass and sends it off to the nearest road.

The Duke began as a gentleman amateur but obviously felt underemployed so, when one of the stalkers went sick, he persuaded the head stalker to let him stalk the beat himself. He would never emulate the professionals but he would be doing something for himself and not just following in someone else's footsteps. He managed almost everything quite satisfactorily, even using an old knife of Prince Albert's for doing the 'garaloch' – it was in a glass case in his study and the Duke is sure he would not have minded. The one problem he never could quite solve was tying the stag to the saddle of the pony.

Soon after he began stalking on his own, the Army were issued with a new rifle, the semi-automatic FN, subsequently known as the SLR. Until then the Duke had been using a standard single-shot, bolt-action sporting rifle. However, as a Field Marshal and Colonel of the Welsh Guards he thought it would be interesting to submit the new weapon to a field test. If it was a good stalking weapon it should be all right on the battlefield as well. There was one untoward incident with this weapon. Out stalking among trees the Duke followed the usual procedure of resting the rifle on the shoulder of his stalker. He bagged the stag but also, apparently, the stalker who staggered off holding his head in agony. Unfortunately the gas port of the self-loading mechanism must have been right against the stalker's ear and he caught the full blast. He was deaf for a day or so but suffered no lasting harm. 'I became very attached to that rifle,' says the Duke, 'and it served me well.'

Since 1967 the Duke has been patron of the Wildfowlers' Association of Great Britain. Wildfowling is not like most shooting. It takes place at dawn or dusk; it is solitary; it is cold; and there is usually a gale blowing. It sounds like very Outward Bound entertainment. The Duke has done it in Canada with a host, recently recovered from whooping cough, who insisted on trying to attract his prey by quacking at them. This was a failure. In India he had a bad day at Barratpore, near Delhi, and a better one with a young Zulfikar Ali Bhutto, recently appointed Foreign Minister of Pakistan by General Ayub Khan. Mr Bhutto set the Duke up in a hide on an island in the middle of a swamp, complete with carpet, table, chair and a human retriever who waded into the water after every victim, carefully slitting its throat even when it was already very obviously deceased.

His favourite wildfowling country, however, is the Norfolk coast. Here he once went punt-gunning with the actor James Robertson Justice, the large red-bearded portrayer of Sir Launcelot Spratt in the long-running series of 'Doctor' films. Most punt-gunners are professionals, but Robertson Justice was one of the few amateurs who owned his own gun, a massive shotgun mounted on the bows of a twenty-foot-long wood and canvas punt very low in the water. It was an unsuccessful day in terms of birds shot, but, says the Duke, 'in spite of the cold and wet and general discomfort, I was glad to have had the experience'. He was fond of Justice who owned some land in Sutherland. The Duke stayed there and remembers the actor's peregrine falcons hunting for grouse.

The Duke seems to thrive on cold, wet and general discomfort. He also enjoys pigeon shooting – he once bagged two hundred in a single evening during a blizzard in Suffolk – and grouse – 'not just a question of hitting the grouse but of missing the neighbouring guns at the same time. This is a real hazard.'

The size of the bag is not what matters. Sound management, accurate shooting, clean killing are the criteria. 'I do not mind missing,' he says, 'but I hate wounding birds.' And even if there is nothing to shoot at, it is always a pleasure to be 'in' the countryside. The 'in' is essential. The Duke is a participant, not a spectator.

Land, air and sea all appear to be equally appealing to him, though I have put his flying activities under travel rather than sport. His earliest conscious memory of sea is not of the waters off Corfu but of the western Atlantic rolling on to a French beach. Berck-Plage perhaps. There he paddled but he did not swim. This came later at the pool at Wolfsgarten – a curious circular pool within an octagonal shell, built in the 1900s by the Grand Duke Ernest Louis of Hesse and surely one of the oldest in Europe. Princess Margaret of Hesse und bei Rhein told me she thought it was the first-ever German swimming pool. It has no shallow part and is a uniform five foot in depth which, says the Duke, may explain why he did not leap in until comparatively old. 'If the attempt had failed,' he says, 'my life would have been entirely in the hands of some much older cousins. I expect they would have fished me out before it was too late but, as I know only too well what a nasty little boy I was, I think that had I failed to surface they might have well have been tempted to look the other way.'

He excelled in the Cheam swimming pool – an indoor pool, which made it unusual among English prep schools of the period – and at Salem enjoyed swimming in Lake Constance. There was no pool at Gordonstoun, the Moray Firth was too cold for him, but he did learn life-saving at the public baths in Elgin city. In the large and well equipped pool at Dartmouth he played water polo and was taught a highly dubious life-saving technique which involved removing your trousers underwater, tying knots in the legs and then inflating them. Happily this was never put to serious test. During the war he played

water polo in the harbour at Trincomalee on an oily pitch which covered both teams in a thin film of discharge; watched fish throughout
the Mediterranean with a pair of underwater goggles purchased in
Athens; and tried body-surfing in Australia. In 1949 he borrowed
Lord Mountbatten's water-skis in Malta and had two aqualung lessons
in the pool at Buckingham Palace though he only twice managed to
dive in the sea itself – once among the kelp weed off the coast of
Scotland and once off Barbados. Diving needs opportunity and practice and there was never enough time.

Messing about in boats had always been easier for him than messing
about in, or under, the water. He originally took to a German
Faltboot in order to avoid hated walking expeditions at school in
Salem. The Faltboot was a collapsible canoe in two large bags, one
containing the rubber skin, the other full of sticks and frames. Assembly was complicated and involved fraught tempers and pinched
fingers. One summer term he and some fellow-pupils paddled their
Faltboots across Lake Constance and then drifted languidly all the way
to the Reichenbach Falls where Sherlock Holmes met Moriarty. They
returned by train.

At Gordonstoun, seamanship was a vital part of the curriculum
under the supervision of Lieutenant-Commander Lewty, RN, Retd.
Lewty was a stern but accomplished taskmaster and the Moray Firth
an ideal if exacting training ground. Those were primitive times and
there was no changing room at Hopeman harbour, which was a long
bicycle ride from the school. It was after long sodden journeys back
from the sea that he was first told that it was impossible to catch cold
if you were wet with seawater. 'I can only say,' he adds, 'that experience proved this to be so.'

By the time he arrived at Dartmouth he was such an accomplished
small-boat sailor that he was one of only two cadets in his term
allowed to skipper the college cutters and whalers. They would sail
down the River Dart and then race in the beautiful estuary which
older television viewers may recognise because it was the setting of
that long-running nautical soap opera, *The Onedin Line*.

Once, tacking alongside another cutter, captained by their Term
Officer, Lieutenant-Commander Campbell, he suddenly found himself
on a collision course with his senior. The rules of the sea are quite as
explicit as the Highway Code and Prince Philip had the right of way.
On the other hand the Lieutenant-Commander, in the Duke's words,
'had more stripes'. It was a ticklish situation and a less pugnacious
competitor than Prince Philip would have yielded precedence. Not

him. 'For reasons best known to himself, he did not give way and although I tried to go under his stern, I clouted him just about where he was sitting in the stern-sheets.' Commander Campbell never mentioned the incident, knowing presumably that he was in the wrong. It was a cheeky thing for a young cadet to do but entirely in character. He always plays to the rules but he plays very hard and he has never given way.

'I have never known a cooler man,' says the former Conservative Member of Parliament Sir Reginald Bennett, who sailed with him at Cowes for many years. Close shaves at close quarters were the order of the day whenever the Duke was at the helm. Even in those Dartmouth days he was adventurous to a point which, to less intrepid mortals, looks positively foolhardy. And just as he seemed almost to enjoy getting thrown off his horse, so he had few qualms about being a man overboard.

In an attempt to get these rather cumbersome boats to go faster he developed a technique which nautical readers may understand better than I do. It involved 'keeling against the tiller to hold it to leeward while pushing the mizzen boom to windward with one hand and holding the sheet with the other. The only snag about this system was that I had no hands left to hold on to anything.' This sort of 'look-no-hands' sailing is always liable to end in tears, even if you are royalty, and one day a wave lifted the boat up and threw him over the side. Somehow he managed to hang on to a sheet and pull himself back on board. The rest of the crew were so preoccupied that they never noticed their captain's brief absence.

In 1947 the Island Sailing Club of Cowes, on the Isle of Wight, gave him and Princess Elizabeth a Dragon-class yacht as a wedding present. It was the first royal sailing yacht since George V's J-class *Britannia*. The wedding present was painted dark blue and he christened her *Bluebottle*. ('Dragonfly' . . . 'bluefly' . . . 'bluebottle' . . . was the royal line of thought.) For years he sailed her competitively in Cowes Week. He and his regular crew, the great and colourful local boat-builder Uffa Fox, became almost synonymous with this most famous regatta in the British yachting calendar.

It was Fox who persuaded the people of Cowes to give him one of the first Flying Fifteens, which was a new design of his. Prince Philip called her *Coweslip* and took her to Malta where he spent many happy hours sailing her up and down the local creeks. He also persuaded Fox to put together a sailing hydrofoil. Fairey Marine on the Hamble River designed the foils and Fox christened her *Fairey Fox*. The foils never really worked and were abandoned. However, he and Fox sailed her competitively against conventional cruising yachts, even winning the Dainty Cup with her. This was thought by their rivals to be 'not playing the game' because the *Fox* was really just an outsize dinghy. The Duke and Uffa Fox had to agree.

The best known of his yachts was *Bloodhound*, a pre-war twelve-metre designed for ocean racing. The Duke had her re-rigged with a new alloy mast and boom and a new engine. He raced her at Cowes and for many years cruised the west coast of Scotland in her with Prince Charles and Princess Anne. These were happy days. However, she became expensive to run and, in any case, most of the time she was lent out to others. After their visit to Norway in 1969 he and the two elder children had a final voyage in *Bloodhound* and then she was sold.

In recent years the Duke's competitive sailing has been done in a succession of yachts, all called *Yeoman* and all owned by his friend and fellow sailing enthusiast, Sir Owen Aisher, the founder of the Marley Tile business.

*Bluebottle* is now retired at the Royal Naval College, Dartmouth, where she is much cherished and occasionally taken out for a gentle sail. *Bloodhound* is a sadder story. Of all the Duke's boats, she is the one which inspires the greatest nostalgia, not just in him but in the rest of the family too. When I mentioned her to the Princess Royal she said that by chance she had found *Bloodhound* in the West Indies a few years ago. The yacht was in a bad way: ill-maintained, thoughtlessly altered, her paint peeling, her dignity impaired. Princess Anne said she felt as if she had been physically assaulted and it was all she could do to restrain herself from going on board to remonstrate with the owner. *Bloodhound* was a part of her life, a happy memory of family sailing with her father, and it really hurt her to see the old lady so neglected.

In the spring of 1990 the Duke asked his old sailing chum, Reggie Bennett, to see if he could find her. After a long search Bennett did find *Bloodhound*, languishing in Poole Harbour. Prolonged negotiations with the owner ensued and when I last saw him, Bennett was cautiously optimistic about finding someone – not the Duke – to buy her and restore her to her former self.

He *is* a sporting prince and sport in many different forms has always been a vital part of his life. It has brought him relaxation and kept him young; it has led to laughter and the love of friends; and it has informed much of his public life. Active participation has meant that he can help in running organisations such as the Award Scheme, the International Equestrian Federation or the Royal Yachting Association with real authority. I hesitate to say that it is the most important single facet in his life but it is impossible to understand him without realising how much of his life has been spent being thrown off horses and carriages and boats; how much time he has devoted to stalking through forests and across moors, always alive to some new sight or sound or smell. To the office-bound and the sedentary, who make up most of our population, these preoccupations of the Duke may seem incomprehensible and even frivolous. He, on the other hand, would find a life divided – like so many people's – between the desk and the TV impossible to contemplate.

# 17

# 'Laughter and the Love of Friends'

'From quiet homes and first beginning,
Out to the undiscovered ends,
There's nothing worth the wear of winning,
But laughter and the love of friends.'

*Dedicatory Ode*
HILAIRE BELLOC

The popular image of the Duke of Edinburgh is one of almost unrelieved tough masculinity yet time and again, as I met those who knew him, I would be told stories about his kindness and concern.

As a young equerry back in the 1950s, John Severne misread the day's schedule and let through a typing error which made nonsense of the timings. Early that morning the Duke's voice came blasting down the intercom.

'How on earth do you suppose we're going to get from the Palace to Herstmonceux in an hour?'

'I . . . er . . . oh . . . sorry, sir.'

'Quick, get my car out. And warn the Royal Observatory that we're going to be late.'

'Yes sir.'

The Duke took the wheel of his Lagonda and drove fast to Sussex.

He likes to drive fast as everyone who has ever been driven by him will testify, but despite a speedy journey they were still behind schedule when they finally arrived.

As they got out and approached the waiting reception line the Duke half turned to his shamefaced equerry and said, 'If anyone asks why we're late, tell them it's my fault.'

An acquaintance, a middle-aged man with a young family, suddenly discovered that he was suffering from terminal cancer and had only weeks to live. He was a yachting man with a fine record of voluntary work in the sailing world and the Duke had got to know and like him through his links with the Royal Yachting Association and the Royal Yacht Squadron.

As soon as he heard of the man's illness, a handwritten, no-messing-about letter of cheer and sympathy went speeding off to the hospital, later followed by the insignia of a Commander of the Royal Victorian Order – an award reserved for service to the Royal Family.

When I went to Wolfsgarten to see Princess Margaret of Hesse und bei Rhein I got an urgent call from the Duke's office asking if I would act as a messenger and carry a small package from the Duke. It turned out to be a set of video recordings he had made of a TV series on the Russian Revolution which he thought the Princess might enjoy.

None of these three incidents, I admit, represents massive self sacrifice or vast efforts of imagination and in a way that is the best reason for repeating them. They are 'grace notes', small indicators of sensitivity and kindness, and above all a capacity for friendship of a spontaneous nature which is at odds with those – a considerable number – who think the Duke 'unknowable'.

A short essay the Duke has written on the subject of friendship is also revealing. He wrote it as a tribute to his old friend, the Maharaja of Jaipur, and it appeared in the front of a small volume, privately published in 1972 by Lillian Lutter, Principal of the Maharani Gayatri Devi Girls' School, in the Maharaja's own state of Jaipur.

He obviously found it difficult because, 'Friendship is such a personal and unpredictable quality. It's not based on careful assessment and it seldom comes in for analysis.' An interesting judgement. The Duke reads widely, but he does not read novels, especially modern ones. A pity. They are much given to musing on personal relationships and friendships. 'Jai was a friend,' he writes, 'but I never stopped to consider why he was a friend or what his friendship meant. All I know is that it was always a pleasure to meet him again and to be in his company. It was a delight to stay with him and as a guest he was always welcome whether it was a grand occasion or in a small party.' In a sense this is unexpected, because generally speaking one of the most remarkable points about the Duke is that he seems to question *everything*; I would not, therefore, have expected him to enjoy a real friendship without from time to time holding it up to the light.

Of his friend the Maharaja, he thinks that if he were to read a perceptive biography he might be able to point to certain character-istics and say that those were the ones he recognised and liked about him. That, however, would still only be half the story because he thinks friendship has a quality that goes beyond rational description.

In the particular case of 'Jai', he says he 'gained immeasurably from his friendship in all sorts of circumstances; in the things we did to-gether, like playing polo or shooting or just sitting and chatting under the moon in Jaipur or in a country house in England.' The image of the Duke and the Maharaja chatting under the Jaipur moon reminded me of an earlier, much younger Duke watching the capercailzie strut at dawn in the woods near Salem. There is a lyrical, almost sentimen-tal element in his make-up which is not often apparent, but is none the less important for being concealed.

As the Duke says, one is affected differently by different people. He finds that 'some annoy and irritate, some are stimulating, others again are happy and entertaining.' In the Duke's case his own response communicates itself, sometimes all too obviously. For example he ex-udes an almost animal antipathy to anyone 'wet', whereas he seems to warm instinctively to people who are extrovert and decisive. I have had one particular dinner he attended described independently by two different witnesses. One is a confident, self-assured, successful man, who said he thought the Duke 'sensible and entertaining'. The other is a quiet, sensitive soul, who thought the Duke 'an unsympathetic bully'. They were both meeting the Duke on the same occasion and the same terms, yet they reacted quite differently and in a sense inevi-tably. The Duke obviously liked one and not the other.

However, his reasons for so liking the Maharaja of Jaipur had noth-ing to do with virility. 'To me,' he wrote, 'Jai had a serene quality, a sort of cheerful calm, which may well have been exasperating for some, but to me it was a most endearing and enjoyable characteristic. He combined with that a very rare quality in men, he was supremely civilised. Kind and modest, but with an unerring instinct for the highest standards of human ambition and behaviour.

'Perhaps this is a prejudiced view but then friendship is prejudice.'

Questions about his friends are common even among those whom I originally thought were close to him.

'Why me?' one man responded when I asked if I might talk to him about the Duke.

'He suggested it,' I answered.

'Oh,' he said. But he sounded puzzled. He had not thought he knew the Duke well enough to be of interest.

Obviously friendship is important to the Duke. Vide, as he would say, the above. Yet even in a close friendship there is a part of him which stays private. Never, for instance, did he discuss his personal affairs with Michael Parker, even though Parker had always shared his own marital problems with his friend. He was a sympathetic ear, but never, apparently, one to vouchsafe too many confidences himself.

The Parker friendship seems quite significant. It has lasted from the Second World War and is still intact, though because Parker lives near Melbourne, Australia, the two see each other less often than they might like. When they first met in the war, Parker, like the Duke, was a displaced person; he was also outspoken, devil-may-care, hail-fellow-well-met, and a good sport. He kept wicket to the Duke's off-breaks; he liked to throw small aeroplanes into loops and spins; he enjoyed cheeking Churchill; he made the Queen laugh. What more could you ask? His premature departure from the Duke's employ was one of life's little tragedies.

Parker had been a Thursday Club regular and he was also a soul-mate of Uffa Fox, for years the Duke's sailing companion and also a convivial drinking, yarning and singing chum. Fox was one of the great builders and sailors of small boats, an Isle of Wight man who revolutionised the world of dinghy racing with his *Avenger*, built in 1929. Peter Scott, the painter and conservationist, son of Scott of the Antarctic and a friend and mentor of the Duke, was one of Fox's early patrons.

It was Fox who introduced the Duke to Sir Reginald Bennett at the dry dock in Greenwich when they were preparing it for the clipper, *Cutty Sark*. Bennett, who succeeded Fox as the Duke's sailing companion, was also, as an undergraduate at New College, Oxford, the founder of the Imperial Poona Yacht Club. This was a cocked snook at the colonial bores of the day who talked interminably about 'the good old days in Poona'.

The club's rules are bogus, replete with such items as 'For "white" read "black" and for "coloured" read "coloured" throughout', 'No memsahib, male or female is eligible', and 'At Tiffin the Senior Officer Present shall take the chair if there is one.'

The club crest is two red spheres on a yellow ground. In 1955 Fox, a new member, invited the Duke to a 'frightful piss-up at the Royal Corinthian'. The Duke asked Reggie about the club crest.

'All balls,' said Reggie. 'Just like the club.'

The Duke joined immediately.

He is identified on the membership list as 'The Maharaja of Cooch Parwani' which can be very loosely translated as the Maharaja of not a lot. When an American member, Buzz Mosbacher, skippered his boat to victory in the America's Cup, the Duke sent him a telegram, saying 'Poona is proud of you. Cooch Parwani.'

Other members include his kinsman, ex-King Constantine of Greece, the holder of an Olympic yachting Gold Medal, and Robin Knox-Johnston, the first person to sail single-handed non-stop round the world. Sir Alec Rose, the Portsmouth greengrocer and another intrepid round-the-world sailor, was also a member until his death in 1990. The members are therefore serious sailors with an unserious side to them. They like to let their hair down at 'tiffins' and 'durbars'; they like to drink and sing, and have a robust good time; and the Duke enjoys this too. It sounds like guest night in the wardroom or a night out with the boys. They are united by a love of sailing and an ability to excel at it; also by a fierce sense of loyalty so that no one has ever told tales out of school. This sort of boisterous, undemanding, high-spirited recreation is the perfect antidote to the still stuffy atmosphere of Court life.

Alas, these days the Duke is seldom able to make the Imperial Poona 'tiffins' and 'durbars'. He is always somewhere else and this is, in a sense, the story of his life. Time and again those who seem closest to him say that they only see him once a year or less. He sees far more of his valet, Barry Lovell, than he does of his sister, Princess Sophie; far more of his pilot, Geoff Williams, than of his son, the Prince of Wales; almost as much of his secretary, Brian McGrath, as he does of his wife, Her Majesty the Queen.

'He has a lot of acquaintances,' says Mike Parker, 'but his life hasn't always enabled him to build up friends. He's going round the world at such a lick.' An exaggeration perhaps, but it is true that the Duke's constant motion does mean that he can't see some of his friends very often. 'And remember,' continues Parker, 'that his constant job is looking after the Queen in first place, second and third.'

This point about 'looking after the Queen' is one which everyone who has worked for the Duke hammers home inexorably because they feel that it is not only crucial to his role, but also widely unappreciated. 'He's been a *marvellous* consort to her,' said one senior retired courtier, not otherwise lavish with his praise especially where the Duke is concerned. Another former employee said, 'It was always absolutely vital that nothing must go wrong in his household that would reflect badly on the sovereign.'

The nature of the relationship between a husband and wife is almost impossible for any third party to understand, but that between a Queen and her consort is doubly so. Prince Albert is quoted by the author, John Pearson, in a thoughtful essay on the Duke on the role of consort as he saw it. Albert thought that he

should entirely sink his own individual existence in that of his wife; that he should aim at no power by himself or for himself; should shun all attention, assume no separate responsibility before the public, but make his position entirely part of hers and fill every gap which as a woman she would naturally leave in the exercise of her regal functions.

The Duke's role is not as extreme as that but there *are* aspects of his relationship with the Queen which can perplex outsiders. When his former equerry, David Alexander, stayed at Balmoral in a small house party, he was struck by the degree of formality which surrounded the Queen, even behind closed doors. And, he pointed out, there are more closed doors at Balmoral than in most places, doors behind which none of us will ever penetrate. That summer there were fewer than ten guests staying at the castle, but even in this intimate gathering, the Queen always arrived last for drinks before dinner and no one left a room until she did. On one occasion the Duke arrived later than his wife, and found it necessary to bow formally and say, 'I'm very sorry I'm late.' Then he helped himself to a drink and the atmosphere became recognisably that of any Scottish house party.

The point is that at one and the same time the Queen is Elizabeth, daughter, wife and mother, a woman like any other, *and* the anointed sovereign. To those of us brought up outside royal circles and life at Court this is a paradox which we find difficult to reconcile. For the Duke, by blood more royal even than his wife, and brought up in a royal family, it presents no problem. 'You've got to remember,' said one expert, 'she's been *anointed*.' A fact courtiers and true royals never forget. In fact they take it for granted and regard deference as no more than ordinary good manners.

This necessary formality can be mistaken for coolness and distance. Insiders say this is nonsense. All those I spoke to who have observed the Queen and the Duke together at home or on holiday, and not on public duty, say that they make a well-knit team, consulting regularly and with mutual respect and affection, laughing a lot at the same jokes (and the same people), and generally presenting a picture of marital accord which most of us do not see. It is true that their duties often take them away from each other — the Queen does not go on World Wide Fund for Nature trips; the Duke does his best to avoid visits to stud farms in Normandy or Kentucky. But they spend at least as much time together as any other couple who are both fully employed in different occupations. Luckily, too, they often go on jobs together, as one is reminded when looking at the cabin of the Queen's Flight aircraft. There is the Duke's seat, dark blue, adjustable, and there, right opposite, is the Queen's identical one. They fly together, face to face and almost knee to knee.

His immediate family has always been important to the Duke. Mike Parker, who was close to him in the Clarence House days, emphasises time and again what a happy family life they had together and how, no matter how busy they were, the Queen and the Duke always set aside time each day to be with Prince Charles and Princess Anne. The Princess Royal herself agrees emphatically and makes the point that the Duke was always very careful to be with the children at bedtimes, something she herself has tried to do now that she has children of her own. She and her brothers accepted that they had to spend time being looked after by people other than their parents but 'Nanny was always *nanny*, never some sort of surrogate parent.'

The Duke's relationship with his daughter is popularly supposed to be the closest of any between him and his children, though you would expect people to say that of a father and an only daughter. Certainly she talks of him not only with real affection, but also just the right smidgen of eye-rolling exasperation when she recalls the odd irreconcilable disagreement. The particular one she mentioned to me concerned some arcane matter of equine veterinary practice, in which her own experience turned out to be quite unlike that of her father. The matter was rapidly dropped. Father and daughter, of course, have close working links now that she has taken on both the International Equestrian Federation and the Royal Yachting Association. She says she cannot possibly run the former with the hands-on dedication that her father managed all those years, but it gives them two particular topics to discuss regularly. Like Lord Zuckerman, the Princess is a keen admirer of his analytical mind. If you ask the Duke for a précis of a book he has just read there is never any need to read it yourself. He does the best book précis of anyone she knows.

All three sons followed his educational footsteps, though only Andrew seems to have enjoyed Gordonstoun and he is the only one to have retained his links with the school and become a member of the governing body. Charles and Andrew both followed their father into the Royal Navy where they obviously enjoyed themselves. Andrew is able to pursue the prolonged naval career that the Duke himself would have liked, though Charles, as heir to the throne, felt compelled to leave the service prematurely and, like his father, after only one single command.

The relationship between the Prince of Wales and the Duke continues to provoke speculation. People always remark on their differences and yet I believe that their similarities – speech, gesture, interests – are almost more striking. It is said that the father is the more abrasive of the two and yet he has his softer side, just as the son can also bark.

Some of their similarities in outlook have taken me by surprise. Architecture, for instance.

Here is a memorandum about a proposed addition to an existing – and historic – building. The writer can see that he is going to lose the argument because 'the architects are more concerned with their own aesthetics' than with the existing building.

Their argument is exactly the one which allowed so many lovely country houses to be ruined during the late 19th century with monstrous Victorian additions at different levels, different scales and everything else . . .

Any addition, if there must be one, should, thinks the writer,

be as inconspicuous as possible and it should not be allowed to distract in any way from the original architecture . . . who ever heard of anyone making a modern addition to a van Dyck or a Rembrandt? The fact that it has been done before is no excuse for doing it again – in architecture, I mean.

Most people, I submit, would recognise this as one of the Prince of Wales's tirades against the architectural profession. In fact it is the Duke of Edinburgh complaining about the proposed new King George VI chapel at St George's Windsor in June 1967. In the event the designs were modified, but that is not the point. The point is that, in expressing his views on architecture, it seems to me that the Prince of Wales sounds very like his father's voice.

There are other areas apart from architecture. Both are keen to encourage young people, particularly those without obvious opportunities; yet they have always done so through different organisations and in different ways. Both have been dedicated and proficient polo players and are keen on equestrian pursuits; yet the Prince of Wales has never become involved with the doings of the International Equestrian Federation. Both are fascinated by religion, yet the Prince of Wales has not developed a close association with St George's House. He seems determined to do his own thing in his own way.

His younger brother Prince Edward has now become very actively involved with the Duke of Edinburgh's Award Scheme, heading a special projects group which has already raised more than four million pounds. The Prince of Wales has always eschewed that sort of close co-operation with the Duke. Prince Edward, incidentally, is now observed to be very close to his father after a hiccup in their relations when he prematurely left the Royal Marines before completing his officer training. His artistic temperament always made him seem an unlikely candidate for that tough, single-minded corps, but he was coping well with the rigours of the course, and his departure remains mysterious. As his father is the Captain-General of the Royal Marines it was an embarrassment for him.

Now, of course, the Duke is a patriarchal figure, although because of the longevity of his mother-in-law and his own comparative youthfulness, he is not usually thought of as the senior member of the clan. It would be fascinating to know the truth about his relationship with the Queen Mother and with his sister-in-law, Princess Margaret. More than one insider – close acquaintance perhaps, rather than friend – suggested that I ought to think hard about what he called the 'very tight trio' at the centre of the family. 'The Queen won't always agree with the other two,' I was told, 'but cross one and you've crossed all three.'

The early years must have been difficult for the Duke because, as the letter King George VI wrote to his daughter on the occasion of her marriage suggests, they *were* a very close, tightly knit family with a shared experience peculiar only to themselves. I sensed a very strong bond between mother and younger daughter when I met them – that sort of laughing telepathy which you usually only get between close members of a family. I could imagine that the arrival of the Duke may have seemed a disruption back in the late forties. Anybody in his position would have been regarded as such and he was not only 'different', he wanted to adapt to changing views and circumstances. That meant ruffling established conventions, shaking complacency, even if it was only by doing such uncontroversial things as installing intercoms and dictaphones. But whatever they may have felt in the past about the interloping Duke it seemed to me that they now viewed him with genuine affection. The affection was evidently tinged with exasperation, but I do not believe there was a single person to whom I talked about the Duke who did not give some evidence of that, however tiny. I mentioned to his mother-in-law and Princess Margaret how the Duke so often, after a church service, took the preacher to task over his sermon. They both laughed at this and the Queen Mother recalled an evidently hilarious sketch done by Hugh Casson one Sunday. It showed the Duke bearing down on the vicar and reducing him to a 'quivering wreck'. The Queen Mother was on the verge of showing me the sketch but thought better of it. However, she did say that the Annigoni sketch at the top of the house was the best portrait of the Duke ever done. The finished picture – not so good – hangs in the Fishmongers' Hall. After lunch we inspected the sketch. I was half wondering if it might work on the front cover of this book. But though it does have an eye-flashing, clenched-jaw quality which captures one aspect of the Duke's character, it is less than fair to the others. 'I think perhaps it is too fierce for the cover,' said the Queen Mother, eventually. 'I don't,' said her daughter, 'I'd buy it.'

Among those who have been on his staff the Duke excites an utterly convincing devotion. 'The best boss I ever worked for,' said General David Alexander. He was run close in this competition by Denis Healey who was Minister of Defence when Alexander was in Whitehall. The comparison between the Duke and Denis is intriguing. Alexander was the Duke's equerry and treasurer in the late fifties. 'But very demanding,' he adds. I don't think that any of the former employees I spoke to would dissent from this view. No one who has ever worked for him would regard him as particularly easy, let alone easy-going, but provided you can manage long hours and keep your end up it is obviously a wonderful experience. Some think him a bully, but sensible people ignore the explosions, which are like sudden squalls at sea – violent for a brief moment but swiftly gone and forgotten.

He lost good friends and relations in childhood and youth. He never saw his father or his English guardian, the Marquess of Milford Haven, after his teens; he lost his sister Cecile and his friend and brother-in-law, George Donatus of Hesse, when still at school; Alex Wernher was killed in the war. Later Mike Parker was taken away from him – different degree of tragedy perhaps, but nonetheless a serious deprivation. Baron, the photographer, died under the surgeon's knife in 1956. Lord Rupert Nevill, a close friend of his and of the Queen, was his private secretary from 1976 to 1982 when he died suddenly at the age of only 58. The Duke has been unlucky with his friends.

He seems to keep up with no one from school. On his stag-night all his fellow diners were in naval uniform but, with the exception of Parker and Lord Lewin, there do not seem to be many surviving naval colleagues. Since then it has not always been easy to make friends. Of course he can be relaxed, amusing company and he obviously does have many acquaintances. He does not, however, seem to give friendship lightly or easily. If not surrounded by barbed wire there is something akin to a moat around him. He keeps his distance.

Human relationships tell us much about character and the kind of people who command our affection, and the degree of affection we are able to give and to attract is revealing. The nature of the Duke's life necessarily condemns him to hordes of acquaintances. He seldom stands still long enough to forge a friendship and everywhere he goes he is the man at the top. Being at the top can be a serious inhibitor of friendship though he inspires among those who work for him a degree of loyalty and affection which I found almost alarming. Like most of us, only I submit more so, his closest relationships are with members of his family, both in England and abroad, and with those relatively few people whom he has known since his early days. To them he remains, in the words of the Wernhers' daughter, Myra, 'A true, true friend. He never lets you down.'

# EPILOGUE

EPILOGUE

# 'Mere Lottery'

'If by the people you understand the multitude, the *hoi
polloi*, 'tis no matter what they think; they are
sometimes in the right, sometimes in the wrong: their
judgement is a mere lottery'
*Essay of Dramatic Poesy*
DRYDEN

In the end there are two pertinent questions to ask as the Duke
nears seventy, and these questions merge and overlap. The first
is one that everyone asks and the second – oddly – hardly bothers
anyone. 'What's he really like?' is the popular first question.
'What's he really done?' is the neglected second. Although I have
followed Sir Hugh Casson's directive and tried to produce a 'loose-fit'
portrait I hope I have already provided enough clues for most readers
to come up with some plausible answers. However, I would like to
collect my own thoughts after a whirlwind few months trying to un-
ravel the Duke even if I run the risk of repeating myself.

'What's he really like?' people invariably ask whenever I admit to having interviewed anyone remotely famous. It is a curious question because
it assumes that the physical experience of actually being in the same
room with 'celebrities', shaking their hands, and exchanging real live
words with them reveals something utterly unlike the image conveyed
by film or television or the printed word. On the whole, my experience
is that the assumption is wrongly based: most people in real life are more
or less like their public image. The better you know them the more complex they become. Sometimes, as you probe away, you discover aspects
of character that belie the impression gained from examining them

through the filter of the media. But the single interview characteristic of newspaper and television journalism is seldom very revealing – particularly if the person being interviewed is a professional, accustomed to presenting a well polished and impenetrable veneer to his interrogators.

In the Duke's case, the first impression is indeed that he seems remarkably like the Duke of Edinburgh. Perhaps he is a little shorter than I had assumed because he is very long in the back. He is also inclined to do a half knees bend when meeting and greeting, almost as if bracing himself against a heavy swell while on deck. This, too, is height-reducing. Sometimes this is deliberate – it can be disconcerting to be talked to from above. Otherwise, physically, he is much as I had expected. Fit, alert, eyes gimletting into you above that beaky nose but plenty of humour at the same time, not only in the eyes but the mouth and the laughter lines.

Turnout, as you'd expect, immaculate without a hint of flashiness. Shoes from Mr Lobb of St James's. 'One of the reasons I am going so well,' he told Lobb when he congratulated the Duke on his fiftieth birthday, 'is that I have always been so well shod'; socks, I am told by the manufacturers, are an antiquated design called the 'Tenova' much loved by the Duke of Windsor and Lord Mountbatten, nowadays only worn by himself, the Prince of Wales and the managing director of Austin Reed, whose subsidiary, Stephens Brothers, makes them, as well as his shirts. Their factory in Blackpool was one of the Duke's visits in 1990. The suit probably came from John Kent, though his Admiral's uniform is made by Gieves & Hawkes, the naval and military tailors who kitted out Lord Nelson and are still the preferred source of suiting for officers of the British armed forces. If you catch a herby fragrance that will be a smell from Penhaligon's, the company first started by William Henry Penhaligon, barber to the court of Queen Victoria. It is the kit, in other words, of an English gentleman, the sort of gear you would expect of an Admiral of the Fleet cutting a dash without being vulgar. If he were flanked by Lord Lewin and Lord Hill-Norton he would not look out of place.

No very great surprises, then, in his appearance. Nor, to be honest, are there huge surprises in his replies to direct questions. I have a feeling I have learned as much about the Duke from reading files and letters, talking to his family, his friends, his acquaintances and his staff as I have done from talking to him face to face. As the Princess Royal said, expressing doubt about whether she should talk to me, 'It's impossible to judge a portrait of oneself and almost as difficult to judge one of a close member of one's family — especially if you're supposed to be exactly like them.' The Duke himself, in saying he would do his best to answer my questions, said that he was 'not exactly the best authority on some of the subjects'.

My first encounter with the Duke was on 19 February 1969. I was twenty-five years old and a feature writer on the *Daily Express*, still just recognisable as the great popular newspaper created in the 1920s and '30s by Lord Beaverbrook. Beaverbrook, who had died a few years earlier, had for much of his life pursued a vicious personal vendetta against the Duke's uncle, Earl Mountbatten of Burma. Various reasons have been put forward for this — a woman, the disaster of the Dieppe Raid in the Second World War, the Beaver's passionate hatred of anyone of German ancestry — but no one has satisfactorily explained it. The two men were both such outsize, not to say conceited, figures that it would have been surprising if they had not been at daggers drawn. To an extent the whole of the two clans — Aitkens and Mountbattens — were drawn into the conflict and in one unguarded moment, on tour in South America, the Duke allowed himself to remark that the *Daily Express* was 'a bloody awful newspaper'. Not surprisingly, the rebuke rankled.

My interview was a sort of mutual olive-branch. Unsurprisingly there were conditions. My interrogation had to be tied to a particular theme so there could be no question of my suddenly throwing in what one might have expected from a Beaverbrook journalist interviewing Mountbatten's nephew. I chose, for obvious reasons, to talk about his own children in particular and his thoughts on young people in general with particular reference to his Award Scheme. Looking at my article now it does seem a little safe and bland, though not without interest.

Content apart, my overriding sense was one of . . . fear is perhaps too strong, apprehension too weak. He was exceptionally professional. A little warm-up to start with. Then he switched on his tape recorder, an old-fashioned one with proper spools rather than cassette tapes, and we were away. Unlike his uncle, Mountbatten, he listened attentively and answered each question as if he were giving it genuine and considered thought. On the one and only one occasion when I interviewed Mountbatten he had virtually ignored the questions I tried to put and instead attempted to tell me only what he wished to say. The Mrs Thatcher approach to the press. That was Mountbatten's style but not the Duke's. The Duke listened to the questions and answered them directly and, as far as I could see, honestly.

But he was still intimidating. In part this lay, I suppose, in his reputation for bawling people out, especially when they ask damn fool questions. In part it was that inexplicable confusion which overcomes even quite normal people when confronted with royalty. It happens to the best of us. And at the time of the interview I was twenty-five, the Duke forty-eight — old enough to be Admiral to my lieutenant, company chairman to my management trainee. So it is not altogether surprising if I found him alarming. Even so, I think there is something in his manner which almost everyone finds alarming.

Sir Hugh Casson, who first met him just after the war in Feliks Topolski's studio, suggested that there was a fundamental insecurity in the Duke which made it impossible for him to resist what he described as 'banter'. In other words, on seeing Casson at some function, he would always say something on the lines of 'I say, Hugh, what a perfectly ghastly tie'. (His views on Sir Hugh's neckware are, however, not uncommon.) Sir Hugh is older than the Duke, knows him well, and as a former president of the Royal Academy is not easily upstaged. The tie seizure, says Casson, is the reflex of a man who is not entirely at ease, not entirely confident. When I was introduced to the Duke by Gyles Brandreth, at a National Playing Fields lunch, the Duke went straight for my jugular. 'What's that tie?' 'Real tennis . . . sir.' 'Ah, real tennis!' And off he went, smiling and muttering 'Real tennis!' He knows about real tennis because his son Prince Edward plays, but it is not his game. Actually that peculiar English custom of wearing a tie that means something is — as the Duke knows — a useful opening for a conversation.

If Casson is right, then he is suggesting that at that 1969 interview I was not the only one who was apprehensive. The Duke was nervous too. This seems an unlikely proposition and yet he would have had every right to be nervous. He was being interviewed by 'a bloody awful newspaper' with a circulation of millions. It could have misfired badly. He certainly did not *seem* nervous to me, yet Hugh Casson was not the only one to remark that the Duke was by no means as self-confident as he can appear. I put the point to his daughter, the Princess Royal, and she said that she certainly did not think him shy but that left to his own devices he would not choose to occupy centre stage. He was not naturally an attention seeker.

A day or so after the 1969 interview I received a transcript from the Palace typed up in that large stately print they used in those days. It seemed a literal reproduction of the Duke's answers. There were few signs of the text having been doctored, but there was one point where I had asked him about the children's education. In answering he had

The official wedding photograph was taken by Baron, a friend of the Duke's and of his uncle Lord Mountbatten.

In the upper left picture the proud parents display the infant Prince Charles, and, a generation later, father and son at Lord Mountbatten's funeral. *Below:* The Duke tends to a barbecue with Princess Anne in 1972. *Above right:* With Prince Andrew, and *(below)*, the Duke and his youngest son, Prince Edward.

'His constant job,' says his old friend and former secretary, Mike Parker, 'is looking after the Queen. In first place, second and third.' *Opposite page:* With the Queen and four of their grandchildren, William, Harry, Peter and Zara in 1987.

For forty years the Duke's energy has been tireless as he travels the United Kingdom and the world. In 1952 he visited the Lancashire coalfields *(above left)*. Ever since it began in 1956 he has toiled in sun and rain for his Award Scheme *(above right)* and contrary to some opinions he has never been afraid to meet the press. In the lower photograph he is seen conducting a press conference in North America in 1966 with the author's father. But he has still not been to see the tribe that worships him *(below right)*.

His life is full of a multitude of different roles, many of them requiring completely different uniforms and outfits. Here, clockwise from the upper right, he is in the regalia of Chancellor of the University of Cambridge and in the uniforms of Colonel of the Welsh Guards – a role he relinquished to the Prince of Wales before taking on the colonelcy of the Grenadiers – Marshal of the Royal Air Force and Admiral of the Fleet.

Prince Andrew, the Duke's second son, has inherited his father's enthusiasm for photography. This picture was taken by him in 1986.

referred to the children, like any normal parent, as simply 'Charles' and 'Anne'. An intrusive hand had inked in the words 'Prince' and 'Princess'. Secretary? Press officer? Equerry? Who knows? At all events, a much more ferocious hand had run several lines through the titles and restored the text to the original. Another tiny indicator, I told myself at the time, of what he's really like. Or of what he would wish me to think he was like?

I never had any reaction to the piece, which made a three-part series in the paper, and that too seems typical of the Palace if not of the Duke himself. Years later I wrote an article for a Canadian magazine. Because it was Canadian and remote from Britain, I allowed myself more *lèse-majesté* than usual and was quite critical, far too critical, in fact, for my wonderfully loyal monarchist aunt in Aberdovey, North Wales, my touchstone for all things royal. There was no official complaint, no sign of displeasure. Later, however, I sent in a routine enquiry to Buckingham Palace and received the usual courteous, more or less helpful reply. A postscript was appended. 'You will be interested to know,' it said, 'that the contents of your recent article in Canada have been noted.' They – and he – are, in other words, masters of the understated, but chilling, rebuke. He welcomes informality. There is apparently no need to end your letters to him with the formal 'I have the honour to remain, sir, your humble and obedient servant'. It is, however, unwise, to be overfamiliar. Nothing will be said but, in the words of his old secretary Jim Orr, 'You know when you have overstepped the mark.'

In 1970 the *Daily Express* sent me to Strasbourg to cover the European Conservation Year conference at which the two main speakers were the Duke and Prince Bernhard of the Netherlands. Environment was not yet the fashionable subject it is today, though even then the Duke was warning of impending crisis and of time running out. I remember, by contrast, Antony Crosland, the Labour Cabinet Minister, who also attended the conference, being irritatingly lofty about privileged people's concerns for dead seagulls and vanishing pandas when for most people, in his view, 'the environment' meant substandard housing.

After the speeches most of the great and the good milled around talking with each other, but the Duke had spotted our small group of British journalists and made a bee-line for us. 'You boys got all you need?' he wanted to know, shaking hands all round. For five or ten minutes he stayed with us, chatting easily about some of the points raised earlier, then said he was sorry but he supposed he ought to get back to the top brass, and breezed off again. It was a thoroughly professional piece of public relations on behalf of conservation. He carried it off with no self-consciousness and not the slightest suggestion of that knee-jerk hatred of the press with which he is normally credited.

This matter of his relations with the press is a puzzle and a problem. It is also, obviously, important because it affects the image he presents to the world at large. I mentioned to the Princess Royal, for instance, that if anyone else had started up his Award Scheme they would be a national hero. She countered this by saying, 'Yes, but to the people who work in the Scheme he *is* a hero.' True enough, but I wonder if the adulation he is accorded by the relatively small number of people with whom he works has made him careless of his reputation in a wider world?

In his early years the press were flattering to the point of being adulatory. The Beaverbrook papers were sometimes an exception to this rule but even they could flatter. They probably overdid the praise – vide the purple prose of Collie Knox, describing the Duke at his wedding. However, somewhere along the line things started to go wrong. Prince Bernhard recalled an incident many years ago in New York where he had to lay a restraining hand on his 'junior partner' because the Duke showed an inclination to sort out some intrusive photographers. 'Please, Philip,' murmured Bernhard, 'let's not stop the party before it has even begun.' There were some spectacular individual spats, with David Leitch of the *Sunday Times* in Morocco, with Terry Coleman of the *Guardian* in West Africa. And, for whatever reason, there was sometimes a simple misreporting or misrepresentation which not only achieved wide and adverse publicity at the time but also found its way into various cuttings files or newspaper 'morgues'. Periodically these old stories are taken out, dusted down and given a fresh airing, maddening the Duke, his friends and colleagues, but acquiring, over the years, the bogus veracity of all much-repeated tales.

Two such incidents in recent years have passed into ducal folklore. The better known of the two took place on 16 October 1986 in the People's Republic of China. The Queen and the Duke were on a state visit and had recently been in Peking, a city of which the Duke at least had formed a dim view. On the 16th, the Duke met a group of British students studying at the North West University in Xian.

It sounds like an entirely characteristic exchange. The Duke was particularly interested in these students, because they came from

Edinburgh University, of which he has been Chancellor since 1953. The students were particularly interested in his views on Peking since they had not yet been there. The Duke told them that Peking was pretty ghastly because apart from the Forbidden City, which he did enthuse over, most of the rest of the town had been ripped down by the people's planners and replaced by people's tower blocks made out of people's breeze blocks. This view is commonplace among Western visitors to Peking. The Duke then asked one student, Simon Kirby, how much longer he was spending in China. Kirby replied that he had some time still to run, at which the Duke laughed and said that he had better be jolly careful or he would come back 'slit-eyed'.

Not being an old China hand I had not heard this line before, but I am told that it is a regular old chestnut and that a reverse form is common currency among Hong Kong Chinese who are given to telling their friends and relations in Britain that if they stay there very much longer they will come back with 'round eyes'. Ho, ho, as *Private Eye* used to say, highly satirical.

There is some dispute about the status of this conversation. The Palace and Foreign Office view was that it was a private exchange and should not have been reported. There were no Chinese present nor members of the press. Journalists who were on the trip say that it was one of those occasions on which two 'rota' members of the press corps had been allowed to be with the royal party. The form on these occasions is that the 'rota' journalists pool information with their colleagues after the event so that the story everyone files home is, in effect, an authorised and agreed version of what took place.

What actually happened was that while waiting for the royal party to visit the museum housing the great army of terra-cotta warriors in Xian, Alan Hamilton of *The Times* heard the distinctive accents of his home town, Edinburgh, cutting through the pervading Chinese voices in the crowded square. On investigation he found a group of Edinburgh students who were in town to learn Chinese. They were obviously intent on talking to the Duke so Hamilton asked if he could come back afterwards to find out what the royal couple had *really* thought about the warriors. Hamilton's experience was that royal press officers were always boringly anodyne. When he returned after the visit he learned from the students that the Queen and Duke had been very excited by the warriors, but that the Duke had been complaining about Peking and had made a remark about 'slitty eyes' (the Duke says he said 'slit-eyed', not 'slitty'). Hamilton, accompanied by the Press Association reporter, Tom Corby, wrote it all down and then they went back to their colleagues in the press bus. The others wanted to know what Hamilton had discovered so he read over the contents of his notebook. His tabloid colleagues were as unmoved by this as he himself until he got to the 'slitty eyes' moment whereupon the whole bus erupted, with hacks and hackettes demanding to be dropped off at the next phone box. 'They all went mad,' says Hamilton. One, Harry Arnold of the *Sun*, universally admired by his colleagues as an amazingly resourceful newshound, managed to prise the students' phone number from the operator, despite the fact that he spoke no Chinese and she no English, confirmed the story and filed accordingly. And the rest, as they say, is history.

Hamilton included the 'slitty eyes' reference in his piece, but threw it away as a laconic aside halfway through. The *Mirror* and the *Sun*, however, gave it the front page. Properly handled, this was the stuff of a rip-roaring, Duke boobs again, international incident. And so it proved. The popular press had a field day; it was a national joke. 'The Great Wally of China' said the *Mirror*; 'the Duke gets it wrong' said the *Sun*. It was huge fun for their readers but not for those involved. Simon Kirby, the student at the centre of the storm, was sufficiently embarrassed to send an apologetic letter to the Palace, and the Foreign Office took the grand mandarin view that no harm was done except to the image of a section of the British press who were judged, by the Chinese, to have been rude to a guest of the Chinese people.

The Duke replied personally to Kirby that December, thanking him for being so thoughtful, wishing him an interesting and enjoyable time during the remainder of his stay in China and telling him:

I certainly do not blame you for all the fuss and humbug your comments may have generated in the British media. It seems to me that on such occasions the press also has a responsibility to show some concern for the national interest. I suspect that any Chinese who may have been aware of what happened were astonished by its behaviour.

You may be pleased to know that the fuss had no effects whatever on my hosts during my subsequent visit to China on behalf of WWF. Very few people were aware of the incident anyway.

It seems improbable that Anglo-Chinese relations could have been harmed by this incident, but it did the Duke no good. The 'slitty eyes' remark is lodged in his file and will be used against him as long as he lives. The whole affair was made even sadder because the conversation with the Edinburgh students had been so relaxed and jolly, and was thought by all who took part to be completely private.

This impression of the Duke as tactless and bad-mannered was given a further push in 1988 when the *Daily Mirror* ran a front-page story headed 'BLIMEY! GET THAT BLOKE IN A UNIFORM OUT OF HERE' together with a photograph of the Duke in Field Marshal's uniform captioned 'Philip: he caused a security flap with his icy out-burst at the airport'. The *Daily Express* also carried the story with a front-page picture and the line, 'The Duke blows his top. Page 3'. According to the *Express*,

Prince Philip the Furious turned the air blue at an airport yesterday. Dressed in full Field Marshal's uniform, he stormed up and down the tarmac and roared at the skies, 'Where's my bloody aeroplane?'

Like the 'slitty eyes' story this, too, has found its way into the canon and is trotted out whenever anyone wants to demonstrate the ultimate awfulness of the Duke of Edinburgh. His latest 'critical biographer', for example, quotes the story as if it were gospel and adds as his last pontifical word on the Duke: 'He will undoubtedly be the last royal male from whom this kind of behaviour is both expected and toler-ated.' Leaving aside the implied question of why this sort of behaviour might be expected and tolerated from a female royal, one needs to know whether the story on which the judgement is based is true.

It appeared in the papers on a Saturday and the following Monday James Denyer, managing director of Newcastle airport, faxed letters to Brian McGrath, the Duke's private secretary, to Richard Stott, edi-tor of the *Daily Mirror*, and to Nicholas Lloyd, editor of the *Daily Express*. Mr Denyer was obviously a very angry man.

For a start the Duke had been nowhere near Newcastle airport on the day alleged. He was at Balmoral and the incident reported on 3 September as having happened 'yesterday' could not have taken place any later than Monday, 4 July, the last time the Duke had been at Newcastle airport. On that occasion he had indeed arrived from Albemarle Barracks in Northumberland as suggested. He was fifteen minutes early and was, according to Mr Denyer, 'in his usual jovial mood'. His aircraft was just arriving, he and Mr Denyer had a jolly chat, walked to the aircraft and the Duke got in, still in 'a happy frame of mind'. Pulling away from the stand the Duke, from his usual position in the captain's left-hand seat, smiled and waved and took off without any evident sign of displeasure. The only people the Duke spoke to were Mr Denyer, the director of operations and his military driver. He never raised his voice. He never said 'bloody' anything. All this was explained to the local *Mirror* reporter by Mr Denyer when he phoned to check the story from head office. In the circumstances Mr Denyer felt an apology was due.

The next day's *Newcastle Evening Chronicle* printed an article headed 'APOLOGIES FOR SLUR' which reported Mr Denyer saying, 'The Duke was extremely upset at these stories, both of which were completely untrue.' Mr Denyer felt they were 'not only a slur on him, but also a slur on this airport'.

A week later the *Express* printed Mr Denyer's letter, under another from a lady in Wales about the lack of hygiene in a hospital canteen. The *Mirror*, however, stood by their story which, claimed its editor, had been 'given to our reporter by an extremely reliable source who personally witnessed the events described in it'. The story was checked twice before publication and once subsequently. The *Mirror* stuck to its guns. 'The question of an apology does not arise.' Mr Denyer stuck to his guns too. 'Total fabrication,' he told Brian McGrath.

Difficult question. Does one believe the Duke, the manager of Newcastle airport and the then Captain of the Queen's Flight, Sir John Severne, who first drew my attention to the story? Or does one believe the *Daily Mirror*'s 'extremely reliable' but nonetheless anonymous source? No contest. But it is the latter whose version creeps into the cuttings file and onto the historical record. This, as any fair minded person must surely admit, is a travesty – a popular word with the Duke.

And then there is the question of the Duke, the press and women. I feel somewhat personally aggrieved about this because ever since it first became known that I was writing a book about him the popular press have been telling stories which suggest that I was about to produce a salacious 'kiss and tell' volume which would reveal the amazing secrets of the Duke's love life. *Private Eye*, the *Evening Standard*, the *Daily Mirror*, and the *Daily Mail* all printed stories to this effect. Sometimes they spoke to me before doing so, sometimes not. In the event, it seemed to make little difference.

The magazine *Private Eye* mentioned the actress Anna Massey in this context. Her uncle, Vincent Massey, was Governor-General of Canada and I knew that she had met the Duke during her uncle's time in office. She confirmed this, writing, 'I don't take *Private Eye*, so didn't know anything about the article. I must say such rumour and gossip really doesn't interest me at all. I don't know how it started as I have only met the Duke once at my uncle's and have never seen him since. So that's really all there is to say.'

Nigel Dempster, in the *Daily Mail*, mentioned the actress Pat

Kirkwood. Miss Kirkwood says that in 1948 she was appearing at the London Hippodrome in a show called *Starlight Roof*. She and the Duke's friend, Baron, the photographer, had been seeing each other for over a year and had arranged to have dinner together after the performance. However that evening Baron phoned the theatre to say there was a change of plan and he would be bringing along two friends. These turned out to be the Duke and another naval officer, Captain 'Basher' Watkin. The four of them met up in Miss Kirkwood's dressing room and then adjourned to Les Ambassadeurs Restaurant where they had a late supper before going upstairs to the Milroy nightclub. There they spent an hour or so chatting and dancing. A good time was had by all, but after this single, innocuous encounter Miss Kirkwood says she and the Duke never again met socially.

The *Evening Standard* produced the name of Daphne du Maurier, the novelist. Miss du Maurier was, of course, the wife of Lieutenant-General 'Boy' Browning, comptroller of the Edinburghs' household. Unfortunately she is dead now, but the author Margaret Forster is writing her official biography with the family's co-operation and has seen all the private papers and spoken to all Dame Daphne's surviving family and friends. She is in a better position to know than anyone I can think of and she says that the suggestion that the Duke had a fling with the novelist is pure fantasy.

No wonder then that the Duke can sometimes appear to be impatient with the press, a section of which seems determined to label him as a tactless, bad-tempered philanderer. 'I certainly believe in the need for a "free" press,' he told me, 'but there is a difference between freedom and licence and between the honest pursuit of truth and the cynical pursuit of thoughtless – even vindictive – sensationalism.'

In both my earlier encounters and in my researches for this book I have always found him well aware of the job I was trying to do and the reasons for doing it properly. I would never describe him as the easiest person in the world but the image put about by the tabloid press seems to me to be not only simplistic but also perverse.

He does not enjoy being written about. Even when Basil Boothroyd submitted the text of his biography twenty years ago he found 'Rubbish!' scribbled in the margin once, and I have had dozens of them. Certain people, certain topics, even certain words seem to make him excited, and everybody I have spoken to about him acknowledges the fact. However, if you keep your head down, stand your ground until the storm is over, and stick to your guns, it seems, usually, to be all right in the end. Having said that, one has to wonder how 'short-fused' anyone else might be in his position. This was a point his old friend Lord Buxton made. Of course, conceded Buxton, he could lose his temper, he could seem irritable, but who wouldn't? The retiring Archbishop of Canterbury, Dr Runcie, made a remark quoted in a Sunday paper which in a sense reinforced Buxton's observation. The worst aspect of his tenure of office, said Runcie, was the permanent need for 'geniality'. No matter how foul you were feeling, no matter how asinine everyone else seemed, there was this wearing necessity of being 'nice' all the time. Small wonder if someone in that position snaps occasionally.

Another misapprehension is that the Duke feels frustrated. The only frustration he even half admits to is about having had to leave the Navy prematurely. Some people agree and think he would have done better to have stayed in, but by no means all. 'He's turned out much better as the Duke of Edinburgh than he would have done in the Navy,' says Lord Buxton. Lord Lewin is of the former persuasion; Lord Buxton of the latter. Buxton is a fan – especially of the Duke's achievements in the fields of conservation. In the Navy the Duke might have spoken out of turn, trodden on toes, and not got on as well as everyone now thinks.

I put the frustration question to Michael Mann, the former Dean of Windsor, domestic chaplain and the Duke's co-author. Mann felt that the Duke has acquired a peace of mind that he did not have earlier in life. 'But,' he adds, 'there's a worm inside the man that drives him on. I don't know that he would ever feel fulfilled, though he might feel content.'

Mann also said that the Duke could never accept anything until he had gnawed it and chewed it to pieces. He, too, emphasised the 'but' factor, which is so evident in the correspondence between himself and the Duke. 'When he's in a corner and he's lost a point, he doesn't stop like other people would and say "yes, well maybe you're right." He goes shooting off on something else . . . but in fact, he'll come back later and he will have accepted. When you're actually in argument with him, he will never admit that he's being convinced. You know he has been convinced if he's changed the subject or changed the line of questioning. He would find it very difficult to say "I'm sorry, I'm wrong".'

Michael Mann gave me an interesting example of this. At St George's House the Duke asked him to run a course for Lord-

Lieutenants. Some thirty of them came and it was a great success. Afterwards Mann commented to the Duke that it was a pity they all had to pay their own expenses. 'If they can't afford to do it, they ought not to think about it,' said the Duke. However, he had second thoughts, and later the Lord-Lieutenants did begin to get some of their expenses reimbursed. But the Duke never admitted to Michael Mann that he had been wrong.

This analysis confirms the Casson thought about insecurity. The really secure person has no trouble admitting his errors . . .

The apparent need always to be seen to be right does contribute to the occasional 'bulldozer' (a Michael Mann adjective) tactics and perhaps to a lack of sensitivity for the people he has bulldozed. Often he seems not to realise that he *is* being a bulldozer and people have not, over the years, always been good at pointing this out to him. 'Sir, with respect, you are being a bulldozer' is a line which too few people have been prepared to try out.

I have spent months discussing him with those who know him best, reading his own words and those of others who have written about him, watching him and studying him. Still he puzzles me. Real humility sits uneasily alongside apparent arrogance, energy and optimism co-exist with sudden douches of cold water, real kindnesses are mingled with inexplicable snubs; certainty and uncertainty, sensitivity and insensitivity, walk hand in hand. He is gregarious, he is a loner; he loves argument, he cannot bear to lose one. On the one hand, he will make a detour of thousands of miles to console the victims of a hurricane; on the other, he once got in such a bate with an equerry who failed to take shotgun lessons, that he stopped the car and ordered him out. These apparent inconsistencies certainly make him intriguing; but they also make him exasperating. He is energetic, mercurial, quixotic, and ultimately impossible to pin down – partly on purpose.

The quality I notice more than any other is exasperation. Perhaps that is because he excites it in me, but time and again watching him chair the Award Council, reading his papers on the train, discussing housing policy with a Glasgow councillor, explaining his ancestry, arguing the meaning of life with the Dean of Windsor, I come up against that same sense of 'Oh why, oh why, can no one understand me?' To him 'the point' of everything seems so crystal clear. He cannot see why the rest of us cannot see this too.

Late at night, as the train rolled south from his Duchy of Edinburgh, I reminded him of the occasion he and Robin Woods, then

Dean of Windsor, had spent two hours wandering around Cambridge University 'incog', like Queen Victoria watching the Trooping of the Colour unobserved. In Cambridge the Duke was 'disguised' in a tweed cap, and, apparently, no one recognised him.

'Who told you that?' he asked.

'Robin Woods.'

'Well, it's quite wrong.'

Oh God, I thought, this is the third time today he's done this. 'If you disagree with *everything* I'm told I'll never get this book written,' I said.

He smiled.

I smiled.

Stalemate.


If as a person he is ultimately unknowable, his achievements are easier to assess.

His contribution to the Monarchy in general and to his wife, the Queen, in particular, is paramount. If supporting the sovereign and nursing the Royal Family into the twentieth century had been his only achievements, that would have been enough. It would not have mattered how many schemes and awards he had founded or how many international organisations he had organised; if he had fallen down on this first essential, he would have failed at everything. For more than forty years, however, he has played his part in one of the world's most public marriages. In public his contribution has been visible, obvious and faultless. He is always there at the great ceremonies of State, holding the Queen's hand, always in a technically subordinate position, yet at the same time always making it clear that he is the Queen's number one champion and defence. 'Vide Albert' – that terse comment of the Duke's – keeps coming to my mind. Different circumstances, different problems, and yet *fundamentally* their situation is identical. They have both had to reconcile a dominant personality with a supportive function.

The consensus among those I have consulted is that the Duke has pulled this off. In the forty-odd years of his membership, the character of the Monarchy and of the Family Firm has changed beyond recognition. When the Duke joined he was, like any bridegroom, an outsider in his wife's family. The fact that he was already 'family' may have been apparent to those on the inside, but not to the general public. Over these last forty years he has, subtly and by degrees, become so much a part of the institution that it is now almost impossible to imagine what it would be like without him.

The Duke himself is resolutely unhelpful in assessing his other achievements, but I would put the Duke of Edinburgh's Award Scheme at the top of the list, because it is the one original creation which really could be said to have captured the public imagination. The Study Conferences are also original, but these only take place every six years; the World Wide Fund for Nature (what a mouthful!) has taken up far more of his time and he has campaigned tirelessly on conservation and ecological issues. The same was true of the International Equestrian Federation. Both organisations grew and prospered under his stewardship and he contributed many original thoughts and ideas to them, but they were not his invention.

These are the most important areas of achievement, but there are countless others, some not nearly as well chronicled as they should be. How many people are aware that he was the prime mover in creating the National Fellowship of Engineering in 1976? Or that, paradoxically, this polyglot European prince is the patron of the English Speaking Union? Everyone knows about the Prince of Wales's painting, for example, but hardly anyone is aware that his father also paints. 'Exactly what you'd expect,' says Sir Hugh Casson. 'Absolutely totally direct, no hanging about. Strong colours, vigorous brushstrokes.' The antithesis – interestingly – of Prince Charles's tentative, delicate watercolours. His work for St George's House, his interest in theology and the whole contemplative, thoughtful side of his nature deserves to be better known, if only to counterbalance the popular image of the hectoring sea-captain megaphoning instructions from the bridge. One has to ask whether his public relations could not have been handled with rather more sophistication.

He has been an object lesson in the arts of regimental colonelcy; a knowledgeable authority on housing policy and mortgage tax relief; a champion of British industry abroad and a constructive critic of it at home; he has somehow managed to be a popular university chancellor while being a deadly enemy of what he perceives as self-satisfied intellectuality; and he has always played as hard as he has worked.

'It's bound to be full of "ifs",' said another writer contemplating this biography. What if he hadn't been exiled? What if his parents hadn't split up? What if he'd stayed at school in Salem? What if he hadn't married the Queen? What if he had not left the Navy?

However, it is not the 'ifs' which really mark the Duke's life and his personality, it is the 'buts'. He's very dogmatic. Well, yes, but

. . . He's tremendously busy. Yes, but . . . He's very kind and thoughtful. Yes, but . . . He's enormously likeable. Yes, but . . . He's very frightening. No, but . . .

I find it very difficult to make any statement about the Duke of Edinburgh without qualifying it and, to me, the most endearing thing about him is that he seems to find it just as hard to do so himself.

'I am not really interested in what goes on my tombstone,' he said.

To which there remains only one possible rejoinder.

But . . .

# Acknowledgements and Sources

I am extremely grateful to the Duke of Edinburgh and all his staff at the Palace: Brian McGrath, Clive Robertson, Malcolm Sillars, Jimmy Jewell and John Haslam; and to Robin Janvrin, press secretary when the idea of this book was first mooted. My special thanks also to Anne Griffiths for all her help in unravelling the Duke's ancestry in the appropriate chapters, and for advising on the family trees, as well as suggesting some unexpected illustrations of one sort and another. Also to the girls in the Duke of Edinburgh's office for their unfailing enthusiasm, courtesy and sense of humour.

Members of the Royal Family who have talked to me include Queen Elizabeth the Queen Mother; the Princess Royal and Princess Margaret; and from Prince Philip's own family, his sister Sophia, Princess Georg of Hanover. Princess Margaret of Hesse und bei Rhein has kindly allowed me to use some of the photographs from her archive.

His former private secretaries, Michael Parker and James Orr, both spoke to me often and at length. I would like to thank them and also other former members of his staff including General David Alexander, RM, equerry and treasurer; and Air Vice Marshal Sir John Severne, equerry and Captain of the Queen's Flight.

Other authorities on the Duke who generously assisted me were Prince Bernhard of the Netherlands, Admiral of the Fleet Lord Lewin, Lord Buxton, Lord Charteris, Lord Hunt, Lord Zuckerman, the Right Revd Robin Woods, the Right Revd Michael Mann, Sir Reginald Bennett, Myra Butter, Sir Hugh Casson, Sir Peter Parker, Major-General Sir Christopher Airy, Major-General Michael Hobbs, Sir

Graham Day, Sir David Smith, David Byatt, Gyles Brandreth, Hugo Vickers, Alan Hamilton, Robert Varvill, Philip Ziegler, Squadron Leader Geoff Williams, Alexander Frater, Alastair Forbes, Peter Linklater, Margaret Forster, Ann Leslie, Delia Gafita and the Writers' Union of Romania, Martine de Geus, Stanley Johnston, David Burbidge, Peter Ustinov, Robin Duchesne.

Others have preferred to remain anonymous and some who are not on this list are identified in the text at the appropriate moment. All those who talked to me did so in the knowledge that I had offered to show the manuscript to Buckingham Palace before publication, but several times people asked me to treat remarks or anecdotes as confidential or unattributable. I have tried to respect these wishes, which sometimes means that I have identified an informant simply as 'an old friend' or 'a former employee'. I know how irritating this can be to the reader and how it can lead to suspicions of fabrication. In this case I do promise that the device is used simply to avoid embarrassment. To all of those who talked to me, my sincere thanks.

I am grateful to Lady Margaret Colville for allowing me to consult the diaries of Sir John Colville, and to Correlli Barnett, Keeper of the Churchill College Archives Centre at Cambridge, where they are held.

Of previous books about the Duke, easily the most informative is Basil Boothroyd's *Philip, An Informal Biography*, published by Longman in 1971. I have, where appropriate, tried to identify other books in the text, but among those I have found particularly useful are:

*Prince Philip. A Family Portrait* by Queen Alexandra of Yugoslavia. Hodder & Stoughton, 1959.
*Towards Disaster* by HRH Prince Andrew. John Murray, 1930.
*George VI* by Sarah Bradford. Weidenfeld & Nicolson, 1989.
*Chips: the Diaries of Sir Henry Channon*, edited by Robert Rhodes-James. Weidenfeld & Nicolson, 1967.
*The Reality of Monarchy* by Andrew Duncan. Heinemann, 1970.
*Queen Victoria's Descendants* by Marlene A. Eilers. Atlantic International, 1987.
*Kurt Hahn. An appreciation of his life and work*. Gordonstoun School, 1976.
*Flannelled Foolishness* by E. R. T. Holmes. Hollis & Carter, 1957.
*The Ascent of Everest* by John Hunt. Hodder & Stoughton, 1953.
*Majesty: Elizabeth II and the House of Windsor* by Robert Lacey. Hutchinson, 1977.
*Elizabeth R* by Elizabeth Longford. Weidenfeld & Nicolson, 1983.

*The Royal House of Greece* by Prince Michael of Greece and Alan Palmer. Weidenfeld & Nicolson, 1990.

*For Starters: The Business of Life* by Peter Parker. Jonathan Cape, 1989.

*The Ultimate Family* by John Pearson. Michael Joseph, 1986.

*Royal Artists* by Jane Roberts. Grafton, 1987.

*A Romanov Diary – the Autobiography of H. I. and R. H. Grand Duchess George.* Atlantic International, 1988.

*An Autobiography* by Robin Woods. SCM Press, 1986.

*Mountbatten* by Philip Ziegler. Collins, 1985.

Of the Duke's own books I have relied most heavily on:

*Selected Speeches 1948–1955.* Oxford University Press, 1957.

*Birds from Britannia.* Longman, 1962.

*Competition Carriage Driving.* Horse Drawn Carriages Ltd., 1982.

*A Question of Balance.* Michael Russell, 1984.

*A Windsor Correspondence* (with the Right Revd Michael Mann). Michael Russell, 1984.

*Down to Earth: Speeches and Writings on the Relationship of Man with his Environment.* Collins, 1988.

*Survival or Extinction: A Christian Attitude to the Environment* (with the Right Revd Michael Mann). Michael Russell, 1989.

# SOURCES

*Prologue: 'Two Truths'*
Private letters, personal observations, and a number of interviews form the basis for this. The Richard Ellmann observations on the function of biography come from a review first published in the *New Statesman* in 1969 and subsequently in *a long the riverrun*, a selection of his essays, published by Hamish Hamilton in 1988 and by Penguin a year later.

*Chapter 1: 'The Grief That Fame Can Never Heal'*
Princess Sophie, now married to Prince Georg of Hanover, is, I

believe, one of only two survivors of this episode. As the other, her brother the Duke, was too young to have any recollection of what happened I have relied exclusively on her first-hand account to me.


*Chapter 2: 'Something Inconceivable'*
Various books listed above gave me the basis of my information about the Duke's family background. In addition I was helped by Princess Georg of Hanover, Princess Margaret of Hesse und bei Rhein and the Duke himself, whose knowledge of his family background is almost as encyclopaedic as that of his uncle, Lord Mountbatten. Anne Griffiths and Hugo Vickers also provided expert assistance from outside the family. Louis de Benois's observation about the Grand Duke of Hesse came directly from his grandson, Peter Ustinov.


*Chapter 3: 'The Seed Sown'*
The story of Prince Andrew's Army career derives almost entirely from his own published account, *Towards Disaster* (listed above and translated from Greek to English by Princess Alice). The Duke himself made a number of useful interpolations, as did his sister, Princess Georg of Hanover.


*Chapter 4: 'From His Childhood Onwards'*
My account of the Duke's childhood up to the time he left Salem and went to Gordonstoun is based on published sources supplemented by interviews with members of his family. At the kind invitation of Princess Margaret of Hesse I visited Wolfsgarten where the Duke often went during school holidays. Some years ago I interviewed one of the last surviving teachers at Cheam, Norman Long-Brown. Queen Alexandra of Yugoslavia's chatty book has a number of amusing and colourful anecdotes about this period, but the Duke has sounded a strong cautionary note about several of them. Princess Alice's letter of 1929 first appeared in a privately published memoir of The Elms by the headmaster's wife, Mrs MacJannet. Prince Michael of Greece's remarks about 'Greekness' come from his book *The Royal House of Greece* (listed above).

## Chapter 5: 'Eccentric Perhaps'

I visited Gordonstoun in 1990 and was shown round the school by pupils and the deputy headmaster, David Byatt. Several of the Duke's fellow pupils, in particular James Orr and Robert Varvill, gave me anecdotes and corroborative evidence, though the Duke's memories did not always coincide with theirs! The story of Berry the butler was told to me by Sir Harold and Lady Zia Wernher's daughter, Myra. James Orr provided me with much material on Kurt Hahn and I have supplemented this with my own recollections of Hahn, both at my parents' home in Buckinghamshire and at Brown's Hotel in London where he often held court. Hahn's remarks on the 'five-fold decay' are taken from an address he made at a meeting at Admiralty House on 21 November 1957, sponsored by the London Committee of the Friends of Gordonstoun.

## Chapter 6: 'The Floating Bulwark'

Dartmouth, the beginning of the Duke's naval career, has been partly explained for me by Admiral of the Fleet Lord Lewin and Michael Parker, both of whom have been patient and long-suffering in attempting to do so. They were both very helpful over other naval matters, too. Marian Crawford, as I hope I make clear in the text, is not a wholly reliable source, but the Duke has been an admirable corrective.

## Chapter 7: 'On the Seas and Oceans'

Lord Lewin and Michael Parker were the chief supplement to published sources for my record of the war years. I have drawn heavily on the Duke's own wartime midshipman's log – also available to Basil Boothroyd – and the Duke has assiduously corrected my frequently erroneous impression of war-time naval service, long periods of which seem to have been more tedious than some accounts suggest.

## Chapter 8: 'An Infinite Debt'

The personal memories of my own friends and relations remain, in some cases, quite vivid about the public events described here, and I have drawn on them to corroborate the usual printed evidence from books, newspapers and magazines of the period. Collie Knox's account first appeared in *The Queen* and was reproduced in the Pitkin Pictorial souvenir, *Princess Elizabeth's Wedding Day*. Michael Parker, who served

with the Duke in the Navy during this period and was employed by
him as equerry shortly before his engagement, was a valuable source
of information for this chapter. So was Lord Charteris, then
Lieutenant-Colonel Martin Charteris, who was private secretary to the
Edinburghs at Clarence House and subsequently private secretary to
Her Majesty the Queen.

## Chapter 9: 'When a Man Marries'

In 1980 I conducted a number of interviews with people associated
with the Duke for the *Telegraph Sunday Magazine*. Some of these are
still living but others, such as Olga Franklin and Basil Boothroyd,
are now dead. At various times I have drawn on material from those
interviews. More recent interviews with Mike Parker, Lord Charteris,
and others were again useful, as were the diaries of Chips Channon
and Sir John Colville. These are always witty and informative and
often offer a useful corrective to the official version of events. As
always, Boothroyd is invaluable in providing the Duke's side of the
story and the Duke himself has also provided me with one or two
further thoughts, as have other members of his family. The story of
Peter Linklater's search for Princess Sophie in post-war Germany came
from the man himself, who wrote to me out of the blue after seeing
an article about my researches for this book in the London *Evening
Standard*.

## Chapter 10: 'Of Crown, of Queen'

From now on I am able to draw on personal recollection to a certain
extent as I was nine years old at the time of the Coronation – and still
have my Coronation mug to prove it! Apart from printed sources and
those mentioned above, I am grateful to Lord Hunt, whose Everest
success was reported on the morning of the day itself. The story of
Churchill and helicopters comes from Mike Parker, as does the one
about Baron and the cuckoo clock. Sir Reginald Bennett told me
about Kim Philby and Ian Macleod. The Cardiff anecdote is from *The
Queen's Year* by L. A. Nickolls MVO, a prolific chronicler of royal
events. It was published by Macdonald and is an account of royal
events in 1954. Other information comes from private interviews,
most of them clearly signposted in the text.

*Chapter 11: 'The Division of Labour'*
The account of the Duke's staff, accommodation, and of his planning meeting are all based on personal observation. I am grateful to Anne Griffiths for guiding me through the Duke's bookshelves.

*Chapter 12: 'Winds of the World'*
The Duke was kind enough to invite me to the State Opening of Parliament and my description is based on first-hand observation. Some of the information on royal ceremonial was acquired in earlier researches for books and magazine or newspaper articles. General Sir Michael Gow, the leading authority on the Queen's Birthday Parade, gave me some invaluable insights, and the Royal British Legion Poppy Factory at Richmond helped me with the Remembrance Day details. The Duke's travels over the years are well documented in both books and journalism, including his own writings. The information about the tribe which worships the Duke came from the author Alexander Frater, who wrote about them in the *Observer Magazine*. The Duke himself was very helpful in dotting some 'i's and crossing some 't's, as well as expanding on the bald details of some of his journeys. My father's papers relating to the 1966 tour of North America are comprehensive and fascinating, even though I have used comparatively few of them. The information about flying comes from Air Vice-Marshal Sir John Severne and Squadron Leader Geoff Williams, as well as from a visit to the Queen's Flight and a flight in one of their Wessex helicopters.

*Chapter 13: 'Blood's a Rover'*
This first-hand description of a typical series of visits by the Duke is based on personal observation and conversations with a number of people along the route. I am very grateful to them, and to those who answered my letters after the journey was finished. I am especially grateful to the Duke for allowing me to travel in the Royal Train.

*Chapter 14: 'And Must Unbend His Mind'*
The story of the setting-up of the 1956 Study Conference is told in Sir Peter Parker's autobiography (listed above), but he was kind enough to fill in some details for me and also lent me the two-volume report published shortly afterwards. Lord Hunt and the present direc-

tor of the Award Scheme, Major-General Michael Hobbs, both helped me to understand the Award Scheme. I also have my own memories of this and visited two Award events more recently – the General Council in Northampton and a Gold Award ceremony at St James's Palace. The National Playing Fields Association, like the Award Scheme, produces copious and professional publications and I am grateful to its chairman, Gyles Brandreth, for inviting me to a function at which the Duke presided and for filling me in on details of the way in which the Association works.

### Chapter 15: 'Between the Scylla and the Charybdis'

The Duke's religious thoughts and activities are based on his own published writings identified in the text and on conversations with two former Deans of Windsor and domestic chaplains to the Queen, the Right Revd Robin Woods and the Right Revd Michael Mann. I am grateful to Stanley Johnson for his independent view on the Duke and conservation and to the staff of the World Wide Fund for Nature for background information.

### Chapter 16: 'The Image of War'

The Duke has written extensively about his sporting interests and he personally lent me a number of unpublished written papers about aspects of these activities. Sir William Becher helped evaluate his cricketing prowess and also drew my attention to the invaluable autobiography by E. R. T. Holmes who played with the Duke on a number of occasions. Sir Reginald Bennett and the Royal Yachting Association have given me additional information on sailing, as has the Princess Royal, who also provided me with some extra thoughts on her father's equestrian activities.

### Chapter 17: 'Laughter and the Love of Friends'

The privately published passage on friendship and the Maharaja of Jaipur was lent by Buckingham Palace. I asked practically everyone I spoke to about the Duke's friendships.

*Epilogue: 'Mere Lottery'*

Anna Massey and Pat Kirkwood here both helped personally and Margaret Forster, as the official biographer of Daphne du Maurier, gave me her view of the author's story. Alan Hamilton of *The Times* and my sister-in-law, Ann Leslie, of the *Daily Mail* were both on the royal visit to China and helped me put the 'slit-eyed' episode into perspective. Otherwise the views and analysis are a distillation of material I have already identified.

# *Appendix*

The Official Appointments of HRH the Duke of Edinburgh

At one point in the narrative I mentioned that the Duke was Colonel or Colonel-in-Chief of various regiments. Brigadier Robertson thought I should identify them and promised to give me a list. This is it. As you will see – and as I explained to the Brigadier – it is too long to be included in a single sentence, or even on a single page.

Boothroyd, in his book, attempted to list every single one of the Duke's involvements, but this today would consume volumes. As it is, the Brigadier's list is an interesting sample.

| *Australia* | *Office* | *Year appointed* |
|---|---|---|
| Australian Cadet Corps | Colonel-in-Chief | 1963 |
| Australian Military Forces | Field Marshal | 1954 |
| Royal Australian Air Force | Marshal | 1954 |
| Royal Australian Navy | Admiral of the Fleet | 1954 |
| Royal Australian Corps of Electrical and Mechanical Engineers | Colonel-in-Chief | 1959 |

| *Canada* | | |
|---|---|---|
| Cameron Highlanders of Ottawa (Militia) | Colonel-in-Chief | 1967 |
| Privy Councillor | | 1957 |
| Queen's Own Cameron Highlanders (Militia) | Colonel-in-Chief | 1967 |
| Royal Canadian Air Cadets | Air Commodore-in-Chief | 1953 |

| Canada | Office | Year appointed |
|---|---|---|
| Royal Canadian Army Cadets | Colonel-in-Chief | 1953 |
| Royal Canadian Regiment | Colonel-in-Chief | 1953 |
| Royal Canadian Sea Cadets | Admiral | 1953 |
| Royal Hamilton Light Infantry | Colonel-in-Chief | 1978 |
| Seaforth Highlanders (Militia) | Colonel-in-Chief | 1967 |

| Chile | | |
|---|---|---|
| Chilean Air Force | Hon. Pilot | 1962 |

| Colombia | | |
|---|---|---|
| Colombian Air Force | Hon. Pilot | 1962 |

| New Zealand | | |
|---|---|---|
| New Zealand Army | Field Marshal | 1977 |
| Royal New Zealand Air Force | Marshal | 1977 |
| Royal New Zealand Navy | Admiral of the the Fleet | 1958 |
| Royal New Zealand Corps of Electrical and Mechanical Engineers | Colonel-in-Chief | 1970 |

| United Kingdom | | |
|---|---|---|
| *Civilian* | | |
| Council of Duchy of Cornwall | Member | 1952–72 |
| Order of the British Empire | Grand Master and First Principal Knight | 1953 |
| Plymouth | Lord High Steward | 1960 |

| United Kingdom | Office | Year appointed |
|---|---|---|
| Privy Councillor | | 1951 |
| Windsor Great Park | Ranger | 1952 |
| *Military* | | |
| Army Cadet Force | Colonel-in-Chief | 1952 |
| The Duke of Edinburgh's Royal Regiment (Berkshire and Wiltshire) | Colonel-in-Chief | 1959 |
| Field Marshal | | 1953 |
| Grenadier Guards | Colonel | 1975 |
| Honourable Artillery Company | Member | 1957 |
| | Hon. Member | 1954–57 |
| Intelligence Corps | Colonel-in-Chief | 1977 |
| Intelligence Corps Association | Patron | 1982 |
| Leicester and Derbyshire Yeomanry PAO Squadron | Hon. Colonel | 1953–75 |
| Queen's Own Highlanders (Seaforth and Camerons) | Colonel-in-Chief | 1961 |
| The Queen's Royal Irish Hussars | Colonel-in-Chief | 1958 |
| Royal Electrical and Mechanical Engineers | Colonel-in-Chief | 1969 |
| University of Edinburgh and Heriot Watt Officer Training Corps | Hon. Colonel | 1953 |
| Welsh Guards | Colonel | 1953–75 |
| *Royal Air Force* | | |
| The Air Squadron | Air Commodore | 1983 |
| Air Training Corps | Air Commodore-in-Chief | 1952 |
| Marshal of the Royal Air Force | | 1953 |

| United Kingdom | Office | Year appointed |
|---|---|---|
| RAF Kinloss | Hon. Air Commodore | 1977 |
| *Royal Navy and Royal Marines* | | |
| Admiral of the Fleet | | 1953 |
| Merchant Navy | Extra Master | 1954 |
| Personal ADC to King George VI | | 1948–52 |
| *USA* | | |
| Royal Marines | Captain General | 1953 |
| Sea Cadet Corps | Admiral | 1952 |
| Ancient and Honourable Artillery Company of Massachusetts | Hon. Member | 1952 |
| Confederate Air Force of Harlingen, Texas | Hon. Colonel | 1976 |
| Harris County, Texas | Deputy Sheriff | 1963 |
| Honourable Order of Kentucky Colonels | Hon. Colonel | 1967 |
| The Great Navy of the State of Nebraska | Admiral | 1958 |
| Los Angeles County | Hon. Deputy Sheriff | 1966 |
| San Francisco Port Authority, the Order of Maritime Merit | Grand Commander | 1968 |
| *West Indies* | | |
| Trinidad and Tobago Regiment | Hon. Colonel | 1964 |

# Index